DHARMA LAWS
and
Law Seers of India

DHARMA LAWS
and
Law Seers of India

DR. USHAKAR JHA

MOTILAL BANARSIDASS
SINCE 1903 IN INDOLOGY

MOTILAL BANARSIDASS PUBLISHERS
PRIVATE LIMITED • DELHI

*First MLBD Edition : Delhi, **2017***
First Edition : Delhi, 2014

ISBN : 978-81-208-4158-1

Also available at
MOTILAL BANARSIDASS
41 U.A. Bungalow Road, Jawahar Nagar, Delhi 110 007
8 Mahalaxmi Chamber, 22 Bhulabhai Desai Road, Mumbai 400 026
203 Royapettah High Road, Mylapore, Chennai 600 004
236, 9th Main III Block, Jayanagar, Bengaluru 560 011
8 Camac Street, Kolkata 700 017
Ashok Rajpath, Patna 800 004

MLBD Cataloging-in-Publication Data
Dharma Laws and Law Seers of India
by *Dr. Ushakar Jha*
Includes 3 Appendices and Bibliography
ISBN : 978-81-208-4158-1
I. Hinduism II. Ancient Indian Law/Sources
III. Law Seers of India IV. Jha, Dr. Ushakar
V. Jha, Sadan

Published by
Motilal Banarsidass Publishers Private Limited
www.mlbd.com • mlbd@mlbd.com
Printed by Avantika Printers (P) Ltd.

Dedicated to
Our respected parents

LATE PT. DIVAKAR JHA
LATE SMT. HARESHWARI DEVI

Whose love and blessings
we are proud of.

Whose love and blessings
we are proud of.
not to kill,
not to lie,
not to steal,
to keep body clean,
not to restrain the senses,
these are in short the laws
proclaimed by seers for humanity.

Table of Contents

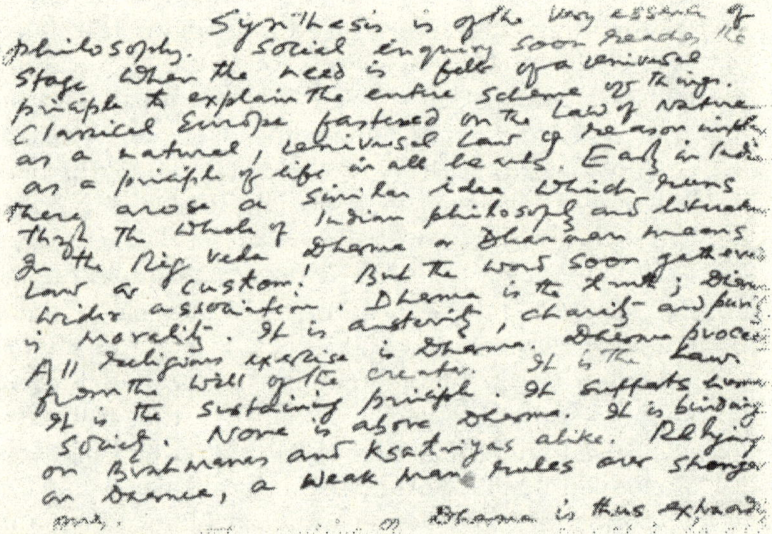

Synthesis is of the very essence of
philosophy. Social enquiry soon reaches the
stage when the need is felt of a universal
principle to explain the entire scheme of things.
Classical Europe fastened on the law of nature
as a natural, universal law of reason with[illegible]
as a principle of life in all levels. Early in India
there arose a similar idea which runs
through the whole of Indian philosophy and literature
In the Rig Veda Dharma or Dharman means
law or custom! But the word soon gathered
wider association. Dharma is the truth; Dharma
is morality. It is austerity, charity and purity
All religious exercise is Dharma. Dharma proceeds
from the will of the creator. It is the law.
It is the sustaining principle. It supports human
society. None is above Dharma. It is binding
on Brahmanas and Ksatriyas alike. Relying
on Dharma, a weak man rules over stronger
and. [illegible] Dharma is thus expanded

Preface

ॐ गं गणेशाय नमः

ॐ नमो भगवते वासुदेवाय

नारायणं नमस्कृत्य नरंचैव नरोत्तमम्।

देवीं सरस्वतीं व्यासं ततो जयमुदीरयेत्।।

Three religions of the contemporary world have come down to us from pre-historic times. These are Hinduism, Zoroastrianism and Judaism. In the course of their long history, they have received tremendous shocks and all of them prove their survival by their internal strength. However, Judaism failed to absorb Christianity and was driven out of its place of birth by its all-conquering daughter. A handful of Parsees is all that remains to tell the tale of their grand religion. In India, sect after sect arose and seemed to shake the religion of the Vedas to its very foundation. But, like the waters of the seashore in a tremendous earthquake it receded only for a while, only to return in an all-absorbing flood, a thousand times more vigorous. When the tumult of the rush was over, these sects were all sucked in, absorbed and assimilated into the immense body of the mother faith (Vivekananda, I:6).

The Hindus have received their religion through revelation in the form the Vedas. They hold that the Vedas are without any beginning or an end. By the Vedas, no books are meant. They mean the accumulated treasure of spiritual laws discovered by different people at different times. Just as the law of gravitation existed before its discovery, and would continue to exist even after humanity becomes forgetful of this law, so is the case with the laws that govern the spiritual world. The moral, ethical and spiritual relation between soul and soul and between individual spirits and father of all spirits was there before their discoveries, and would remain irrespective of whether we remember or forget them.

The discoverers of these laws are called Rishis and we honour them as perfect beings. Hindus believe that God is a spirit. Him, the sword cannot pierce. Him, the fire cannot burn. Him, the water cannot melt. Him, the air cannot dry. Hindus believe that every soul is a circle whose circumference is nowhere. But whose centre is located in the body. Death means the change of this centre from body to body. Here, the soul is not bound by the conditions of matter. In its very essence, it is free, unbounded, holy, pure and perfect. But somehow or the other, it finds itself tied down to matter, and thinks of itself as matter (Vivekanand, I:9).

It is not that the Vedas proclaim a dreadful combination of unforgiving laws. Not an endless prison of cause and effect either but that which is placed at the head of all these laws. In and through every particle of matter and force, stands one 'by whose command the wind blows, the fire burns, the clouds rain, and death stalks upon the earth'.

And what is His nature? He is everywhere, the pure and formless one, the almighty and all-merciful. 'Thou art our father, thou art our mother, thou art our beloved friend, and thou art the source of all strength: give us strength. Thou art He that beareth the burdens of the universe; help me bear the little burden of this life'... Thus sang the Rishis of the Vedas. And how to worship Him? Through love. 'He is to be worshipped as the one beloved, dearer than everything in this and the next life' (Vivekananda, I:9).

It is the same light coming through glasses of different colours. And these little variations are necessary for the purpose of adaptation. But in the heart of everything the same truth reigns. The lord has declared to the universe in His incarnation as Krishna, 'I am in every religion as the thread through a string of pearls. Wherever, thou seest extraordinary holiness and extraordinary power rising and purifying humanity, know thou that I am there.'

In religion there is no caste; caste is simply a social institution. The relation between Hinduism (by Hinduism, Swami Vivekananda means the religion of the Vedas) and what is called Buddhism in the present day is nearly the same as the relation between Judaism and Christianity.

Whatever be the position of philosophy, whatever may be the position of metaphysics, as long as there is such a thing as death in the world, so long as there is such a thing as weakness in the human heart, so long as there is a cry going out of the heart of man in his very weakness, there shall be faith in the God.

On the philosophic side, the disciples of the great master dashed themselves against the eternal rocks of the Vedas and could not crush them and on the other side they took away from the nation that eternal God to which every man and woman clung so fondly. And, the result was that Buddhism had to die a natural death in India, the land of its birth. Buddhism lost its reforming zeal, that wonderful sympathy and charity for everybody, that wonderful heaven which Buddhism had brought to the masses and which had rendered Indian society so great that a Greek historian who wrote about India of that time was led to say that no Hindu was known to tell an untruth and no Hindu woman was known to be unchaste.

He further elaborated, "Hinduism cannot live without Buddhism, nor can Buddhism without Hinduism. Then a realization dawns upon us that the Buddhists cannot stand without the brain and philosophy of the Brahmins, nor the Brahmins without the heart of the Buddhists. This separation between the Buddhists and the Brahmins is the cause of the downfall of India. Let us then join the wonderful intellect of the Brahmin with the heart, the noble soul, and the wonderful humanising power of the great master because they base their philosophy on the Dharma" (Vivekananda, I:43).

The east with its swarming hordes is living a listless life from century to century; the west is with its energetic individualistic impulses, but without any consistent philosophy of civilization. They meet each other. This collision threatens to accentuate the reactionary forces to strengthen autocracy and brute forces to weaken everything that bases itself on reason, reflection and individual rights. While some presaging spirits cherish the hope that eastern thought will yield a harmonising principle to the life of the west, others abandon themselves to the fear that the world is destined to be driven back into another period of darkness in which intelligence will slumber and brute force reign supreme.

'Ideas rule the world' is a phrase coined in the west, but its truth is felt more keenly by eastern than by western minds. For in the east, ideas dominate so much that the impractical ones often become the most fascinating. Today, however, in India, practicality is gaining ground and germinating thoughts are taking shape which will rule not only the imagination but the actions of the new generations. The birth is being witnessed of what has been called New India. We experience a unique coming together of ideas and practices, non-worldly and material, practical and impractical.

In this new India, it was my heartfelt curiosity that has enabled me to put before you a humble submission in the form of a book. The purpose is to quench the thirst of people like me in the new millennium, an era that is destined to witness *vasudhaiva kutumbakam*- converting the world as one family.

This is a book on ancient laws and law seers. There is no dearth of books on this subject. In spite of my sincere efforts to know just the basic facts about our sacred books and the law seers with whom our lineage is associated, I do not think I will ever be able to fully understand them. I was handicapped as I was not well versed in Sanskrit and my attempt to get a single comprehensive handbook covering the field and easy to grasp was unsuccessful.

With the blessings of the Lord, I could venture to peep into several religious books to get a glimpse of the sacred literature that constitutes the foundation of Dharma (or the law as we know it in our contemporary context) and the seers who have shaped this corpus. At the beginning itself, I must clearly state that I have nothing original in this effort. However, my commitment is to provide an overview of the Hindu philosophy related to Dharma. This philosophy is quite different from western philosophy and it symbolizes our culture and heritage.

In this endeavour, I offer my salutations to the sacred feet of Bhagwan Shankara, who is the abode of Vedas, Srutis, Smritis, Puranas and of compassion, and who forever accomplishes the good of the world.

श्रुति स्मृति पुराणानाम् आलयं करुणालयम्
नमामि भगवत्पादम् शंकर लोक शंकरम्।

The readers may find many lapses in the book but I am sure they will pardon me, and I shall be happy if it makes one understand the core of our heritage and follow them in their day to day lives. This will be a great tribute to the seers and saints of the soil who have shaped the nation and whose blessings hold India high.

If we desire peace we must follow the path of Adhyatm based on our *Dharma*. Come forward, blessings of the Goddess Durga will bestow on us in the new millennium.

उतिष्ठत जाग्रत प्राप्य वरान्निबोधत

In this excercise for me, inspirations are many- I salute Sri Chandrasekharendra Saraswati, the then Sankaracharya of Kanchi Kamkoti Peetham, whose *The Guru Tradition, The Hindu Dharma* and *The Vedas* form the base of this present book. To the rest, I simply pray to God for His Blessings to them.

व्यासाय विष्णुरूपाय व्यासरूपाय विष्णवे।
नमो वै ब्रह्मनिधये वसिष्ठाय नमो नमः।।

I hail Thee, Vyasa again and again,
Thou, God in human frame,
Thou, Scion of Vasistha's ancient race,
It is from Thee that all knowledge springs.

15.01.2000 Makar Sankranti.

PART – ONE

DHARMA: A WAY OF LIFE

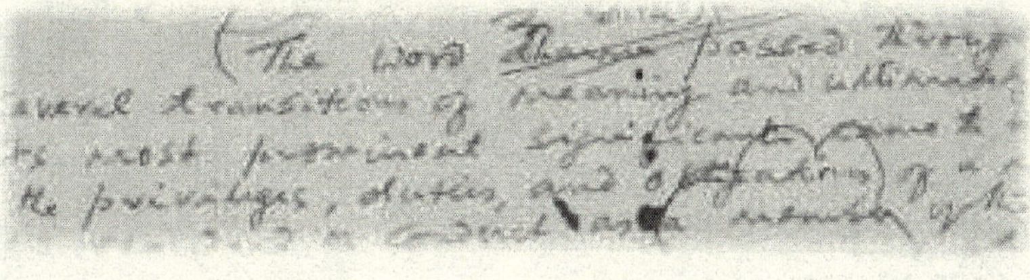
(The word Dharma passed throug
everal transitions of meaning and ultimat
ts most prominent significance came
the privileges, duties and obligations of a

1.
Dharma and the Philosophy of Humanism

The Concept of Dharma

Synthesis is the very essence of philosophy. Social enquiry soon reaches the stage when the need is felt for a universal principle to explain the scheme of things that human society inhabits. Classical Europe fastened on the law of nature as a natural and a universal law of reason implanted in the form of a certain principle of life in all hearts. In ancient India, there was a similar idea which runs through the whole of Indian philosophy and literature. Dharma is that Idea. In the Rig Veda, *Dharma* or *Dharman* means law or custom (Macdonell and Keith, I: 390). But the word soon gathered wider association. Dharma is the truth; Dharma is morality. It is austerity, charity and purity. Any religious exercise is Dharma. Dharma proceeds from the will of the creator. It is the law. It is the sustaining principle. Dharma supports human society. Nothing is above it. It is binding on Brahmanas and Kshatriyas alike. By relying on Dharma, even a weak man can overpower stronger ones.

The notion of Dharma is extraordinarily wide and equally vague. It is best summarised as the ruling force, the harmonizing principle, the foundation of social order. Chandogya Upanishada (23.1-2) informs that there are three branches of the law: sacrifice, study and charity constitute the first; austerity is the second and to dwell as a Brahmachari in the house of a tutor is the third (Max Muller,

1:35). There is a passage in the Satpatha Brahmana (5:3:3:10) in which after a sacrifice, Varuna Dharmapati, (the lord of the law) makes the king lord of the law. This is truly the supreme state, when one is lord of the law and whoever attains that supreme state, to him they come (in the matters of law). Therefore everyone comes to Varuna Dharmapati. But the lordship of the law here means the lordship of justice (Max Muller, 41:71).

Following extracts quoted from the works of the foremost exponents of the science of polity in ancient India reflect their views. Yet, the evident exaggeration of the universal scope and purpose of such science cannot be overlooked.

मज्जेत् त्रयी दण्डनीतौ हतायां सर्वे धर्माः प्रक्षयेयुर्विबुद्धाः।
सर्वे धर्माश्रमाणां हताः स्युः क्षात्रे त्यक्ते राजधर्मे पुराणे।।
सर्वे त्यागा राजधर्मेषु दृष्टाः सर्वा दीक्षा राज राजधर्मेषु युक्ताः।
सर्वा विद्या राजधर्मेषु युक्तः। सर्वे लोका राजधर्मे प्रविष्टाः ।।

With the end of *Dandaniti,* the triple Vedas sink and with Vedas depart Dharma. When traditional State Ethics depart, the Dharma of ashramas vanishes completely too. In politics are realized all the forms of renunciation. In politics are united all the sacraments, in politics is combined all knowledge: in politics is centered the entire world (*Mahabharata: Shanti Parva,* 63:28-29).

धर्ममर्थं च कामं च प्रवर्तयति पाति च।
अधर्मानर्थं विद्वेषानिदं शास्त्रं निहन्ति च।।

This science brings into being and preserves spiritual good, material well being and pleasures. It also destroys spiritual evil, material loss and hatred (*Kautiliya Arthasastra,* XV: 72).

राजधर्मान् विशेषेण कथयस्व पितामह।
सर्वस्य जीवलोकस्य राजधर्मः परायणम्।।

त्रिवर्गो हि समासक्तो राजधर्मेषु कौरव।
मोक्षधर्मश्च विस्पष्टःसकलोऽत्र समाहितः।।

The code of royal duties is the essence of the whole living creation. The three-fold end of human existence as well as the goal of salvation is fixed in the code of royal duties. O son of Kuru! All the religious rites are enshrined in the code of royal duties; in the code of royal duties is united all the learning; in the code of royal duties is centered the entire world (*Shanti Parva,* 56:3-4).

क्रियैकदेशाबोधिनी शास्त्रमयानि शान्ति हि।
सर्वोपजीवकं लोकस्थिति क्रिन्निष्ठास्त्कम्।
धर्मार्थकाममूलं हि स्मष्टतं मोक्षप्रदं यतः।।

Other branches of learning enlighten people on only one aspect of their activities. Nitishastra (on the other hand) is the source of subsistence for all classes, and it maintains the established usage of men (*Shukraniti* 1.4-5).

The word Dharma has passed through several transitions of meaning and ultimately it's prominent significance came to be in the form of privileges, duties and obligations of a man, his standard of conduct as a member of the Aryan community, as a member of one of the castes and finally as a person at a particular stage of life. The king Janaka echoed the conception of Lord of Dharma is this way:

लहसा यज्ञेष्ठु प्रत्यक्षा सा*लहसा परिकील्ततता।
उपाधियोगतो लहसा नान्यथेति विनिर्णयः।।

Janaka advised that the Vedic way of living was to be followed by all means. In this way of living there were checks for all. The violation of the Vedas (as done by the Bauddha) causes the loss of Dharma i.e *Varnasrama Dharma* (Ganguly, 20).

The Vedic religion usually propagates an optimistic life, a life in which all the four stages are to be given proper attention. But in the Upanishads, we have a somewhat pessimistic point of view and therefore the Upanishadic writers championed the realization of knowledge and detachment. The Bauddha and the Jains also emphasized renunciation or *sanyasa.* So far as fundamental principles of life are concerned (charity, pity, purity and nonviolence), there is little quarrel between the Vedic thinkers and the champions of these sects.

Emperor Ashoka in one of his inscriptions (second pillar edict) has defined Dharma (Dhamma) in this way:

कियं चु धम्मेति?अपासिनवे बहुकयाने दया दाने सच सोचये।
कियन् तु धर्म इति। अल्पाति नाभम् बहुकल्यानम् दया दानम् सत्यम् गौचकम्।

The same has been repeated in the seventh pillar edict of Ashoka (line 10 of the Delhi Topra version). The implication is that by avoiding sin as far as possible (literally by committing acts of small sins only), performing various works of welfare to others, and by observing the rules of charity, mercy, truth and purity, Dharma may be acquired. Most of these precepts are prescribed for Buddhist adherents in works like *Singalovada Sutta* in the *Dighanikaya* (ibid, 21).

It is in this sense that the word seems to be used in the well-known exhortation to the pupil in the *Taittiriya Upanishad* (I, II): 'Speak the truth, practice (your own) Dharma.' It is in the same sense that the *Bhagvad Gita* uses the word Dharma in the often quoted verse स्वधर्मे निधनं श्रेय:'. The word is employed in this manner in the Dharmashastra literature. The Manusmriti (1.2) tells us that the sages requested Manu to impart instructions in the Dharma for all the varnas. The *Yagyavalakya Smriti* (1.1) employs it in similar fashion. In the *Tantra-Vartika* too we are told that all the Dharmasastras are concerned with imparting instructions in the Dharma of varnas and ashramas (सर्वधर्म सूत्रणां वर्णाश्रमधर्मोपदेष्ठित्वात्) Medhatithi commenting on Manu says that the expounders of Smritis dilate upon Dharma as five-fold, that is, Varna Dharma, Ashrama Dharma, Varnaashrama Dharma, Naimittika Dharma (such as prayaschitta) and Guna Dharma ('to protect' as the duty of a crowned king, whether kshatriya or not).

Hardatta in his commentary on Gautam Dharmasutra (19.1) and Govindaraj on Manu (2.25) also give the same five-fold classification. Similar is the case with Bhavisya Purana (Brahma-Parva, 181, 10-15) which sets out this five-fold Dharma. The Gautam Dharmasutra (19.1) says उद्रो वर्णधर्मष्ठचाश्रमधर्मष्ठच and proceeds to explain prayaschittas (i.e. Naimittika Dharma). The Apastamba Dharmashastra begins with अथात: समयाचारिकान धर्मम् व्याख्याम:। We shall expound the Dharma relating to the practices based on convention and the conventions are settled by those who are conversant with Dharma and the authorities and not merely by anyone. The Apastamba Grihyasutra begins with अथ कर्माण्याचरद् यानि गष्टहयन्ते। Pointing that actions are श्रुतिलक्षण और आचारलक्षण. In the above cited line of Apastamba Dharmashastra, samaya has several meanings, as Amara says, समय: ष्टापथाचारकाल सि)ान्त संविद:।

——— It may be noted that Mitakshara on Yagyavalkya (1.1) after mentioning the five-fold Dharma and illustrating them, adds a sixth category *sadharana Dharma*–duties common to all men (including even chandalas) such as ahimsa and quotes a Vedic passage in support, न लहस्यत सर्व भूतानि. Slightly different enumeration of virtues to be cultivated by all men are found in Gautam Dharma Sutra (VIII:23-25), Matsya Purana (52:8-10), Manu (X: 63) and in Yagyavalkya (1.1.22) (Kane, II: 10-11 and V:1023-24, 1637 and 1648). It may be noted that the Arthashastra of Kautiliya (1.2.3) prescribes ahimsa, satya, shaucha, anasuya, anrsamsya and kshama for all men. सर्वेज़ां लहसा सत्यं ष्टौचमनसूया*नृष्ठांस्यं क्षमा च। (Kane, I: 4). It is in this sense that the word Dharma is being taken. Efforts are being made to elaborate the sources of Dharmasastra and the implications of it. Here our focus has been on *achara* and *vyavahara* (code of conduct).

From the earlier given extracts, particularly from the first illustration (*Shanti Parva* 63:28-29) it is quite evident that Dharma is closely connected with the traditional state ethics and quite vital to the governance.

Dharma and Dandaniti

यथाहि रष्ठमयो*श्वस्य द्विरदस्य्(कुष्ठाो यथा।
नरेन्द्र धर्मो लोकस्य तथा प्रग्रहणं स्मष्टतम्।।7।।
उदयन् हि यथा सूर्यो नाष्ठात्यष्ठुभं तमः।
राजधर्मास्तथा लोक्यांनिक्षिपन्त्य ष्ठुभां गतिम्।।7।।*(Shanti Parva, 56:5&7)*

In its origin, the science of governance is older than the state itself. The world began with a golden age of perfection when no government was needed. This was followed by a period of sin and darkness. The Gods were distressed and supplicated Vishnu to rescue the world (Prasad, 22). Vishnu first composed a stupendous treatise on life and government and then instituted a king, that is, the government or state (*Shanti Parva*, LIX: 28-29). Historically and philosophically, the idea that the theory of government was prior to the institution of government cannot be sustained, but it shows how clearly Hindu thinkers realized the need of law and regulation as the foundation of human society.

तानुवाच सुरान् सर्वान् स्वयम्भूर्भगवांस्ततः।
श्रेयो*हं चिन्तयिज़्यामि व्येतु वो भीः सुरर्ज़भाः।।28।।
ततो*ध्यायसहस्राणां ष्ठातं चक्रे स्वबुि)जम्।
यत्र धर्मस्तथैवार्थः कामष्ठचैवाभिवल्रणतः।।29।।*(Shanti Parva, 59:28-29)*

Dandaniti is relevant here while discussing the theory of governance. Dandaniti is understood as the science of administration dealing both with the functions and the machinery of government (Dikshitar, 1). All coercive authority is vested in the king who was expected to act impartially and administer the laws with a view to maintain life, property, and discipline among his subjects. Danda preserved the four orders and defined the limits of the activities of individuals as well as social groups. Danda or coercion was thus conceived to be the basis of Rajya or political society. The Vedic thinkers like their modern counterparts regarded it as the primary principle in the evolution of the state (Bandopadhyaya, I: 283).

According to the ancient thinkers, dandaniti is the term employed in the Mahabharata to denote what has been translated by some scholars as political theory. Literally, it means the science of coercion. Viewed in the context as a whole, it is best rendered as the science of governance. In consonance with the general trend of Hindu social thought, it is viewed predominantly as an art. As such, dandaniti claims precedence over all other branches of study. As the reins check the steed, or as an iron hook controls the elephant, dandaniti keeps the world under restraints. It destroys every evil as the sun destroys darkness.

The concept of Danda was one of the most important political ideas propounded in ancient India. This world is brought to righteousness through Danda, the baton of punishment, hence the science of kingship is called Dandaniti, and it is pervasive in the three worlds of Gods, men and demons. Dandaniti controls the four varnas so as to lead them on to the performance of their duties. When it is employed by the ruler properly it makes them desist from adharma (unrighteousness). The Nirukta says that 'Danda' is derived from the root *dad* meaning 'to hold'. It also suggests the root *dam* as the origin of Danda. Gautam remarks, "They declare that the word Danda is derived from the verb *damyati* (the restrains); therefore he shall restrain those who do not restrain themselves". Other texts also agree that Danda is by its roots, restrains and punishes (Sharan, 24).

The great importance of Danda can be realised from the fact that individuals as well as state could make achievements only under the rule of Danda, and they could preserve as well as increase their attainments so long as Danda ruled. Manu has called Danda the king or the real ruler. It is Danda that rules the subjects, it is Danda that protects all, it is Danda that keeps awake, and guards people when they are asleep; and hence the learned style Danda itself as Dharma (Dikshitar, 10).

असम्मोहाय मर्त्यानामर्थ संरक्षणाय च।
मर्यादा स्थापिता लोके दण्डसंज्ञा विष्ठाम्पते।।(*Shanti Parva*, 15:10)

Danda has also been characterized as the God Brahma:

दण्डो हि भगवान् विज़्णुर्दण्डो नारायणः प्रभुः।
छ्यवद रूपं महद् विभ्रन्महान् पुरुज़ उच्यते।।(*Shanti Parva*, 121:23)

Arjun has explained the meaning of 'Danda' in the Mahabharata. According to him, the laws meant to keep the people civilized are Danda. For Manu, Danda comes from Brahma and it has been placed as Dharma.

तस्यार्थे सर्वभूतानां गोप्तारं धर्ममात्मजम्।
ब्रह्मतेजोमयं दण्डमसष्टजत् पूर्वमीवरः।।(Manu, 7:14)

State and Non-State Nature: Matsyanyaya

Hindu thinkers tried to understand the state by differentiating it from the non-state. There is an inherent and underlying dichotomy here in the Indian political thought. The method these thinkers used was logical as well as historical. First, they tried to investigate the particular ways in which the state analytically differed from the non-state. Secondly, they tried to visualize how the pre-state condition developed into that of the state, that is, how the state grew out of the non-state. The chief solution to both of these problems was found in the doctrine of Matsyanyaya–the maxim that the larger fish devours the smaller.

Now, what is the non-state? The same question was asked by the philosopher of Europe thus: 'What is the state of nature?' And the answer from ancient India is identical with that coming from Europe (Sarkar, 509).

Richard Hooker (1554-1600), in his book *Of the Laws of Ecclesiastical Polity* (1593) propounded that the state of nature is a state of strife. The *Leviathan* of Hobbes (1588-1670) declares similarly that the state of nature is a state of war, and a state of the rights of the might. The non-state is thus conceived as a war - 'all against all', an 'anarchy of birds and beasts', or 'a regime of vultures and harpies', as John Stuart Mill remarked. Scholars have maintained that this Hobbesian 'Law of Beasts and Birds' and what Ludwig Gumplowicz (1838-1909) who is one of the founders of European Sociology, terms as 'nature-process' is basically the Indian maxim of the larger fish devouring smaller ones. In such a situation 'should there be no ruler to wield power on earth?', asks the Mahabharata:

अदास: क्रियते दासो ह्रियन्ते च बलात् स्त्रिय:।एतस्मात् कारणाद् देवा: प्रजापालान् प्रचक्रिरे।।
राजा चेन्न भवेत्लोके पष्टथिव्यां दण्डधारक:।जले मत्स्यानिवापक्ष्यन् दुर्वलं बलवतरा:।।
अराजका: प्रजा: पूर्वं विनेष्ठुरिति न: श्रुतम्। परस्परं भक्षयन्तो मत्स्या इव जले ख्र
ष्ठान्।। (*Shanti Parva*, 67:15-17)

राजमूलो महाप्राज्ञ धर्मो लोकस्य लक्ष्यते।
प्रजा राज भयादेव च खादन्ति परस्परम्।। (*Shanti Parva*, 68:8)

The strong would devour the weak like fish in water. It is said that in days of yore, people were ruined through anarchy, devouring one another like the stronger fish preying upon the feebler.

स राजा पुरुज़ो दण्ड: स नेता ष्टासिता च स:।
चतुर्णामाश्रमाणां च धर्मस्य प्रतिभू: स्मष्टत:।।
दण्ड: ष्टास्ति प्रजा: सर्वा दण्ड एवाभिरक्षति।
दण्ड सुप्तेजु जागल्त्त दण्डं धर्मं विदुर्बुधा:।।
समीक्ष्य स धष्टत: सम्यक् सर्वा रंजयति प्रजा:।
असमीक्ष्य प्रणीतस्तु विनाष्टायति सर्वत:।।
यदि न प्रणयेद् राजा दण्डं दण्डयेस्वतन्द्रित:।
ष्टूले मत्स्यानिवापक्ष्यन्दुर्वलान्वल वत्तरा:।।(डंदनए 7रू17.20)

In the Manu Samhita, likewise we are told that 'the strong would devour the weak like a fish' behave in the water and there will be a virtual reversion to the non-state (if the king is not vigilant enough in punishing those who deserved to be punished). The Ramayana also describes the non-state as one in which people devour one another like fishes do. A few details about the non-state condition are furnished in the Matsya Purana: the child, the old, the sick, the ascetic, the priest, the woman and the widow would be preyed upon should Danda or punishment fail to be operative at the proper time (*Matsya Nayaya*, CCXXV: 9).

The idea of the fish–like struggle for existence was thus a generally accepted notion in the 'floating literature' of ancient India. It acquires an important place in the political treatises also. Kautiliya too observes in his *Arthasastra* that Matsya Nyaya prevails if the state is not formed.

दुज़्प्रणीतःकामक्रोधाभ्यामज्ञानाद्वानप्रस्थपरिव्राजकानपि कोपयति किम्ंग पुनर्गष्टहस्थान्। अप्रणीतो हि मात्स्यन्यायमुद्मावयति।बलीयानबलं हि ग्रसते दण्डधराभावे।तेन गुप्तः प्रभवतीति। (*Kautiliya Arthasastra*, 1:4)

'In the absence of the punisher, the powerful swallows the powerless'. Kamandak (500 AD), who generally follows Kautiliya, writes in his Nitisar that in the absence of punishment (Danda), the destructive or ruinous Matsya Nyaya operates and because of mutual animosity among people, it ultimately leads to the disruption of the world (Kamandaka, II: 40).The doctrine was not confined within the circle of academicians and theoriticians, we find it prevalent even among the diplomats and practical statesmen from 9th century onwards. In the declaration of Dharmapala of the Pal dynasty of Bengal, we are told that it was 'in order to escape from Matsya Nyaya' that is, from being absorbed into a larger kingdom that the people 'made his father Gopal accept the sovereignty' (Sarkar, 510).

This theory of the non-state or the state of nature has had important bearing on other doctrines of Hindu Political philosophy. Matsya Nyaya, for instance, is an expressive term in India's legal phraseologies. In Raghunatha's (15th century) *Laukika Nyaya Sangraha* we find Matsya Nyaya coupled with Sundopasunda Nyaya. In this analogy which is based on the Pauranic allusion- the demons Sunda and Upsunda were brothers like Pyrochles and Cymochles in Spenser's Faerie Queen. They quarrelled over the nymph Tilottama and destroyed each other in the contest. Matsya Nyaya arises, as Raghunatha explains, under two sets of conditions. Firstly, there must be a conflict between a powerful and a relatively a weak unit. And secondly, the latter must have been crushed and obliterated by the former. He says that it is frequently referred to in the Itihas and Puranas. He quotes the following passage from Vasistha: 'by this time that Rasatala region had become extremely sovereignless, i.e. an anarchic non-state, characterized by the ignoble Matsya Nyaya'. Vasistha's verse is elucidated by Raghunatha with the gloss that 'strong fish began to put an end the lives of the weak'.

The non-state, is then, a state of anarchy, one in which the 'tyranny of robbers' has full sway, where 'justice is non-existent, and the people prey upon one another'. It is considered as the greatest evil.

राष्ट्रस्यैतत् श्त्यतमं राज्ञ एवाभिज़थ्चनम्। अनिन्द्रमबलं राज़्ट्रं दस्यवो*भिभवन्त्युत॥2॥
अराजकेज़ु राष्ट्रथ ज़ु धर्मो न व्यवतिज़्ठते।परस्परं च खादन्ति सर्वथा धिगराजकम्॥3॥
तस्माद् राजैव कर्तव्यः सततं भूतिमिच्छता ।न धनार्थो न दारार्थ स्तेज़ां येज़ाम राजकम्॥12॥(*Shanti Parva*, 67:2-12)

We are informed that the pleasure of wealth and wives is impossible under such circumstances. Only the robber is happy in such a state. Even his happiness is precarious because 'a single man is deprived of his loot by two, and the two are robbed of theirs by several combined'. 'A free man is made a slave' and 'women are assaulted'. The psychology of men in the state of nature is brought out in the Shanti Parva of the Mahabharata establishing the following causal nexus: Then foolishness or stupidity (moha) seized their minds. Their intelligence being thus eclipsed, the sense of justice (Dharma) was lost. Cupidity or temptation (lobha) overpowered them next. Thus sprang up the desire (Kama) for possessing things not yet possessed. And this led to their being subjugated by attachment (raga), under which they began to ignore the distinction between what should and what should not be done. Consequently, there appeared sexual license, libertinism in speech and diet, and indifference to morality. When such devolution set in among men, Brahman (the idea of godhead) disappeared and with it Law (Dharma) too.

The phenomenon of government founded on human psychology and general trend of thought in this regard seems to have been the same across the world. In ancient China, Hsun Tze (305-235 BC) rebuked the principles of Mancius (373-289 BC) who postulated the 'original goodness' of human nature. According to his counter-theory, 'man is by nature wicked; his goodness is the result of nurturing.' Chinese philosophers also claim that the ancient rulers understood the native viciousness of man ... and therefore created morals, laws and institutions in order that human instincts and impulses might be disciplined and transformed (Sarkar, 511).

In the western world, Seneca (the stoic philosopher, Lucius Annaeus Seneca: 4BC-65AD), 'looked upon the institutions of society as being the results of vice, of the corruption of human nature. They are conventional institutions made necessary by the actual defects of human nature.' The doctrine of human depravity and the natural wickedness of man were entertained by the church too. The idea that the institution of government was made necessary by sin and the thought that it is a divinely appointed remedy for sin continued and developed by St. Augustine and St. Gregory the great. This was emphatically restated by the ecclesiastical and political writers of the period from the 9th to the 13th centuries, and it found a champion in Pope

Hildebrand, Gregory VII (1073-1085) (Carlyle, II: 143-6 and III: 97,105 and187).

The verdict of political thinkers from ancient India on the nature of man is identical. According to Kamandaka, men are by nature subject to passions and are covetous of each other's wealth and wife (Kamandaka, II: 42). 'Rare', says Manu, 'is man pure or sinless (by nature)'.

अधात्काक: पुरोडाष्ठांश्व च लिहया)विस्तथा।
स्वाम्यं च न स्यात्कलस्मष्ठिचत्प्रवर्तेताधरोत्तरम्।।21।।
सर्वो दण्ड जितो लोको दुर्लभो हि ष्ठुचिर्नर:।
दण्डस्य हि भयात्सर्वं जगद् भोगाय कल्पते।।22।।(Manu, 7:21-22)

The lower ones tend to usurp the places of the higher. People are prone to interfere with the rights of others and violate morals and manners. This is certainly not to say that in India there was no golden age of Saturn (or Kornos) as mentioned in Greek mythology (an age defined by pristine purity and bliss). The Mahabharata precedes the dogmas of Father Lactantius and other Christian theologists by over a millennium when we find Mahabharata saying: at first there was neither state nor ruler, neither punishment nor anybody to exercise it. The people used to protect one another through innate righteousness (Dharma) and sense of justice. But as among the stoics and canonists, the 'fall' of mankind is accounted for in India also on the basis of a postulate of sins, the loss of true religion, moha, stupidity and such vices.

न वै राज्यं न राजा*सीन्न च दण्डो न दाण्डिक:।
धर्मेणैव प्रजा: सर्वा रक्षन्ति स्म परस्परम्।।14।।
पाल्यमानास्तथान्योन्यं नरा धर्मेण भारत।
खेदं परमुपाजग्मुस्ततस्तान् मोह आविष्ठात्।।15।।

....

....

विप्लुते नरलोके वै ब्रह्म चैव ननाष्ठा ह।
न ष्टाच्च ब्रह्मणो राजन् धर्मो नाष्ठामथागमत्।।21(*Shanti Parva*, 59:14-21)

On the whole, therefore, it is not a roseate romantic conception of human tendencies and instincts that the Mahabharata offers. We read in the Smriti Parva, 'by nature men tend to overthrow one another. Left to itself, the whole world would be in a mess' like a devil's workshop. As a rule, men are used to behave like creatures that cannot see one another when the sun and the moon do not shine or like 'fish in the shallow waters' or like 'birds in places safe from molestation' where they can fly at one another's throats in a suicidal strife. Men, we are told, normally acknowledge only one right, and that is the right of might. The wives, children, and food of the weak are liable to be seized perforce by the strong. 'Murder, confinement and persecution constitute the eternal lot of the propertied classes'. The very phrase, 'This is mine (*mamedam*), may be lost from the vocabulary, and *Mamatva* or ownership become extinct'.

The natural tendency of human relation, again, is towards sexual promiscuity. The formation of marriage alliances or of stable societies is not instinctively prompted in man as he 'is' (his natural state). And if possible, he would shirk even agriculture, commerce and other means of livelihood, preferring a state of slothful ease and the primrose path of dalliance (*Shanti Parva,* 68: 10-11, 14-15, 18-21).

In the political anthropology of the Mahabharata such is the natural man or man as nature made him. Therefore, instead of postulating with the writer of Emile that 'all things are good as their author made them, we must also see that everything degenerates in the hands of man', or finding reason to complain of 'what man has made of man'. The political theorists of ancient India set a high premium on the institutions and conventions that make up the civilization. In fact, as they say it is to 'educate' man out of the deplorable mire of primitive license and beastly freedom that government has been instituted. The state is designed to correct human vices or restrain them and open out the avenues to a fuller and higher life. And all this is possible only because of Danda (Sarkar, 513).

The Doctrine of Danda

In all discussions of political theory therefore, the doctrine of Danda occupies the foremost place. Some writers have even termed their treatises on politics and statecraft as Dandaniti or the science of Danda. In the Manu Samhita no other category is calculated to command greater attention than the Danda.

तस्यार्थे सर्वभूतानां गोप्तारं धर्ममात्मजम्।ब्रह्मतेजोमयं दण्डमसृजत्पूर्वमीश्वरः।।14।।
देवदानवगन्धर्वा रक्षांसि पन्नगोरगाः।ते*पि भोगाय कल्पन्ते दण्डेनैव
निपीडिताः।।23।।(Manu, 7:14-23)

For, is not Danda 'divine', God's own son, the protector of all beings as powerful as law itself? Indeed, it makes all created beings stick to their respective duties (*SwaDharma*). This is like the 'virtue' of Plato or 'functions' of the neo-Hegelian philosophers like F.H. Bradley (1846-1924), Bernard Bosanquet (1848-1923) and Benedetto Croce (1866-1952), and it makes them cooperate with one another in procuring the enjoyment (*bhoga*) or happiness of all (Sarkar, 1921:88). The division of travail (of work) of which Durkheim speaks is brought about by Danda as per the prescriptions of Manu. Further, it governs, protects, and watches; and last but not the least, it is identical with law. To crown it all, the whole world is rectified by Danda and even the gods and demigods are subject to its authority.

Danda as interpreted by Manu is obviously the very principle of omnipotence, comparable to the *majestas* of Jean Bodin (1530-1596) or the *Summa potestas* (highest power) of Hugo Grotius (founder of modern natural law theory: 1583-1645). It is the abstraction of that power whose concrete embodiment is Aiswarya (Lordship), Swamitva (ownership) or sovereignty in a state which is explained by John Neville Figgis (1866-1919) as the real 'divine right' of kings. It is absolute with jurisdiction over all and it is not controlled by any entity. To use a very recent category Danda is the most important feature of *staats rason* (reason of state), an expression of *Machtpolitik* (power politics) and marked by *autolimitazione* (self-limitation) in the sense of Georg Jellinek (1851-1911).

In the Hindu political thought, Danda is a two-edged sword and cuts both ways. On the one hand, it is a terror to the people and is a corrective of social abuses. It is a moralizer, purifier, and civilizing agent. As the Nitisar (Kamandaka, II, 40.2) observes, it is by the administration of Danda that the state can be saved from a reversion to Matsya-Nyaya and utter annihilation, and it is by Danda that people are set right. It is through fear of punishment, according to *Sukranitisar* (IV: 1) that people become 'virtuous' and refrain from committing aggression or indulging in falsehood. Danda is efficacious, moreover, in causing the cruel to become mild and the wicked to give up wickedness. It can subdue even beasts and it frightens the thieves and terrifies the enemies into submission as tributaries, demoralizes all those who are wayward. It is also good for preceptors and can bring them to their senses, should they happen to be addicted to an extra dose of vanity or become unmindful of their own duties. Finally, it is the foundation of civic life, being the great reserve of all virtues and all the 'methods and means of statecraft' would be fruitless without a judicious exercise of Danda. Its use as a beneficent agency in social life is therefore unequivocally recommended by Sukra (Sarkar, 514).

But, on the other hand, Danda is also the most potent instrument of danger to the ruler himself. The improper administration of Danda, says Kamandak, leads to the fall of the ruler. Manu does not hesitate to declare that Danda would smite the king who deviates from his duty, from his 'station in life'. It would smite his relatives too along with his castles, territories, and possessions (Manu, VII: 28-30).

दण्डो हि सुमहत्तोजो दुर्धरष्ठचख्नतात्मभि:। धर्माद्विचलितं हन्ति नष्टपमेव सबान्धवम्।।28।।
ततो दुर्गं च राज़्ट्रं च लोकं च सचराचरम्। अन्तरिक्षगतांष्ठचैव मुनीन्देवांष्ठच पीडयेत्।।29।।
सो*सहायेन मूढ़ेन लुब्धेनाख्नतबुि)ना। न ष्टाक्यो न्यायतो नेतुं सद्रेन विज़येज़ु च।।30।। (Manu, 7:28-30)

The common weal depends, therefore, on the proper exercise of *summa potestas*, the *Aiswarya*, the *staatsrasan* as Manu would not allow any ill-disciplined man to be the administrator of Danda. The greatest amount of wisdom accrued from the 'help of councilors and others become the essential pre-condition for handling this instrument. And here is the logical check on the eventual absolutism of the *Dandadhar* (Punisher) in the theory of sovereignty as developed in ancient India. In the two-edged sword of Danda, we encounter on the one hand, *staatsrason* (interest of the state) and on the other, *sithickkeit* (morality, virtue, Dharma etc.). The conception of this eternal polarity in societal existence is one of the fundamental contributions of political philosophy of the ancient Indian to the human thought (Sarkar, 514).

According to Shanti Parva, property (ownership) does not exist in the non-state (Matsya-Nyaya). In the non-state man can possess or enjoy, but they do not own. Essence of property consists in *mamatva* or *swatva*, that is, ownership. It is one's ownness that underlies the magic of property. To be able to say *mamedan* (this is mine) about something constitutes the very soul of owning or appropriation. This proprietary consciousness is created in men for the first time by the state through its sanctions and Danda (Mahabharat, XII: 68.13-29). In Danda rests the very foundation of human liberty and progress. This is the standpoint of Hindu political philosophy as well as of modern idealism in European philosophy (Redano, 278-82).

Dharma and the State

Property is the first acquisition of man through the state. His second acquisition is Dharma. Doctrine of Dharma is like the doctrine of *mamatva*, an essential factor in the theory of the state, and both have their foundation in the doctrine of Danda.

Danda is a very elastic term. It has more than one meaning. It really admits of almost all the ambiguities associated with the term 'Law' as analyzed by Thomas Erskine Holland (1835-1926) in his jurisprudence. For the purpose of political theory, we may confine ourselves to the import of Dharma as law, justice, and duty, as somewhat new values of life.

The doctrine of Dharma, then, enunciates three propositions: first, the state differs from the non-state as a law-giving institution; secondly, the state differs from the non-state as a justice-dispensing institution; and thirdly, the state differs from the non-state as a duty-enforcing institution.

In Matsya-Nyaya, there is no law, no justice and no duty. The state is the originator of law, justice and duty. Dharma (law) is the creation of the state and the state as such has the sanction of Danda. Theoretically, therefore, every Dharma, if it is nothing but Dharma is ipso facto, what should be called positive in the Austinian sense (John Austin: 1790-1859; known for his Theory of Sovereignty). Dharma is obeyed as Dharma only because of the coercive might of the state.

Ramsay Muir in his book, *Nationalism and Internationalism*, has remarked, "Law and Liberty are the bones and blood of western civilization and it is their conflict that marks the characteristic feature of European History. It is the strife after liberty that keeps law alive and progressive: it is the restraint of law that prevents the eager claim for liberty from ending in chaos. The two are independent. One supplements the other". Prof. Ilyas Ahmad, on the other hand, says, 'It was the absence of liberty in the east that made Eastern governments irresponsible. Despotism and their law mean tyranny' (Ahmad, 189). But this statement is not true. In fact, there ought to be no antithesis between law and liberty. A progressive law is the very condition of liberty and law means a system of regulations which ought to be obeyed by the community, not because it is a divine command or the will of an irresponsible master, but because the community feels that it would be to its advantage to do so. Unquestioned submission is not obedience. It is slavery. It is the spirit of criticism (which is in other terms liberty) that forces law to keep pace with the times. The law ought not to be static and liberty ought not to be its sleeping partner. Law would be dynamic and flexible in character as liberty ought to be a living spirit, eternally vigilant, and a constant guide.

From the very beginning of speculation, the conception of law has been associated with the conception of the state and as such the philosophy of law has been related to political philosophy. Political Science is said to be related to jurisprudence–The Science of Law. Political Science deals with government and its organisation, and law- legal machinery is but a part of its mechanism. Jurisprudence has often been regarded as a branch of Political Science, for the law whether it is statutory or controversial, civil or criminal, private or public, falls in every sense within the scope of the state and therefore of Political Science Jurisprudence. This in its widest application has always been coterminous with legal philosophy. And legal philosophy is much more than analytical jurisprudence which is but a part of it. Jurisprudence in its restricted sense deals with formulated law. Legal philosophy is a critical study of formulated laws. Jurisprudence determines what is lawful. Legal philosophy considers the problem of the nature of law. Jurisprudence considers the structure and function of law. Legal philosophy traces the underlying principles and causes of law. Jurisprudence centers itself on the consent of law. Legal philosophy takes into consideration the spirit of law (Berolzheimer, 183-84).

As Krause has said, "Legal philosophy is the science of law and state in pure reason", or as *Lession* puts it, "it is the doctrine of the realization of the idea of the good in human will; and therefore it is a vision of Ethics, it touches economics and it deals with the promise of the state." It is the systematic study of the origin, content and import of conception of law in connection with the considerations of the principles of government. As Roscoe Pound puts it, it has forever taken a leading role in the study of human institutions and this can be easily seen from the five-fold task which Mc Donald says legal philosophy must always attempt. In the first place, it must trace the origin of law to its sources in human nature. Secondly, it must connect law with the society and circumstances of the times in which it originates, or exists. Thirdly, it must analyze the ultimate elements of law such as: it should show if force is an essential element. Fourthly, it must state the laws of its growth; and finally it must discriminate between Ethics and Law.

Origin of Law

In this sense, the philosophy of law has always been unquestionably mixed up with political philosophy as the latter has also been intertwined with the philosophy of law; and as political philosophy has always been conditioned by time, place or conditions of political phenomena in the same sense legal philosophy has been determined by prevailing circumstances.

The theorists have recognized the following four schools of law: firstly, as Bryce tells us, there is the school which has always found the origin of law in compulsion or fear. The Sophists in Greece were the first to regard justice as the interest of the strong and as such the laws of the state were based on the peculiar interests of the governing class and many had no choice but to obey them because of compulsion. Laws in this sense were nothing but commands of political superiors to political inferiors. This view of law was taken up and developed in modern times by Bodin, Hobbes, Bentham and Austin and has come to be known as the Analytical School of Jurisprudence.

Secondly, there is another school which has found the origin of law in agreement or reason. The Greeks regarded law as the common spiritual substance of the community, the result of common agreement. Even Socrates is said to have refused to break the laws simply because he had made a covenant with them to obey them. In modern times, Rousseau made use of this view and defined law as an act of general will, the resolution of the whole people. Similarly, in Kant, the law is an expression of the legislative will of an individual. But side by side with this view of law as embodying 'reason', there developed from the very beginning a tendency to look upon nature, in some sense, as the source of reason. Thus, the Greeks differentiated between conventional and natural. The state and laws were, to them, right by convention and not by nature. The Romans similarly began to call enacted law-*Lex* and law by nature-*Ius.* This tradition of regarding laws of nature as embodiments of reason continued throughout the middle ages and was made use of in modern times till the fall of Contract Theory that eventually led to its abandonment. Nevertheless, the idea of regarding the laws of nature as the embodiment of highest moral principles has led to examination and justification of laws on the basis of their ethical validity. This is the Philosophical School of jurisprudence.

Thirdly, there is the Historical School of Law which does not regard law as the command of the sovereign, but that which has grown in the course of time. They trace the origin of law in the customs, traditions and habits and manners of the people. Savigny (Friedrich Carl Von) was the chief exponent of this school, and Sir Henry Maine its great luminary.

Fourthly, there is Pragmatic School of Law which bases laws on the satisfaction of our social wants and regards them as expression of our social solidarity. Leon Duguit is the greatest representative of this view.

Purpose of Law

A distinguished American Legal theorist Roscoe Pound (1870-1964) has explained the purposes of law in the following ways: firstly, laws have been made to keep the peace in the given society and peace has always meant the maintenance of status quo. This was true of Greece where the chief function of law was to maintain the balance in the social contribution in so far as everybody had an appointed function to perform. This was also true of Rome and similarly of the middle Ages.

Secondly, laws are necessary to provide what we call an equality of opportunity to all individuals. This phase begins with the 16th century. The ancient and the medieval conceptions of law were based on natural inequalities of individuals. The sixteen century conception came to be based on equality, meaning like freedom of will and the power of conscious employment of one's faculties (inherent in all men). It went therefore against traditional restrictions.

Thirdly, this conception of law as the maintenance of natural equality easily passed into the maintenance of natural rights, that is, it was no longer directed against any traditional restrictions on the personality of individual: it asserted personality itself as its basis. It took its stand on the free moral worth of the individual who should assert himself to his maximum with due regard to the good of community. Lastly, the end of law has come to center on individual wants, rather than individual wills or personalities. People emphasize the maximum satisfaction of wants and not the maximum self assertion. Pound has noted twelve different senses in which the term 'Law' has been used:

(a) Laws are divinely acclaimed rules for human action. This was true of Mosaic Law... The Ten Commandments and is still true of the Muslim Law.

(b) Laws represent a tradition of the old customs which has proved acceptable to the Gods and hence point the way in which men may walk with safety. This was true of Egyptian law as well as that of the Greeks.

(c) Laws are the recorded wisdom of the wise men (of old age) that learned the safe course or the divinely approved course for human conduct. This was true of Ancient India and, in fact, is more or less universally true of patriarchal state of civilization wherever it existed.

(d) Laws represent a philosophically discovered system of principles which express the nature of things, to which therefore man ought to conform. This was the basis of the laws made by the *jurisconsults* of Rome.

(e) Laws are a body of ascertainments and declarations of an eternal and immutable moral code. Such were the so called laws of nature.

(f) Laws are a body of agreements among men in a politically organised society based on their relations with each other. This was particularly true of Greece.

(g) Laws are a reflection of the divine reason governing the universe ... a reflection of that part which determines the 'ought' addressed by that reason to human beings as moral entities in distinction from the 'must' which it addresses to the rest of the creation. This was the view of St.Thomas Aquinas (1225-1274) in the middle ages.

(h) Laws are the commands of the sovereign authority in politically organised societies which tell how men should conduct themselves, therein, resting ultimately on whatever basis was held to be behind the authority of that sovereign. This was true of Greece and Rome and is still true of our modern analytical jurisprudence.

(i) Laws are a system of precepts discovered by human experience whereby the individual human being will/may realize the most complete freedom possible consistent with the freedom of will of others. This forms the basis of Historical School of Law.

(j) Laws are a system of principles discovered philosophically, and developed in detail by jurists' writings and judicial discussions, whereby the external life of man is measured by reason, whereby the will of the individual in action is harmonized with those of the fellow men. This was the chief contribution of Bentham and the basis of many a cases of law since the 19th century.

(k) Laws are a body of rules imposed on man in society by the dominant class for the time being in furtherance of its own interests. This view has been chiefly held by those who have studied law and society from t h e economic point of view. The economic interpretation of history has made the state a class state, and its law, a class law.

(1) Laws are the dictates of economic and social laws with respect to the conduct of men in society, discovered by observation, expressed in precepts and worked out through human experience of what would work and what would not in the administration of justice. (Pound, 60-67)

Holland remarks that law is that which is not necessarily commanded, but which can also be enforced. Holland defines Law as 'a general rule of external human action enforced by a sovereign political authority'. This will apply to all kinds of laws: permissive, constitutional or international. Law in this sense is more than command. It is an expression of common will, an epitome of social solidarity and a manifestation of the moral idea of right.In short, we can say that

a) Law is a rule of human action which means that the order or uniformities of the physical world (as distinguished from the world of man) do not come under its scope.

b) As a general rule, it is not a particular order to an individual.

c) It must relate to external action. Thoughts of men, their motives and intentions cannot be controlled.

d) It must be enforced by a determinate authority and this authority must be sovereign. Thus, the sovereignty of God (who is also determinate does not come in for the sovereign), a sovereign must be a political sovereign, that is, a human being.

Dharma as Law and Morality Combined

In all primitive societies and early civilizations, religion, law and morality could not be differentiated. In Egyptian morals 'truth' was the fundamental element, and truth and charity were also the cardinal principles on which law was based. 'Truth' was the law according to which verdicts were pronounced in divine court of the dead and so was the case in human courts. For this reason, the presiding officer of the highest Egyptian tribunal was made to wear the badge of office called truth suspended from his neck (Berolzheimer, 3).

Similarly law and morals cannot be separated in the Vedic Aryan civilization. The word Dharma particularly includes both law and morals. Service and sacrifice to Gods, obedience to state, love of family and the purity of social life could only be explained through Dharma. In this way Ilyas Ahmad clarifies that according to Berolzheimer, it becomes the sum total of pious duties. The four commandments, together with five injunctions form the core of Aryan ethics. These four commandments are:

Thou shalt honour the Gods; thou shalt honour thy parents; thou shalt honour thy country; thou shalt honour the guest especially when he stands in need of protection.

To these are added the five injunctions: "Thou shalt keep thyself clean; thou shalt hold thy senses in check, in particular not violate; thou shalt not kill; thou shalt not steal; thou shalt not lie" (Berolzheimer, 38-39; Ahmad, 203).

The Greeks also did not differentiate between law and morals. Life in the Polis was a life of virtue and the great purpose of the Polis itself was a moral life, a good life. In Plato, the state is a moral being and every individual has to look after social morality. The laws are expression of disinterested reason so that justice in the community may be assured. Similarly, in Aristotle, the great function of the state and its laws remains the attainment of a life of virtue. It is only in the city of Rome that we find a complete separation of law and morals. The reason was that Rome was an agricultural country and its laws were made to suit the daily wants of its citizens so that there was no necessity of seeking an ethical basis for law; but when the city state began to grow and other people came under its sway, the Greek ideas of natural law with its corollaries of good conscience and equity made their appearance and the *Jus Gentium* ('Law of Nations') came into being. Roman law came to be based on ethical foundations, and since then the partnership of law and morals has seldom been abandoned.

Having gone through the meaning of words, Danda, Dharma and Law, we can summarize that in ancient European theory, law is the embodiment of eternal justice. According to *Demostenes* (4th century B.C.), laws are the gifts of the Gods and the discovery of sages. In Aristotle's conception, law is the rule of God and reason. Stoics like Cicero and Seneca believed that law lay in the hearts of all men. The doctrine of 'natural law', of law as the 'kings of all things', was maintained by jurists, such as *Guius* and others, whose views are codified in the *Digest of Justinian.* It was the theory also of Celsus and other church fathers. In medieval European (Teutonic) theory, so far the theory which is independent of the tradition of Roman jurisprudence, law was not 'made' or created, but it existed as a part of the national, local or tribal life (Carlyle, I:235; Comme, 84-100; Sarkar, 516). The modern theory of law in Europe may be said to have originated in the 16th and 17th centuries. With Bodin and Hobbes with their analysis of sovereignty has since become classical. However, Austin is recognised as the father of analytical jurisprudence. According to this view, law is the command of the sovereign enforced by a sanction.

Thus there are two theories of law: first, law as uncreated or original, existing either as a part of universal human conscience and taught by 'natural reason' or as a custom among the people; and secondly, law as created by law-makers, as something which is to be obeyed, not because it is just, good or eternal, but because it has been enacted by the state. Both these conceptions are to be found among the speculations of political philosophers of ancient India.

The ethical conception of law as dictated by conscience that is, as *jus natural*, has a long tradition in Indian thought. In the *Brihadaranyaka Upanishad* (1.4.14) law is identical with truth and as powerful as the king. It is of course the creation of God. Brahman (God), as told, was not strong enough, so to compensate the lack of strength he created the most excellent Dharma. There is nothing higher than the law. Thenceforth even a weak man rules the stronger with the help of the law (as with the help of a king). Thus, the law is what is called the truth. And, if a man declares what is truth, they say, he declares the law; and if he declares the law, they say, he declares what is true. Thus, both are the same.

According to Apastamba, law is what is universally approved in all countries by men of three twice born castes who have been properly obedient (to their teacher) and who are aged, of subdued senses, and neither given to avarice nor hypocrisy (*Dharma Sastra*; 1.7.20.8). In the Manu Samhita again, law is whatever is practiced and cherished at heart by the virtuous and the learned who are devoid of prejudices and passions.

विद्वद्भ: सेवित: सद्भिर्नित्यमद्वेषरागिभि:।
हृदयेनाभ्यनुज्ञातो यो धर्मस्तं निबोधत: (Manu, 2.1)

Vasistha Dharmashastra (1.5.6) and Baudhayana Dharmasutra (1.1.1.4-6) also hold the view that law is the practice of the *shishta*, that is, those whose hearts are free from the desire. The *shishtas*, that is, passionless and unavaricious persons are obviously analogous to the sages of Demonsthenes.

The sacred law has been settled by the revealed texts and by the tradition (of the sages). On failure of (rules given in) these (two sources) the practice of the *shishtas* has authority. But he whose heart is free from desires (is called) a *shishta* (Vasistha: 1.4-6). The practice of the *shishtas* stands third.The fourth *shishtas* are those who are free from envy, free from pride, contended with a store of grain sufficient for ten days, free from covetousness, and free from hypocrisy, arrogance, greed, perplexity and anger.

Shishtas are those who, in accordance with the sacred law, have studied the Veda along with the appendages, know how to draw inferences from that and are able to adduce proofs perceptible by the senses from the revealed texts (Baudhayan, 1.1.1.4-6).

In the *Yagyavalkya Samhita* (*Yagyavalkya Smriti,* 1.7) law is defined as Sadachara, that is, the practice or conduct of good men, what seems pleasant or good to one's self, and the desire that springs from mature consideration. In the Vyavahara Darpan, law is described as something eternal and self existent, the king of kings, far more powerful and right than themselves. In these two definitions, we have once more, the oriental counterpart of Greek, Stoic, Romans and *Patristic* conception of law as morality (Sarkar, 517).

In Hindu analysis, Dharma also came to be defined as positive law. The conception of law as *Rajyam Aagya* in Kautiliya's language, that is, as command *Rajyam Aagya* enforced by sanction, finds clear expression in the writings of Narada, Sukra and Jaimini. In the Narada Smriti (Narada Smriti, 1,2), it is said that the performance of duty having fallen into disuse, positive law (vyavahara) has been introduced, and that the king as superintending the law is known as *Danda-dhara* or wielder of Danda, the power to punish. The sanction is definitely mentioned in the Sukra Nitisar (*Sukra Nitisar,* 1) according to which the sovereign should categorically state in his command that he would surely destroy by severe punishment those offenders who after having heard his decrees would act contrary to them. In order that the law may be seriously recognised as command, Sukra stipulates that the greatest amount of publicity should be given to it. For instance, it is the duty of the sovereign to have the laws publicly announced by sounding state drum or have them inscribed in esplanades as written notices. The documents embodying these commands (Shasan-patra) are to bear the king's signature, date etc. Laws (thus being promulgations of the state, as mentioned in the Sukra Nitisar) help the king become the maker of the age, the cause of time, and of good and evil practice. Since the ruler is the dictator of virtues and vices, people make it a point to practice law by which the ruler is satisfied with. Besides, as the law is upheld, by sanction, it can be understood why Sukra advises the sovereign to make use of this terrible weapon (Sarkar, 517) in order to maintain the people (each one in his proper sphere). The same idea of positive law is expressed by Jaimini in the very definition of Dharma. The Mimansa-Sutra declares चोदनालक्षणोर्थो धर्मः (*Mimansa Sutra*, 1.1.2). Dharma is that desired object which is characterised by command. Jaimini has also examined the reason why that which is determined by a command should be obligatory. He analyses the reason as lying in the fact that 'the relation between the word of command and the purpose to which it is directed is eternally efficacious'.

Thus, law is not purely the will of the stronger. It is a rule of abstract justice or right reason. It is not fixed but it is always growing and changing, thus attaining a perfect harmony with the highest moral inspiration of men... not sacred and unchangeable and therefore not static but dynamic, always meeting the demands of the situation (Ahmad, 204). Law is the child of morality, not morality the offspring of law. The theocratic states have always maintained the latter view and therefore their law has always remained unprogressive. In modern society, law tries to adapt itself to the varying and growing demands of public morality. Law is not a mere command from one side: it is for the common advantage. Hence, it is not mere force or fear of punishment that obliges men to obey it; it is clear duty of every man to cooperate in its enforcement, as it is meant for common good. It is in no sense to be evaded, but one protected, maintained and respected because it is a moral obligation. Because it is a thing of common concern, people no longer emphasise the sovereignty which it issues, but the fact that the wisest members among us seek to have a hand in its making and enacting for the benefit of humanity as a whole.

Pujya Sri Chandrashekharendra Saraswati Swami has very clearly elaborated the word Dharma. In his book *Hindu Dharma* he writes that Dharma is that which makes us lead a disciplined life so far as this world is concerned. The Brahman is related to the other world (Paraloka). The ordinary man (jiva) arrives at the stage in which he is capable of inquiring the Brahman only through the pathway of Dharma which is constituted by the pathway of *Karma* or action. The Purvamimansa which constitutes the Karma Marg (Path of Karma) is an inquiry into Dharma and into leading a life according to Dharmashastras. And the purpose of Uttarmimansa or Vedanta is inquiry into the Brahman and realising it. Although the Vedanta was taught extensively in the schools, it did not mean anything more than taking an interest in the subject. The students were not to be immediately involved in the pursuit of the goal of Vedanta. When a student became a grihastha or householder, he lived a worldly life, in accordance with the tenets of Dharma. It was only after he became mature, he was qualified for full involvement in Atmashastra (the Atmashastra that he had learned earlier merely for outward knowledge and not for actual realisation). Narada was not an ordinary being. Because of his extraordinary nature he was inspired to know and realise the Brahman soon after completing his education. He passed from the brahmacharyasram itself (without becoming a household) to the state where he was qualified for Brahma-Jnana. Narada apart, the type of education was such that an ordinary man did not stray into aDharma (unrighteousness). By adhering to Dharma–and with devotion–he became interested in Atma-Vidya (Saraswati, 78).

It is perhaps because of his understanding of the instinct of man and the need for human actions to be inspired by Dharma that the famous poet Nilakantha Dikshit said that if, even after born a man, one does not have any sense of discrimination, it would be better for such a person to be born an animal, since animals are not subject to law that controls the senses. It is further said that our rishsis knew that 'all except God will perish'. That is why one must be cautious that man with his capacity for discrimination must be able to grasp the truth that Atma is not different from the Brahma. The Atma has neither a beginning nor an end. Every individual goes through a succession of births and determined by his Karma. He either sinks further and further down or rises further and further up. But in life after life the Atma remains untainted.

Dharma and the Social Order

So far we have analysed the concept of Dharma as central to a disciplined life. We have also seen how it is in the root of the distinction between state and non-state nature. The most important and original contribution of our authors to the idea of the social order consists in their development of the late Vedic concept of law (Dharma). Dharma is being held the crown of the social structure under divine dispensation and is identical with the abstract principle of truth. The authors conceived Dharma explicitly for the first time in the concrete sense of the sum total of the distinctive duties of the constituent units of the social system. These units were comprised of the four castes (varnas) and the four orders (ashramas) as well as the individual king. This involves the conception of a law of social order which is supreme over its members. The Dharmasutras seek to enforce the observance of this principle of Dharma by old and new sanctions.

The world in which we live, the moves that guide our daily behaviour and the aspirations we envision for the future have been shaped not by the conquistadores of history but by a handful of great thinkers in the fields of philosophy, religion, economics and political theory. In the fundamental sense, the society will come not out of laboratories of science or the halls of legislation but out of the minds of creative geniuses in these ideational fields. Emerson, an American scholar, very appropriately said, 'Not he is great, who can alter matter, but he who can alter my state of mind.' These are the people who have shaped Dharma–the law which controls the working of the society and humanity since the human being came into existence.

But despite the importance of these great thinkers, they appear to have been relegated to a secondary position in our times. Perhaps this is a result of materialism of our age–our preoccupation with the production and consumption of material possessions and our emphasis upon activity and achievement, rather than upon contemplation and reflection about such matters as our goals and purposes in life. Once an educated person was defined as an individual who voluntarily indulged in more thinking than what was required for his own survival. The scholar championing this definition also declared that by this standard there are only a handful of educated people.

Meaning of Dharma

Justice P.S. Mishra in his Foreword to *Hindu Dharma* points to a difference of opinion even among the learned as to the meaning of the word Dharma. The word is derived from 'dhr' to uphold, sustain or nourish. The seers often use it as the mental perception and realisation of God. The Taittiriya Upnishad also uses it with 'satya' and 'Dharma'. It exhorts students to speak the truth, and practice Dharma (सत्यम वद् धर्मम् चर). According to Sankara Bhagvatpada, 'satya' means speaking the truth and 'Dharmam' means translating it (satya) into action.

सत्यमिति यथाष्ठास्त्रर्थता स एव अनुज्ठीयमानः धर्माणामा भवति।

In this connection, the explanation given by K. Balasubrahmania Aiyar is relevant: "An analysis of the significance of these three words *Rta, Satya and Dharma* brings out clearly to us the fundamental basis of Dharma as the ideal for the individual, while Rta denotes the mental perception and realisation of truth; Satya denotes the exact true expression in words of truth as perceived by the mind, Dharma is the observance, in the conduct of life, of truth. In fact, Dharma is the way of life which translates into action the truth perceived by the man of insight as expressed by him truly. In short, Rta is truth in thought, Satya is truth words and Dharma is truth in deed".

To sages, Dharma and satya are inter-changeable words and their goal is–as it has always been–to rise higher so as to realise Him who alone is the Truth. For them there is no pursuit higher than that of practising truth in thought, word and deed.

'Bhutahitam' is Sri Sankaracharya's answer to the question (that he himself raised), 'Kim satyam'? It means that truth (or truthfulness) is what is spoken for the well-being of all living beings. To the question: 'Ko Dharmah'? His answer is, अभिमतो यः ष्ठिाज्टानाम् निजकुलीनम्। It means that Dharma is that which is determined by the elders and by learned people.

Of the four Purusharthas or aims of life, Dharma is always mentioned as the first, Artha second, Kama third, and Moksha as the last. The four stanzas of Mahabharata that together go by the name of 'Bharat-Savitri' contain these profound truths: Dharma is eternal but neither happiness nor sorrow is eternal; the atma is ever-lasting but not that which embodies it; and from Dharma arise Artha and Kama. They also contain Vedavyasa's lamentation: 'With uplifted arms spring Artha and Kama. Why is Dharma then not practised?' According to Sri Saraswati, the Mahaswami-Dharma is our only protection (Mishra, IX).

Duty of the King

It was looked upon as the duty of the king in ancient India to see that his country was not ravaged by epidemics. The king was primarily held responsible for national calamities. In the language of Sanskrit politics, this truth was expressed by saying that for the sins of the king, the people suffered. If the king by his avarice or policy had kept the mass of the people always in the state of Semi-Starvation such a people would fall on easy prey to all diseases; for which the king was primarily responsible. If through neglect and want of foresight, the king failed to sink wells, dig tanks, and erect reservoirs of water to fall back upon in seasons of drought resulting from famines. It was said that the sin of the raja had caused the famine. In short, while all private sufferings were rightly attributed to the sin of the individual, public calamities were attributed to the sin of the king and the king alone; and never to any individual sin.

The ancient sages of India did not rest content with the surface causes of things. They penetrated deeper and with the universal formula of monism they declared that all partial laws whether laws of nature or laws of morality–the Ritam and Satyam–were manifestations of one supreme law; and were intricately interwoven with each other. One could not break with impunity a moral law without bringing confusion in the working of the physical laws–for both these laws were worked by the same divine agency of the Devas. The harmony of seasons would be broken if there was discord in the moral world. A selfish and self-seeking people must suffer from the whims of a fickle and variable nature. Even the history of Hebraic nations affords many proofs to this truth. The moral sins of Sodom and Gomorrah brought about the physical destruction of those cities. The same was the case with Babylone and Nineveh. In modern times, the destruction of San Fransisco is attributed to the same cause-moral occupation by some pious souls.

A wise king therefore looks, not only to the physical

welfare of his people, but to their moral welfare also. A government that neglects the religion and moral education of its people suffer from calamities, if there be any truth in the saying that Ritam and Satyam are the same physical and moral laws but different aspects of the one single law.

The following saying by Bhisma from *Shanti Parva* shows that calamities have their roots in the maladministration of the state (*Shanti Parva,* 141:9-10):

राजमूला महाबाहो योगक्षेमसुवष्ढटय:।प्रजासु व्याधयष्ठचैव मत्वां च भयानि च।
ख्रतं त्रेतां द्वापरं च कलिष्ठच भरतर्ज़भ।राजमूला इति मतिर्मम नास्त्यत्र संष्ठाय:।।

O mighty-armed one, the peace and prosperity of subjects, profuse and seasonable rain, diseases, death, and other calamities, all depend on the king. I (Bhishma) have no doubt also in this that the setting of Krita, Dvapara, Treta and Kali, all depend on the King's conduct.

Thus a virtuous king brings Krita Yuga (the Golden Age) among his people and a tyrant the contrary. The four ages also are nothing but symbols of good and bad administration by the king.

Thus in chapter 69 of the same Parva, we find: 'When the king rules according to 'Dandaniti' (The Constitution laid down by Brahma for the state) the Krita age is said to flourish'. But when the king violates any portion of the Constitution, other ages set in according to the extent or degree of violation.

दण्डनीति परित्यज्य यदा कात्स्न्र्येन भूमिप:।
प्रजा: क्लिष्ठनात्ययोगेन प्रवर्तेत तदा कलि:।। (*Shanti Parva*, 69:91)

Dandaniti— The Megna Carta

This Dandaniti was the real Magna Carta of our liberties in ancient times. The mode how this constitution was first obtained from Brahma is placed in chapter 59 of the Shanti Parva of the Mahabharat. The Rishis Brahaspati and Sukra abridged the voluminous works of the Brahma. All kings, however despotic, were bound by this constitution and there are cases recorded in the Mahabharata where the kings got into trouble by their disregard of the Constitution. Thus King Vena was the first who was killed by the Brahmana because he broke the Divine Constitution. 'Vena, a slave of anger and malice became impious and tyrannical towards all creatures. Brahmavadin Rishis killed him.' When the king abandoning the Constitution in its entirety, oppresses his subjects, then the age that sets in, is called Kali: then diseases appear and men die untimely. Wives become widows and people become heartless. The clouds do not rain in season nor do crops grow in abundance (*Shanti Parva,* 69:91-92).

This also shows that calamities are due to maladministration that is they rage when the sovereign does not act constitutionally.

If the sovereign acts unconstitutionally, then even the seasons get out of joint; summer months become cold and vice-versa. There are droughts, floods and pestilential epidemics (*Shanti Parva,* 90:37). In modern times, weakness is considered a sin but not so in Ancient India. We find that the weakness is a real elemental force in which everything is finally established and the eyes of the meek, of the Muni and of the venomous snake should be considered as unbearable. Do not therefore meet the weak as you would meet an enemy. Meekness is more powerful than even the greatest power. That power which is scorched by weakness is absolutely rooted out (*Shanti Parva,* 91:17).

Justice P.B. Gajendragadkar has elaborately explained the role of law in the modern context in the article "Majesty of Law". He remarks, "The Constitution of India heralds the birth of a new and historical epoch in the history of India. It has pledged the country the task of security to all its citizens-justice, social economic and political" (Gajendragadkar, 414). The ideal of a welfare state is based on the evolution of a new social philosophy. The state now accepts the responsibility of meeting all legitimate demands of social and economic justice, and meeting these demands, the state has to fight inevitably what the Beveridge Report has so picturesquely described as the 'giants of idleness, disease, squalor, and want'. In pursuit of this ideal, the state rejects the doctrine of unmitigated economic individualism and the theory of Laissez-faire on which it is founded. As Friedmann has observed, the effect of adopting a new social philosophy is the transformation of the free economic society in which the state is a glorified policeman, but otherwise a disinterested spectator, into a controlled society in which the state is an active participant in the economic and social life of the citizen (Friedmnn, 251).

In order to appreciate the expanding role of law in a modern democratic welfare state, it has become essential to reconsider the philosophy and principles of law and to redefine the rule of law itself. Mr. Justice Gajendragadkar further says that the problem posed by the planned economy of a welfare state can be reasonably solved only if the need of planning and the force of law on which it tends to rely are reconciled with the claim of individual freedom. The Majesty of the Law was never more eloquently described than by the Brhadaranyaka Upanishad. Therefore there is nothing higher than law. So a weak man controls the strong man by law, just as if by a king. Verily that which is law is truth; therefore, they say of a man who speaks the truth, 'he speaks the law', or of a man who speaks the law, 'he speaks the truth'. Verily, both these are the same thing (*Brihdaranyaka Upanishada,* 4-14).

It is true, as Maitland has observed that races and nations do not always travel by the same road and at the same rate. Even so, a comparative study of ancient laws in the world has disclosed a number of remarkable affinities. Henry Maine (1822-1888) showed, on the one hand, that legal ideas and institutions have a real course of development as much as the general and species of living creatures, and in every stage of that development, have these normal characteristics; on the other hand, he made it clear that these processes deserve and require distinct study and cannot be treated as mere incidents in the general history of the societies where they occur (Gajendragadkar, 415). The general conclusion reached by Maine with regard to the characteristics of ancient law has now been broadly accepted as correct. 'If, by any means, we can determine the early forms of jural conceptions', observed Sir Henry Maine, 'they will be invaluable to us. These rudimentary ideas are to the jurist what the primary crusts of the earth are to the geologist. They contain potentially all the forms in which law has subsequently exhibited itself' (Maine, 2-3). According to Maine, the earlier notions connected with the conception of law are those contained in the Homeric words, 'Themis' and 'Themistes'. When a king decided a dispute by a judgment, the judgment was assumed to be the result of the divine inspiration. Themistes are really the award themselves assumed to have been divinely dictated to the judges, According to Grote, 'Zeus of the human king on earth is no law-maker but a judge,' and his judgments, divinely inspired, constitute law. It is fairly certain that in the earlier stages of the human race, no trace of any legislature in modern sense of the term, or even of any author of law can be found. At that stage, law has not reached even the footing of custom, properly so called. 'It is rather a habit,' as Maine observes. It is, to render a French phrase, 'in the air'.

The next stage in the development of ancient law witnesses the transfer of authority to pronounce judgements, from king to aristocracies. Military and religious oligarchies appear on the scene and though the authority of the king was not superseded, and the judgement pronounced by the king was the result of the consultation held by the king with members of the military and religious oligarchies. Maine's theory is that in the East these aristocracies became religious, while in the West, they became civil or political (Gajendragadkar, 416). This era of aristocracies succeeding the era of the king may be regarded as a feature of the growth of law in the Indo-European family of nations. Even during this era, the aristocracies do not purport to make the laws. Their claim is based on the monopoly of the knowledge of laws giving rise to customary law. In this sense during this epoch the stage of customary law can be said to have been reached.

The study of Roman law shows that the period of customary law in due course led to the era of jurisprudence. This era may be called the era of codes. The Twelve Tables of Rome can be treated as the best representation of this era. The Twelve Tables deal rather with adjectival laws and not with substantive laws. Even during this early stage of development of ancient law, students of history notice that, whereas law tends to be stable, and seeks to make the social structure steady and enduring, changing social environment exercised pressures for a change, and an attempt appears always to have been made to bridge the gulf between the letter of the law and the needs of the changing social structure.

Justice P.B. Gajendragadkar further remarks that there is another feature of all ancient law which is very remarkable. Law does not make any distinction between religion, ethics, or morality, on the one hand, and the provision of what may be called the positive law, on the other. Though in its progress, the legal order appears to have tried to meet the new demands arising out of a multitude of unsatisfied social desires, human agency did not claim the authorship of law. Its origin continued to be divine. The Mosaic Law or Hammurabi's Code or the Manu Smriti, each one in its own way, claimed to be based upon divine inspiration. Demostsenes gave to the Athenian jury four reasons why men ought to obey the law. He said, "Men ought to obey the law because 'Laws are prescribed by God, because they were a tradition taught by wise men who knew the good old customs, because they were deductions from an eternal and immutable moral code, and because they were agreements among men, binding them because of a moral duty to keep the promises" (Pound, 22). Similarly, it is recorded that Cicero believed that justice and the whole system of social life depended upon the God and Man's belief in them. The law, according to Roman ideas, rested upon the double foundations of divine regulation and human ordinances (Vardachari, 33).

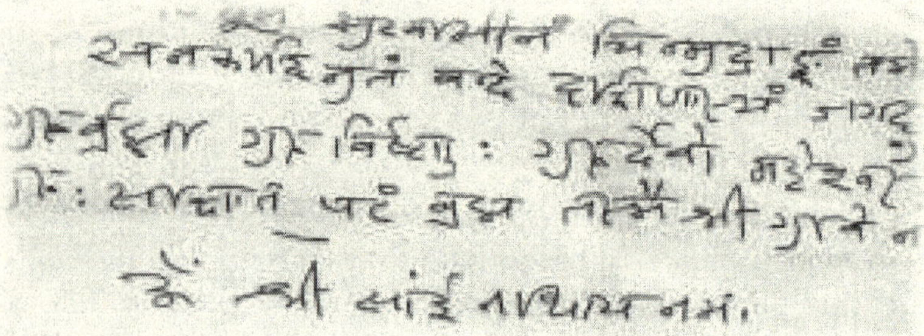

2.
The Goal of Dharma

The goal of Dharma is universal welfare. The great man who produced works on Dharmashastras did not have a trace of self-interest in them and had nothing but the thought of happiness of all creatures. These treatises are the authority on which Dharma is founded. As people find the forms of things, the image with their eyes, as they perceive sound with their ears, so we can know Dharma with the help of Dharmashastras.

The Veda (Shruti) is the root of all Dharma. After Sruti comes Smriti. The Smriti consists of the notes based on the Shruti. It is the same as the Dharmashastra. Another guide for Dharma is the example of lives of great men. The Puranas provide an account of how great men conducted themselves. There is 'sistachar' to guide us which is a set of rules derived from the lives of the virtuous people of noble character. Not every one's conduct can be a guide to us. The individual whose life is an example for the practice of Dharma must have faith in the shastras, and must live in accordance with these ordinances. Besides, he must be free from desire and anger. The conduct of such men is sistachar. Another authority or guide can be revelations made through our conscience in a state of transparency.

In matters of the self, Dharma and religion, Vedas are in the forefront as our guide. Dharmashastras come next. After Dharmashastras is the conduct of the great sages of the past. In the fourth position is the example of virtuous people of our own times. Conscience occupies the last in determining Dharma.

Pujya Saraswati teaches us that we must consult our conscience only as the last resort when we have no other means of knowing what Dharma is with reference to our actions. Why is conscience called one's "Manahsakshi"? Conscience can only be a witness, not a judge. A witness often gives false evidence. The mind, however, does not tell untruth, indeed it knows the truth of all things. ' No deceit can be hidden from the heart (mind)', says Auvvai. Conscience may be regarded as a witness. But nowadays, it is brought in as a judge in Dharmic matters also. As a witness it will give us a true report of what it sees or has seen. But on the basis of that, we cannot give a decision on 'what is just' with any finality. Guided only be conscience, every body will believe 'what I think is right'. How can this be justified as the verdict of Dharma?

It is only when there is no other way left, then you tell your mind- 'you have seen everything as a witness now, tell me your opinion'. The mind belongs to each one of us as individuals. So it cannot be detached from our selfish interests. The place it has in one's personal affairs cannot be given to it in matters of religion. On the question of Dharma the opinion of sages/seers alone is valid as they were concerned with universal welfare and transcended the state of their individual concerns (Saraswati, 121).

Wealth as Guru's Blessings

Of the four aims of life–Dharma, material acquisitions (Artha), desire (Kama) and liberation (Moksha) –we seek gratification of Kama alone (in the form of pleasure, love etc.). To satisfy our desires, we keep fighting for material objects. We must strive towards obtaining liberation through the practice of Dharma which will then end our compulsion to run after money and material goods and will lead us towards the eternal bliss (Saraswati, 115).

The Guru alone can give us the wealth, the treasure that is ever-lasting. That which does not accompany us on our departure is not wealth. True wealth is that which prevents us from returning (which means it is that wealth that liberates us from the cycle of births). It is that wealth that unites us inseparably, indissolubly, with what is eternal, the Paramatma.

This wealth called Jnana is received as the blessings from the Guru. It is imparted to us in the form of Guru's upadesha, and it neither diminishes with the passage of time nor has it to be added to by our own effort. The wealth received as a blessing from the Guru grows and makes us to grow with it.

The happiness derived from such wealth is ephemeral. The jnana received as a blessing from the Guru alone is 'nityaananda' or eternal bliss.

No amount of devotion on our part will be commensurate with the great good that is bestowed on us by our Guru. That is why it is said that we must be as devoted to the Guru as we must be to be the Iswara.

One must have the same high devotion for the Guru as one has for Iswara, so says the verse. (The verse is from Svetasvatara Upanishad though it also occurs in the Gurugita): स्य देवे परा भद्रिः, यथा देवे तथा गुरौ। तस्येसे कथिते ह्यार्थत प्रकाष्ठान्ते महात्मभिः।। (as mentioned by Saraswati, 198). It goes on to maintain that the inner meaning of the Upadesa of the Guru is revealed in its entirety only to such a high-soul disciple (the disciple who is a Mahatma). Since the disciple who is as devoted to the Guru as he is to Iswara is described as a 'Mahatma', it means that through this devotion he gains the knowledge of the self (Atmajnana). The sloka declares that the upadesa of the Guru remains burning as light in such a student with a high soul. तस्यैते कथित ह्यार्थात प्रक्षान्ते महात्मनः।

Ahimsa as Dharma

According to the Manu Smriti, Ahimsa is the foremost Dharma that is common to all. It is included in the Yoga, the control of mind. Ahimsa means much more than what it is meant generally as non-injury; it implies not harming others even by thought or word.

Pujya Saraswati says that, by nature, none of us wants to cause any harm to other people. But we retaliate in anger when some one harms us. When our own children set fire to our house in all innocence we do not want to punish but try to extinguish the fire first and thereafter take care to see that the children be kept away from fire and other dangerous objects. We must learn to think that all those who cause us pain are like these children. If a person tries to hurt us, we must lovingly prevent him from doing so. We must not bear any ill-will against him or think of retaliating. This is true ahimsa (Saraswati, 702).

He further says that mind is like a demon. But think what wonders the demon–the *vetala*–accomplished for Vikramaditya after he had been brought under control. The mind will do us unlimited good if it is made subservient to us. Anjaneya (Hanuman) acquired his immense strength and was able to perform so many great and good deeds only because he had conquered his mind. The mind's power is immeasurable. All the cosmos is the work of the supreme Goddess and in this creation of hers even the mind of a tiny ant pervades the entire universe. Many great men, many yogis, have stated that they were able to control the mind by adhering to true Ahimsa, anger will naturally give away, the mind will become clear and will easily be controlled.

Though the chief aim of the non-violence is to control mind and action there is another unexpected benefit that it brings. It is called *Avantara Prayojana.* Think of people who come to the *math* to see the Puja. But with that they also listen to the devotional music and see people whom they had not seen for long. You also listen to the discourse. All these belong to the category of *Avantara Prayojana.* Thus if a man practices true non-violence (by body, mind and speech), he will be rewarded with a benefit that he had not expected. In his presence all creatures will forget their ill-will and cease to cause harm to any other creature. अलहसा प्रतिज्ठयाम् तत्सन्निधानवैरत्याग:(*Yoga Sutra*, 112.35).

The presence of men who are practitioners of ahimsa transforms the psyche of even cruel people. This also means that when a man is full of love he can make other people also loving, and this is an Avantara Prayojana. A Sannyasin must observe total non-violence. He must not even pluck a leaf from a tree and must not do violence to plants by cooking them. It is because of the rule of absolute non-violence that is enjoined unto him, there is an interdiction on his performing rites in the sacred fire. Tending a fire for the conduct of a ritual might unwittingly make us responsible for the destruction of some insects. It is because the Sannyasin cannot perform Agni ceremony that his body is not cremated but interred when he dies. When he is initiated into Sannyasa he takes a vow that he shall never be the cause of fear to any creature.

We are told *Ahimsa paramo Dharmah* (Non-violence is the supreme Dharma). Buddhism and Jainism impose total non-violence on their followers. Hinduism does not make non violence mandatory except in the case of ascetics. In Hinduism, an exception to the general Dharma of non-violence is made in the case of a righteous or just war and in a sacrifice in which some times animals are killed. It is to fetch the divine power to the earth and to appease the Gods that animals are sacrificed in Yajnas. It is our belief that the animals so sacrificed will attain a high state that they cannot otherwise through their own efforts. Altogether it means the good of the animals and the welfare of the world.

In a war, heroes of the army sacrifice themselves in the cause of their nation. Is it not better to lay down one's life for the sake of others than fatten oneself doing nothing?

It is easy to proclaim oral allegiance to the principle of non-injury but difficult to practice it. Quarrels and disputes are inevitable in the world. In dealing with them, action that is apparently violent may have to be taken. In reality such action is not to be regarded as violent. The intention or purpose is important here, not the action itself. Certain types of violence are justified according to the shastras and not considered sinful because such violence is committed not for our personal delight but in pursuance of our duty towards society, that is, the offering of an animal in sacrifice, sentencing a murderer to death, killing an enemy in war.

If a religion makes the practice of non-violence universally applicable it will be problematic to observe it under all circumstances. Those who find it not practicable to follow the rule of ahimsa are liable to sin. The Hindu religion has taken a more realistic view on the question. Buddhism imposes total non-violence on its followers. But what do we see in practice? In all those lands where Buddhism has a hold the armies take part in fighting. Besides, almost without exception, everybody is a meat-eater in these places.

If a great Dharma or principle is made common to all, in the end it is likely to lead to a situation in which no one will respect it in practice. In Hinduism, the rule of absolute non-violence is meant only for the sanyasi. Following this example, Brahmins and Vaishnavas in regions like Gujarat, and Saivas in the South (like Vellalas) practise ahimsa without being bound by any shastric injunctions. They have voluntarily adopted the principle and practised it from generation to generation. Influenced by the example of sattva guna of ascetics, these communities have become vegetarians on their own. And following their example (and without being compelled to do so), other castes too abstain from meat on the days like the new moon, on the day of shraddha and also on the days sacred to various deities. When a principle is imposed only on a few (as it is difficult to make it universal), it becomes an ideal for others for whom it may not formally apply; they try to practise it as far as they can. Non-violence is a samanya Dharma (a Dharma common to all) in Hinduism. It is observed as an ideal on specific occasions; adherence to it is not practicable always.

In Vedic Dharma, the definition of ahimsa is the absence of ill-feeling in all action (Saraswati, 702-704). Pujya Guru further remarks that truthfulness means mind and speech being well-integrated. The wise say that speech being at variance with the mind is untruthfulness.

God has given man the gift of speech so that he may give expression to his thoughts and feelings. If what we speak is at variance with what we think (with our mind) God will take away the faculty of speech from us in our next birth,that is, we will be born in the animal kingdom (Saraswati, 705).

There are exceptions made in our shastras to the rule of absolute non-violence: in waging a war to preserve Dharma, in offering animals in sacrifice. Are there similar exceptions to the rule of truthfulness? 'You will say, perhaps, none. But, as a matter of fact, there are'.

The Pujya Guru continues, "In any locality there must be a number of undesirable characters. Let us suppose that a certain citizen is annoyed with such characters and gives open expression to his anger. He is outraged. That other man is guilty of such and such crime; he keeps recounting the misdeeds of the bad elements. In doing so, he is being truthful, that is, speech and mind is in accord. But the expression of his feeling serves no purpose. Neither he nor the community is benefited. It is a futile kind of accord–that of his speech and mind–and it cannot be called truthfulness."

Take the example of another man. He is full of evil thoughts and, if he gives expression to them, can he be called truthful? No. Thus truthfulness is not merely an accord between mind and speech. It means voicing good thoughts, thoughts that are beneficial and are liked by people: सत्यम् भूतहितम् प्रियम्। Doing good in thought, word and deed is truthfulness. All that does ill is untruthfulness. It is not enough that you speak to a man about what is good for him. You must speak with affection, and the one to whom your words are addressed must find them acceptable. If you speak harshly nobody will listen to you even if you mean good. Thus words that serve no purpose do not constitute the truth. Your speech must be beneficial, and at the same time, capable of bringing happiness to the man to whom it is addressed. This is truthfulness.

The wise say, "May he speak the truth. May his speech be pleasant. May he not speak the truth that is unpleasant. And may he not speak an untruth that is pleasant."

सत्यं ब्रूयात् प्रियं ब्रूयात् न ब्रूयात् सत्यमप्रियम्।
प्रियं च नानष्टतं ब्रूयाद् एज़ धर्मः सनातनः।।(*ManuSmriti*)

A mind that is subject to desire and anger will not give rise to words that bespeak affection and cause well-being. Truthful words are the product of a mind free from desire and anger.

What is truth then? Thought and speech must be in accord; the mind must be serene; and the words spoken must be pleasing, and one's speech must do good to the speaker as well as the listener.

For a man rooted in truth there is an Avantara prayojana, an incidental benefit, gained from his speech. Since such a person habitually speaks the truth, his words will become truth. Such a man will never deliberately utter a lie. But, if unwittingly or out of ignorance, he commits an error while speaking, that error will come out to be true. The blessing as well as the curse of a great man comes true because of the force of their innate and habitual truthfulness. This is the 'incidental benefit' they derive from their habit of truthfulness. But truthfulness must not be practised with the intention that what one speaks must come true. Power such as this is earned unintentionally and unconsciously.

The Duty of a Man

A man will purify himself completely if he performs the forty samskaras and adheres to principles like non-violence, truthfulness, non-covetousness, cleanliness and also controls his senses. He will then develop the maturity and wisdom to find out his true self, Iswara and ultimate reality.

All human beings must express the gratitude to their fathers and to the Gods.They are indebted to their fathers, and should perform rites to the Gods. We must serve our fellow creatures to the best of our abilities and extend hospitality to at least one guest a day. This is atithya. Then, there is Brahmayajna to perform, the word Brahma here denotes the Vedas. Brahmayajna means chanting the Vedas and making others chant them. This duty is carried out by a few on behalf of all. One of the rites common to all is bhutayajna, demonstrating our love to all creatures, feeding them etc. Pitriyajna, devayajna, manusyayajna, bhutayajna are some of these rites which all are duty bound to perform in one way or the other. (Saraswati, 708)

If each individual does his work according to Vedic Dharma and does it in the spirit of dedication to Isvara he may be said to be performing Brahmayajna.

Mother Veda says, 'Matri-devo bhava, pitri-devo bhava' (mother is a deity, father is a deity). Auvvai, who brings us the essence of the Vedas, observes: अन्नायुम् पितावयुम् मुन्नारी दैवम् Mother and Father are the deities first known.

We must treat our parents with respect and do all we can to keep them in comfort. We cannot make sufficient recompense for all the sacrifices they make on our behalf. After they depart from this world we must without fail offer libations to them and perform shraddha, all in shastric manner. Though they ridicule the idea of performing shraddha, even reformers have agreed that we must care for our dead parents.

In the state of workless-ness, love, devotion and jnana are not bound by any rules. But when an action has a purpose behind it you have to respect the rules pertaining to it.

Every family must perform Pooja to Iswara. The Law has created the entire cosmos for our sake. Our sense organs take delight in the various objects in creation. The Lord must be worshipped in every home. He must be invoked and known as the creator of all beings and things. If we keep doing so, we will in due course have the wisdom not to use in Pooja things not fit to be offered to Him.

Annadana or the gift of food is one kind of service or *paropakara.* We talk of service to the poor, social service and so on. Today, all this is done with much fanfare and publicity. In the past the needy were served naturally, without making any noise. Service comes under *Purta-Dharma* and it includes digging wells and ponds for the public, feeding the poor, building temples for spiritual well being of the people and laying out gardens to name a few. We must try to please the Lord with the very hands and feet that he has given us–we must do so by serving others and by treating all as one treats oneself.

A man can be fortunate in many ways. But there is nothing that makes him more fortunate than the opportunity he has of serving others.When we serve our family we are not conscious of how we help it. We must learn to help people who are not our kin–other families, our villages or home town, our nation, indeed all mankind. We have so many problems ourselves, we suffer so many hardships, and we have so many worries and cares. We must not, however, mind serving others in the midst of all our difficulties. We will forget our problems when we are immersed in the work of helping others. There is a saying, 'Feed milk to your neighbour's child, your child will be nourished'. The Lord will raise us up from our troubles when we do good to others. However, it is not with such consideration of profit that we must try to help people in difficulties. We must not worry about how others will benefit from our work, but consider how we will become naturally pure. Also we must think of the happiness we will experience by serving our fellowmen.

Service should not be confined to mankind but must be extended to the animal kingdom. In the old days, ponds were dug exclusively for cattle and stone pillars were installed here and there for them to scratch themselves. Everyone must feed at least one cow everyday with a handful of grass. This is called 'gograsam' and this act is extolled in the shastras.

Conducting sacrifices, offering oblations to the fathers and performing shraddha must be regarded as an extension of the service we do in this world to the denizens of other worlds. These rites must be gone through with chanting mantras.

There must be many others like us, many groups, who want to get engaged in social work. It would be ideal if the efforts of all were brought together under one body or one group of like-minded members. Care must be taken that association so formed does not break up; it must be managed honestly with proper enforcement of discipline. Those who do philanthropic work must be men of courage and enthutsiasm, they should be those who take praise and blame equally.

Pujya Saraswati remarks, "Krishna Paramhansa was playful. But all his playfulness was an outward phenomenon, for inwardly he served others all the time. How sportingly did he save people from trouble, and many were helped by him. To protect the cowherds, the Child Krishna lifted up the big Gobardhan mountain. And, again, as a little child, he danced on the hoods of the dreaded Kaliya that poisoned the Yamuna. It all seemed child'play- all the heroic acts he performed to save the people of Gokula. Nobody sported like Krishna, but at the same time nobody served mankind like him;it was not worldly service alone that he did. He served mankind by imparting Jnana. As the preceptor of Arjuna and Uddhava alike he taught great truths. All this he did with a smile. Whatever he did was with utmost ease. Those who have taken up the work of serving humanity must be inspired by his example (Saraswati, 716).

We keep aloof from the outside world when we are ritually impure. We must regard any day on which we fail to do any service to others as a day of impurity. Parameshwara is the father of all creatures. By serving our fellow men we serve the Lord. This is the message of Tirumular in his Tirumantiram. It means serving people is equal to worshipping the Lord.

We must not fail to perform sacrifices to the celestial beings, offer libation to our forefathers and perform shraddha. In the ancient times, apart from these, our ancestors did Puja to the Gods, fed guests and performed Vaisvadeva, rites meant for all creatures. One must have some idea of these rites even if one does not perform them.

To sustain ourselves, we cause harm to so many creatures. We take pride in keeping our house clean but we forget that every household is butchery. According to Dharmashastras, it is not just one slaughterhouse but five butcheries together:

पंचसूना गष्टहस्थस्य वर्तन्ते हरष्ठच
खण्डनी पाज़णी चुल्ली जलकुम्भ उपस्करः।

Khandani is used to cut vegetables; it stands for one type of butchery as vegetables also have a life. The second butchery is represented by the grinder or pounding stone. We mercilessly grind corn, pulses etc. There are objections raised by meat-eaters about vegetarian food. They tell us, 'Like the goats, cows and fowl that we eat, vegetables and cereals also have life'. Though there is no difference between them, there is a difference in the degree of violence done to vegetables and animals. Plants have life and feeling like humans but they do not have the sensation of pain to the same degree as animals and birds have. This has been scientifically established. Also, but for certain leafy vegetables which we uproot to consume as food, most other vegetables are obtained from plants without killing them: it is like removing our nails or hair. The plants suffer only a little pain. Pain even to this degree will not be caused if we eat the fruits of these plants after they drop ripe. As for the cereals they are harvested only after the crop is ripe and dry.

There is one more argument in favour of vegetarianism. In the global context only certain types of meat like lamb, beef, and pork are accepted by different communities as edible. Horse meat is not usually eaten. During World War I and II, when the question arose as to whether the soldiers could be fed horse meat, the non vegetarians themselves opposed the idea. People who think it civilised to eat birds and animals condemn tribes in some remote lands who eat human flesh as barbarous and call them cannibals. We must tell meat-eaters who remind us that vegetables also have life that vegetarianism promotes sattvic qualities. Unavoidably, for the sake of existence, we have to keep at home instruments of butchery like the khardavsi, pesani etc.

The third butchery is represented by the culli or the kitchen fire. Many insects perish in the cooking fire. An ant crawls about the oven or the fire-place and is burnt. Sometimes when we keep a pot, on the floor or the shelf an insect or two get crushed. In the summer, insects arrive seeking wet places, for example, where vessels are kept. The water-pot is also included among the objects of butchery. Then there is the Upaskara, the broomstick. Many tiny insects are killed when we sweep the floor. Thus there are five instruments or objects of butchery in our home.

We cause pain to, or kill, even harmless creatures. It is said that to live, to sustain ourselves, we have to keep hunting so many living things. But it all seems unavoidable. We do not kill deliberately. There is an explanation for the sin committed unwittingly. It is the prayaschita of vaisvadeva. We perform this function to ask the Lord to forgive us for our sin of having caused the destruction of various creatures and to pray for their happiness in afterlife. Vaisvadeva is meant for the excommunicated and for all creatures of earth like dogs, crows, insects, etc. This rite absolves us of many sins.

The pancha-mahayaga was conducted by the sages, by the children of Brahma. The five great sacrifices are to be performed uninterruptedly until the deluge. But we have had the good fortune of having broken this tradition.

There are a number of simple rites, the performance of which will free us from inner impurities. From generation to generation our forefathers performed them and earned happiness and contentment. We must follow their footsteps. We do not have to go in search of any way of life, any new doctrine or belief.

We can learn from the great men of past who have left us lessons not only in Atmic matters but also in the conduct of family and social life. For instance, kinship and friendship were based on high principles. When there was a marriage or a social ceremony all friends and relatives came forward to help. It was cultured behaviour at its best and it was not based on any empty outward show. People then were truly and sincerely interested in helping the needy and the poor. Among the relatives in the past there was not much gap between the rich and the poor. And the rich man helped his poor relatives. All this is part of Dharma. The man who helps purifies himself more than the man who is helped.

Now things have changed. The well-to-do do not help their poor relatives. Annadan was part of the noble tradition of the past. If you help a poor man with food or material, he will become happy: there is affection on both sides. Among relatives, there should be no distinction between the rich and the poor.

By constantly serving others, by being companionable to all creatures, our mind and consciousness also become clear. In this pure consciousness, in this pure chitta, we shall see the image of the Lord. We have made our minds muddy with impurities. We must make limpid by being devoted to the Lord and by serving mankind. The Iswar will be within our grasp.

The great guru says, "To live a life inspired by Dharma means coming under a certain discipline and following certain rules of conduct. It is important for people to acquaint themselves with these rules. It would be ideal if they lived according to them on their own because to abide by them out of compulsion is not a matter of pride. Sampradaya or tradition is something that has evolved naturally and it is natural that people adhere to them. Not all the customs and rules making up Sampradaya are written down in the shastras. Anything laid down as a law becomes a matter of compulsion. Nowadays everywhere people are asked to follow this or that. Notices are displayed about this and that. 'Do not magnify the faults of others' says the wise. But if there is something good, a man should speak appreciatively about it". (Saraswati, 721)

Ishwara and the guru alone may be praised directly. Friends and relatives instead of being praised, must be spoken well of to others. A servant may be praised after he has carried out the job entrusted to him. A son should never be praised.

प्रत्यक्षे गुरवः स्तुत्याः परोक्षे मित्रबान्धवाः।
कार्यतो दासभष्टत्याष्ठच न स्वपुत्रः कदाचने।।

It is customary to speak of Kama (desire) and Krodh (anger) together. Krishna Paramatma says in the Gita that desire and anger goad a man into sinful action. (Saraswati, 722)

ध्यायतो विज़यान् पुंसः संगास्तेज़ुपजायते।
संगात्संजायते कामः कामात्क्रोघो*भिजायते।।62।।
क्रोधाद्भवति सम्मोहः सम्मोहात्स्मष्टति विभ्रमः।
स्मष्टति भ्रंष्ठाद बु)नाष्ठो बु)नाष्ठात्प्रणष्ठयति।।63।।(*Geeta* 2, 62-63)

We must be extremely wary of this terrible sinner called anger. A little thought will convince us that we are not in the least qualified to be angry with anybody or to shout at anybody. We are even guiltier than those against whom we turn in our anger. We know this in our heart of hearts. If we are guiltless, we must ask ourselves whether we would have not committed the offence if we were placed in the same circumstances again.We must try our best to keep anger always at a distance.

The purpose of human birth is to live a life full of love for all. No joy is greater than that of loving others. Amassing wealth, acquiring prosperity, earning fame, bedecking one self only gives transient pleasure and no sense of completeness. The happiness that permeates our inner being is the happiness that comes from loving others. When we love others we are not conscious of our suffering the physical extension we make and the money we spend: indeed the joy of loving gives us transcendent feeling. A life in which there is no love for others is a life lived in vain.

Our love for others ends in sorrow. However if there is no love there is no meaning in life. We must create such love that will never change, love that will be enduring. The object of our love must never become separated from us, never desert us. If there were such an object and if we devoted all our love to it we would never be separated from one another–there would be eternal bliss, everlasting fullness.

The Paramatma will never be separated from us. Even if our life departs it will dissolve in Paramatman and become one with Him. Only that love is everlasting which is dedicated to Him. True love knows neither reason nor motive. God loves us for no reason. If he needed a reason he would not give us even a morsel of food. It is Parameshwara who forgives all our misdeeds and protects us. He is all love. It is His love that is manifested in different forms- which is neither based on reason nor on motive.

We must learn to have such love as is revealed through Parameshwara: love that is universal, love that is not based on any reason or interest. If our love is manifested slowly but constantly there will be fullness, tranquility and bliss.

यो विद्याचतुरो वेदान्स(ांगो निज़दो द्विजः। न चेलुराणो संविज़ान्नैव स स्थाद्विचक्षणः।।
इतिहास प्रराणाभ्यां वेदे सभ्रपबष्टंहयेत्। विभेत्यल्पुश्रुताद्वेदो मामये प्रहारज़्यातः।।

(Pargiter,1)

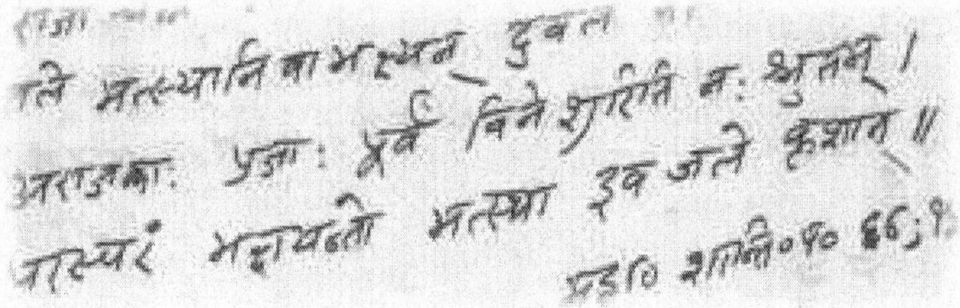

3.
Sources of Dharma

Foundational Factors of Indian Life and Ideas

The Indians belong to the category of peoples who have left their impression upon the pages of history as the founders of original systems of political thought. The foundation of the Indian ideas of state and government was laid at a time and in a region which ensured their indigenous origin. In the long and varied history of the subsequent development and decline, even at the points of closest contact with extraneous systems of thought, there is no room for doubt regarding either the native source of their inspiration or else their national stamp.

The most important factor in shaping the growth and development of India's political thought in ancient times must be sought in the essential genius of her people. A great Indian thinker of our time, Sri Aurobindo has traced the tendencies and characteristics of the Indian genius and their influence upon Indian history and civilization. Aurobindo identifies three basic qualities of India's ancient spirit and characteristic soul. These qualities furnish the key to the rise and decline of her civilization. Among these, first and foremost is her spirituality, the master-key to Indian mind. The next is her stupendous vitality, her inexhaustible power of life and joy, her prolific creativeness beyond all imagination.

Third primary quality is her strong intellectual moorings, at once austere and rich, robust and minute, powerful and delicate, massive in principle and curious in detail (Aurobindo, 8). The decline of India's culture was caused by three movements of retrogression : firstly, 'a sinking of that super abundant vital energy and a fading of the joy of life and the joy of creation', secondly, a 'rapid cessation of the old free intellectual activity, a slumber of the scientific and critical mind as well as the creative institution', and thirdly, 'the operation of spiritual in a dispersed action which replaces the old magnificent synthesis and in which certain spiritual truths are emphasised to the neglect of others'. Radhakrishnan in his *Indian Philosophy* tells us how "the intense spirit of India has enabled it to resist the ravages of time and the accidents of history...The history of Indian thought illustrates the endless quest of the mind, ever old, ever new" (Radhakrishnan, I:24-25). He further argues that the Indian mind "seeks to know the inner truth and the law of all sides of human activity. This intellectual impulse is not confined to philosophy and theology, but extends over logic and grammar, rhetoric and language, medicine and astronomy, in fact all arts and sciences, from architecture to zoology. Everything useful to life or interesting to mind becomes an object of inquiry and criticism" (Radhakrishnan, 27-28).

Passing to another characteristic of the Indian mind Dr. Ghosal notices in the same context its impulse to follow each motive, each specialisation of motive even spiritual, intellectual, ethical and vital, to its extreme point and to achieve its utmost possibility. There was an attempt to know the whole of divine nature and to see beyond nature and into whatever that might be supra divine. When it formulated a spiritual atheism, it followed that to its acme. When it indulged in materialistic atheism, it formulated it boldly and nakedly, without the least concession to idealism or ethics. Illustrating the above from India's attitude towards social ideas and institutions, Sri Aurobindo makes the following weighty remarks: "In life the ideal of opulent living and the ideal of poverty were carried to the extreme of regal splendour and the extreme of satisfied nudity... if it (the Indian spirit) was obliged to stereotype caste as the symbol of its social order, it never quite forgot, as the caste spirit is apt to forget, that the human soul and the human mind are beyond caste... Its spiritual extremism could not prevent it from fathoming through a long era the life of the senses and its enjoyments, and in those too it sought the utmost richness of sensuous detail and the depths and the intensities of sensuous experiences" (Aurobindo, 11-12).

How this Indian sense of balance and rhythm prevented the pursuit of these opposite extremes from resulting in disorder is stated by the same thinker in the following words: "The Indian mind is not only spiritual and ethical, but intellectual and artistic, and both the rule of the intellect and the rhythm of beauty are hostile to the spirit of chaos". He added, "a still more ingrained characteristic, the synthetical tendency, so that having pushed each motive to its farthest possibility the Indian mind returns some fusion of the knowledge it has gained to a resulting harmony and balance in action and institution" (Aurobindo, 12).

U.N. Ghosal has traced out the influence of the factors shaping the growth and development of an ancient social and political theory. He has emphasised the striking reference to righteousness as the essence of Kingship in an old Vedic text. The early Brahmanical works on sacred law (smritis) introduce us to the conception of a welfare state with its programme of universal protection and state relief of the poor and the friendless, its two fold objectives of ensuring freedom from hunger and from want and its standard of complete identification of the ruler with his subjects. These works organically formulate for the first time a remarkable law of the social involving the conception of the kings' government as a branch of the whole duty of this individual. The general attitude of these ancient authors towards the ends of human existence is indicated by the fact that one of them (Apastamba) deliberately rejects the wealth (Artha) in favour of virtue (Dharma). The early schools and authors of the technical science of polity (Arthasastra) indicate a strong tendency towards a materialistic view of life as well as the deliberate sacrifice of morals for political ends. But in Kautiliya, we notice a tendency towards the joint application (in theory if not in practice) of virtue and wealth as the standards of the King's government and a line of state craft honouring as well as violating the moral standards. The complex attitude is maintained in the authoritative teaching of Manu and Bhisma (in the Mahabharat), who inculcate evidently under the impact of Arthashastra thought a composite line of policy based on righteousness as well as on violence. The full force of ethical reaction against the tendencies of the Arthashastra is found in the writings of Buddhist canonists. These authors not only agree in condemning politics as a dismal science based upon the creed of absolute selfishness and ruthless cruelty but plead most impressively for the application of the standard of righteousness to the affair of government. The influence of their elevated teaching upon practical politics is reflected in the celebrated statements of Maurya Emperor Asoka furnishing the key to his internal and foreign policy that all men are his children and that the supreme conquest is the conquest by righteousness.

Regarding the second factor, intellectuality (in the earliest literary works such as the Vedic Samhitas and the Brahamanas), we come across a fundamental concept of omnipotent cosmic or divine law. The early smritis introduce us to the doctrines of profound significance like that of the supremacy of the law of the social order with its combined dogmatic and rational implications and that of the multiple basis of the authority and obligations of the temporal ruler along with its reflection in the branches of state law, the law of penance and the rules of ceremonial purity. Manu and specially Bhisma, while developing the above doctrines add other principles of equal significance such as Bhisma's reasoned plea for the application of the principle of violence as well as righteousness to the affairs of government, his advocacy of a policy of total war accompanied with unscrupulous diplomacy and calculated treachery against the enemy outside, and above all, his statement of the fourfold standard of state craft (namely, the sacred canon, custom, reason, and expediency) with a warning against a strict adherence to the canon in support of his admittedly dubious line of state policy in an emergency. The last statement marks the climax of the application of the smriti spirit of rationalism to politics. The later Brahmanical canonical works continue more or less in the tradition of their predecessors. Meanwhile the Buddhist and the Jain canonists formulate in direct opposition to the Brahmanical dogma of the origin of social order their independent theories of cosmic evolution as well as of the evolution of man and his institution (property, government and society). The greatest single contribution made by our ancient authors to the reasoned treatment of political ideas lies in the schools and teachers of the Arthasastra. This is indicated by their discussion of a large number of principles and problems of government for the first time. We may refer following examples to this estimate of the relative importance of the constituents of the state. These are: their discussion of the methods of recruitment and selection of the officials and the technique of a king's consultation with his ministers; their policy of public security anticipating to some extent the methods of the collectivists as well as the totalitarian states of much later times; their scheme of state planned colonization with the specific object of providing for the military and economic resources to the utmost; their alignments of states in a highly stylised context of the inter-state relations; their selection of the types of foreign policy with the objective of attainment of power and success and specially for achieving progress in the sense of the complete development of a king's resources to the detriment of those of enemy's; their selection of the policy of marching against the enemy based on a balance of the relevant political and military factors with special reference to the question of the intellectual, the moral and the material strength of the two rival kings; their selection of sub-types of treaties in the light of a comparative estimate of the three fold objectives (namely, land, money and ally) of the same, and finally their conception of the dynamic goal of inter-state relation.

Coming to the third and the last factor, namely that of vitality, we have to mention in the first place that the history of Indian political theory begins with our earliest literary works, namely, the Vedic Samhitas and it extends against many vicissitudes of our political fortunes beyond the limits of the ancient times (sources to that effect scarcely available). This means it continued to exist for atleast a period of 3000 years. In the second place, it may be stated that the Indian political ideas and concepts are spread over the whole field of our extensive literature. They are dealt with by the Brahmana canonists in the literature of Vedas, the Smritis, the Puranas, the Mimansas and other works, by the Buddhists and Jain canonical as well as non-canonical writers, by the authors of technical science of polity, by the masters of the classical Sanskrit literatures in the branches of epic and drama and artificial poetry as well as prose romance and folk lore and by the authors of the Tamil classical literature.

If such has been the influence of the three fold characteristic of the Indian genius upon the course of its social and political ideas, no less importance should be given to the tendency of the Indian mind to follow each motive to its extreme point and to sound its utmost possibility. In smriti, the Indian spirit tended to uphold the high and the infallible authority of the Vedas as the source of the sacred law, it proclaimed through some extreme schools of technical Arthasastra the uselessness of the Vedas for worldly success and upheld the claim of politics and economics (or even politics alone) to the rank of science. If the Buddhist canonist thought and Brahmanical Epics of the Ramayana condemned the kshatriya science (Kshatra Vidya) as a dismal science, they pronounced through the authoritative utterances of Bhisma in the Mahabharata the whole duty of the king (Rajadharma) to be the cream of individual and social ethics. If it upheld in the Manusmriti and later works the king's authority as the grand safeguard of individual security and stability of social order, it could conceive in the Buddhist and partly in the Brahmanical thought a golden State of Nature without a king based upon the spirit of philosophical anarchism. If it upheld in the Manusmriti and later works the doctrine of Divine creation and endowment of temporal ruler, it could declare through the chatursataka work of the Buddhist philosopher Aryadeva and through the well-known work on the technical science of polity called the Sukranitisara that the king is a servant of the people subsisting by their contributions. If it inculcated in the king the lesson of the complete merging of his interests with those of his subjects, it could provide for the kings personal safety and security of the state in the line of state craft based upon absolute selfishness. If it is justified in the Brahmanical works on sacred law the Brahman's supremacy over all others by divine admiration, it pushed the Brahmanas to a lower social plane than the Kshatriyas in the works of the Buddhist and Jain canonical literature by contrary theories of the origin of social order.

How the Indian sense of balance and rhythm prevented the clash of these opposite extremes from degenerating into disorder is shown by other examples. It is probably as much to this spirit of balance and harmony of our people as to the ideal of renunciation and the weakness of organisation of the Brahamanical order that we have to attribute the striking fact that this class throughout the history failed to assert its claim to control kings and emperors. We miss accordingly in the Indian theories of the relations of the spiritual and the temporal powers a parallel to the spirit of fierce controversy that raged on this question in the middle ages of Europe. If the Indian spirit imposed upon individuals and groups a comprehensive code of social and religious laws tracing their ultimate source to the Vedas, it knew how to adjust the same to the needs as well as the capacities and sentiments of the people. If it emphasised the principle of kings' authority by reference to his divine origin as well as the fundamental importance of his office and functions, it was no less insistent upon the kings' obligation to protect people on the triple basis of his divine ordination, his subjection to the distinctive law of his order, and his quasi-contractual relations with his subjects following his collection of taxes from the subjects. If it imposed upon the subjects as a duty to obey and honour their ruler, it was no less keen on allowing them to defend their civil rights by force of arms and resist the evil ruler with varying degrees of intensity.

The historical development of political ideas through the centuries is worth mentioning here. To begin with the social factor, the pattern of our social order (dated from the early Vedic times) contemplated the division of society into four primary classes with distinctive status and functions, the Brahmanas at the top representing the spiritual power in striking dissimilarity to the Kshatriyas who represented the temporal power. This principle dominated the form of Indian Social theory through the centuries. The Brahmanas, the Buddhists and the Jains differ in their estimate of the relative status of Brahmanas and Kshatriyas, but they all agree on the fundamental doctrine of social order. It gave rise to the doctrine of the creation of the social order by divine ordination (as in the Brahmanical Theory), or else in the course of a process of cosmic evolution from mythical times down to historical times (as in the theories of the Buddhists and the Jains). The dogma of divine ordination of the social order forms one of the main pillars of the doctrine of the two powers as well as the theory of Brahminical immunities and privileges formulated by the Brahman canonists.

Coming to the political factor, we have to mention that the Indian version of territorial monarchy was derived out of the original Indo-Aryan tribal polity during the period of the Yajus-Samhitas and the Brahmanas, and it was later passed on to the succeeding generations. A second type of polity, namely, that of empire in its different senses of over lordship over vassal states, sole rulership and territorial rule extending to the countries of known natural frontiers, may likewise be traced back to the same period of the Yajus-Samhitas and the Brahmanas. In later times it became the aim of all ambitious kings to achieve this old Vedic ideal. A third type of polity, the republican, can be traced sporadically with the help of historical examples from Northern India across the long stretch of time separating Buddha in the 5th and 6th centuries BC from the early Gupta Emperors in the 4th century A.D. However, in the idealistic conception of the Buddhist canonists the second type of polity left hardly any trace upon our political theory. The problems of republics were discussed from a theoretical or a practical point of view in such different systems of thoughts as those of the early Buddhist canon, Kautiliya's Arthashastra and the Mahabharata, otherwise they are unknown to our ancient political thinkers. The case is otherwise with the first type of polity, that of territorial monarchy.

The Vedic truths refer to the experiences of the seers, which any rational rendering of the reality must take into account. These institutional experiences are within the possibility of all men if only they will to have them. In the branch of state law, while the early smritis conceive the canon and custom (or convention) to be its two fold source, Kautiliya in his great work on the technical science of polity adds two other sources, namely the current (Arthashastra) law and reasoning. Moreover, Kautiliya in this connection lays down the memorable rule that reasoning based on the law prevails in the event of its conflict with the canon and he justifies this by the striking argument that the letter of the canonical text in such a case is regarded as dead. The impact of these ideas on the smritis of Yagyavalkya and his successors is reflected in their statement that the works on the technical science on polity (Arthashastra) and the works on the sacred laws (Dharmashastra) are joint sources of the state law, and that in the case of conflict between two Dharmashastra texts, reasoning based on usage or else injunctions based upon reason will be regarded as authoritative (Ghosal, 3-13).

Tradition as Knowledge

In the last chapter we have seen that Ahimsa and universal love are the two most significant goals of Dharma. A great deal of learning on universal love and its knowledge is invested in the Vedas. As we have also noted earlier that Vedas are accumulated treasury of spiritual laws.The Brahman who knows the four Vedas with the Angas and Upanishads, should not really be regarded as having attained proficiencies if he does not thoroughly know the Purana. He should reinforce the Veda with the Itihas and Purana. The Veda is afraid of him who is deficient in tradition (*Sruta* here means 'tradition'), and such man will do Vedas harm!

Our knowledge of the most ancient times in India crucially rests on tradition. We know from the evidence of language usage that the Aryans entered India very early and established themselves ultimately throughout North India and in the North West of the Deccan- the reason why the history of those times is bound up closely with the Aryan conquests. The Puranas, the Mahabharat and in a minor degree the Ramayana profess to give accounts from tradition about the earliest events. The Vedas, the Brahmans and other Brahmanic literature also supply information. The oldest of these, the Rigveda, contains historical allusions, of which some record contemporary persons and events, but most of them refer to the times bygone and to the persons of the past; and are obviously based on tradition. Almost all the information, therefore, comes from tradition (Pargitar, 1&72).

It is often argued that ancient India has bequeathed to us no historical works. The total lack of the historical sense is so characteristic that the whole course of Sanskrit literature is darkened by the shadow of this defect, suffering as it does from an entire absence of exact chronology (Macdonell, 10).

This is especially true of the Brahamanic literature, for it has been said, 'the Vedic texts, the samhitas and the Brahmanas, are not books with historical purpose, nor do they deal with history' (Keith, 739).

Tradition becomes important in all aspects. It is the only resource since historical works are lacking. And tradition is not an untrustworthy guide either. In ancient times men knew perfectly well the difference between the truth and falsehood as abundant proverbs and sayings show. It was natural therefore that they should discriminate what was true and preserve it; and historical tradition should be considered in this light.

The Aryans could not have established themselves in India without long and arduous warfare. Among the hostile races that possessed the country before them, there were not only rude tribes but also communities in a higher state of civilization. The Aryans not only subdued them, but also gradually cleared much of the country of forests which occupied a large portion of its surface so as to render it fit for themselves, their cattle and their cultivation.

Their wars, their conquests and the founding of the new kingdoms all implied that they were victorious kings, whose lineage and exploits have been sung in many Kshatriya ballads. With the territorial expansion, their religion naturally extended its sphere. Political supremacy fostered religious ascendancy, and rishis and munis protected and fostered by royal power and Aryan prestige spread and propagated their doctrines and observances not only in the countries conquered but also in the surrounding regions beyond the actual Aryan sway. Thus they gradually brought the alien people and tribes under the influence of Aryan beliefs and customs. The aryans met with religious practices and beliefs among the people whom they ruled over or came into lasting contact with, and have assimilated some of them gradually, thus modifying their own religion to a certain extent.

Their victorious career must have given rise to abundant tradition encompassing all kinds. Their tradition must have grown with their territorial expansion. Naturally it was impossible to remember all the accumulated traditions, many were dropped, and only what was important especially that which was interesting to kings, people and priests was preserved. Consequently the principal matters that survived would be (generally speaking) the genealogies of great dynasties, ballads and stories about famous kings and eminent rishis and accounts of the popular religious beliefs and observances. Kings and rishis therefore were the prominent figures; it is mainly with them that ancient traditions deal.

Kings and Rishis

Writing on the difference between Kings and the rishis, Pargiter comments that while kings occupied settled countries and towns the rishis wandered in the woods and hills and in the wild to practice asceticism and a religious life in order to form and enhance their sacred character. The rishi was independent; with spiritual eminence being their aim, they sought God when they were young. A distinguished preceptor, when he had completed his novitiate, was free to establish his hermitage where he pleased or to seek the patronage of some king who might welcome his ministrations. The kings inherited the throne of celebrated ancestors, whose memory and fame they cherished with pride and sought to emulate. The rishis came from well-known families indeed, but that birth right merely entitled them to acquire religious love, and their advancement depended wholly on their own faculties. To maintain their lineage and dynasties was the natural and ardent wish of kings; hence the great desire that is often mentioned among kings to have sons. Rishis perpetuated this sacred lore and fame through their disciples among whom might be their own capable sons (Pargiter, 4).

One indication of this difference is the fact that, while kings are treated genealogically, Brahmanic succession is reckoned by the line of teaching as shown in the lists of religious teachers set out in the Brhadaranyak Upanishad (II, 6; IV, 6; VI, 5) Satpath Brahman (X, 6, 5, 9; Macdonell & Kaith, II: 236). Marriage alliances were matters of high importance with kings and are often noticed. For rishis, though the names of their wives have been preserved, yet very little is ever said about their marriages except when they married princesses; and strange stories are told about rishis, which indicate that the marital relations were not seldom erratic and their lineage by no means pure (Macdonell and Keith, II:84, 259).

The result is displayed in the epics and Puranas on the one side and in the Vedic literature on the other. Sacred lore is the subject of that literature and references to secular matters are generally incidental for the purpose of illustrating some religious points. The ancient portion of the Puranas consists largely of the royal genealogies and Kshatriya ballads while most of their teachings on religious matters were added by Brahmanas later. Dynastic accounts of heroic tales were the principal subjects of the Kshatriya records. Royal genealogies are found in the thirteen Puranas, the epics and the Harivansa; but Brahman genealogies hardly exist and are meagre. The former gives the long list of kings but among rishi families, there are hardly three or four descents. The longest rishi pedigree is that of Vyasa's family with six descendants. Further it is noteworthy that in cases where a king becomes a Brahman, his Kshatriya descent is given up fairly and fully, but the succeeding Brahman pedigree stops short or is dissipated into a mere list of gotra names, as is the case with sage Vishwamitra (*Vayu Puran,* 91, 96-103; *Brahamada Puran,* iii, 66, 68-751; *Brahma Puran,*10, 57-63; *Harivansa* 27, 1460-8 and 32, 1767-72; *Mahabharat,* XIII, 4, 248-59).

Such were the different conditions of king and rishis. The secular business of kings, their wars and exploits naturally had little interest for rishis who dwelt away from the world and were affected little or only indirectly by political changes. On the other hand, though eminent rishis commanded veneration from kings, and their services were at times keenly solicited and handsomely rewarded, the religious doctrines of the rishis lay generally outside the purview of kings unless they were of Brahminical mind. Such was the attitude of the people also at large.The foregoing considerations show that there must have been abundant tradition about kings and their exploits and also much tradition about rishis and their doings; but it is obvious that in such different conditions the tradition about kings and those about rishis must have been correspondingly separate, that is, there must have been two great streams of distinct traditions, Kshatriya tradition and Brahmanic tradition. It is absurd to suppose that all the genuine Kshatriya tradition has been lost or utterly corrupted and that the traditions which we have now are spurious. If the Brahmans could and did preserve their religious compositions with the most scrupulous care and fidelity, it is absurd to suppose the opposite about Kshatriya tradition when there were men whose business it was to preserve such tradition.

The general trustworthiness of tradition is in fact demonstrated wherever it has been possible to test tradition by the results of discoveries and excavations and we should distrust skepticism born out of ignorance. The position is, as asserted by Pargitar, that there is a strong presumption in favour of tradition; if anyone contests tradition, the burden lies on him to show that it is wrong; and till he does that, tradition holds the field.

Pujya Saraswati has drawn our attention towards the dichotomy of life that is caught in between tradition and modernity. He writes that the people are caught between two groups having opposite views. While on the one side there exists the pull of the individuals like us who maintain that they must take the path shown by the shastras; on the other they find themselves persuaded by those reformers who advocate that these shastras should be changed. From a youthful age people nowadays are used to reading reports extolling the changes that go by the name of reforms. This is due to the influence of modern education. However, it is equally true that people have not altogether given up the old customs. A part of the Dharma laid down in the shastras and followed for ages is still seen in our domestic and social life.Thus, we are in a situation where on the one hand, there is the habit formed by custom, and on the other, the habit now being learnt through the new system of education. People are not contented which is the cause misery and misfortune. Always being afflicted by materialistic concerns in daily life, people have completely forgotten the values of the Dharmashastras enshrined by the sages, saints and seers in the ancient age. The peace that once existed can no longer be obtained today. People have more money now. But does that free us from poverty? The claim is that everything is in abundance, that we grow more food than what is needed. Yet there is anxiety everywhere about the supply of essentials (Saraswati, 113).

In place of the old thatched hut or modest tiled house, there now stands a multi-storied building. Then we had just four or five utensils to cook, a basket made of palm-fronds, containers made of gourd shells. Now the house is crammed with all sorts of articles and gadgets that are parts of today's civilized life. People enjoy new comforts and make new acquisitions, yet they are not as happy and contented as their forefathers were.

Armed with scientific temper, secular view of life and specific kind of humanistic spirit, the modern civilization is uprooting age old customs all over the world. This has created a ferment of restlessness. The new world cannot survive as a confused mass of needs and impulses, ambitions and activities, without any control or guidance of the spirit. The void created by abandoned superstitions and uprooted beliefs calls for a spiritual filling.

The modern world is like one body. However, this physical unity and economic interdependence are not enough to make a universal human community. This requires 'a human consciousness, a sense of personal relationships among men. The modes and customs of all men are now a part of the consciousness of all men. Every man has become a spectator of another man. A new humanism is on the horizon. But this time it embraces the whole of mankind' (Radhakrishanan, vii-viii). An intimate mutual knowledge between people is producing an enrichment of world consciousness; yet to our dismay we find that the world is anarchical and unruly. Its mind is in confusion; its brain is out of being. It is due to complete absence of spiritualism in the minds of men. Spiritualism brings solace and people become restful.

Our main education is destined to give a soul to the growing world-consciousness, to develop ideals and institutions necessary for the creative expression of the world soul, to transmit these loyalties and impulses to future generations and train them to be world citizens.

Even now there are people who at heart long for a life of peace lived according to the old traditions. But they do not have the courage to give up either the trammels of modern life or the feeling of pride in the changes affected under the reformist movement. They are in the awkward predicament because they are not fully committed either to the traditional way of life or to the new.

It is important to realise the reason why we should remain true to the shastras. It is not because they represent the views of the seers but because they contain the rules founded on the Vedas which are nothing but what Iswar has ordained. That is the reason why we must follow them. If we are not obsessed with making money there will be plenty of time to think of the Lord. And peace, contentment and happiness will reign.

[illegible]

The notion of [illegible] vague. But it is [illegible] with and after [illegible] the [illegible] summarised as the ruling force, the harmonising [illegible] the foundation of the social order. "Three principles, the foundation of the law; sacrifice, study are three branches of the first, austerity the second, and charity are the [illegible]."

[illegible] Macdonell & Keith, Vedic Index, I, 390

4.
Arthashastra or Dharmashastra

Realising the Ideals of the Puranas

The experience constituted by the Vedas and manifested as the memory is Smriti or Dharmashastra. Smriti does not become Smriti without its Vedic root.The sages who had mastered the Vedas composed the Smritis. What we call smritis make up Dharmashastra. *Vedo' khila Dharmamulam/ Smritisile ca Tadvidam.*

The Smritis must be looked upon as an authority over the time we live in as well as having significance that transcends the time because they are founded on the Vedas. The sages had intuitive knowledge of the Vedas. They did not compose them; they saw them. There was no intellectual effort on their part in this. '*Srutim Pasyanti Munayat*'. The sages see the Vedas.The eighteen sages who mastered the vedas with this super human power are: Manu, Parasara, Yagyavalkya, Gautam, Harita, Yama, Vishnu, Sankha, Likhita, Brahaspati, Daksa, Angiras, Praceta, Samvarta, Acana, Atri, Apastamba and Satatapa.

The noble characters who figure in the Puranas serve as ideals for all of us to follow. The Puranas and the epics give a dominant place to devotion. The devotion we imbibe from the Puranas is the part of the Vedas also. Manu says, वेदो*खिलो धर्ममुलम. The Vedas are the root of all Dharma.

It is for our benefit as well as for the benefit of the world, says Sri Krishna that we must live according to the tenets of the Shastras: *Tasanatdhastram Pramanam the Karyanarya-*

vyarasthitan (The shastras are the authority on what you must do and must not).

यः ष्टास्त्र विविध मुत्सृज्य वर्तते कामकारतःान स सि)म वाप्नोति न सुखं न परां गतिम्।।
तस्माच्छास्त्रं प्रमाणं ते कार्या कार्य व्यवस्थितौ।ज्ञाताष्टास्त्र विधानोद्रं कर्म कर्तुमिहार्हसि

(*Bhagwat Geeta*,16:23-24)

The eight gunas or qualities are:

Daya : Love for all creation

Shanti : Patience

Anasuya : (Non-Jealously)

Saucha : Cleanliness

Anayasa : To have a feeling of lightness, to take things easy.

Mangala : Must be Cheerful

Akarpanya : Is opposite to miserliness.

Aspruha : Being without desire.

By performing rites again and again and by constantly endeavouring to acquire the Atmic qualities one will eventually become desireless."It is not enough, he says, to be attached to Iswara who is without attachement and be free from other attachments. You must be able to sever yourself from the attachment to Iswara Himself". Buddha calls desire as thirst. The Core of his teaching is the conquest of desire.

All religions have one common ideal that is, worship of the Lord, and all of them proclaim that there is but one God. The God accepts devotion irrespective of the manner of our worship, whether it is according to this or that religion. The Vedas proclaim: "The wise speak of the one Truth by different names" (एकम् सद् विप्रा बहुधा वदन्ति). Sri Krishna says, "In whatever way or form a man worships me, I increase his faith and make him firm and steady in that worship".

ये यथा माँ प्रपद्यन्ते तांस्तथैव भजाम्यहम्।
मम् व॥मानुवर्तन्ते मनुज़्याः पार्थ सर्वष्ठाः।। *(Bhagwat Geeta, 4.11)*

The important thing is for the followers of the various faiths to live in harmony with one another.The goal must be unity, not uniformity.The traditional account of the formation of the Dharmasastra or the Arthasastra as given in the Mahabharat is as follows:

Brahama, the creator, was the author of a work in 1,00,000 sections on the topics of Dharma, Artha and Kama. God Shiva as Vaisalaksha reduced it to 10,000 sections in consideration of the brevity of human life. Indra brought it down to 5000: and finally, Indra's work called Bahudantak was reduced by Brahaspati to 3000 and by Usanas still further to 1000 sections.

There was none to administer– every body was happy and there was peace everywhere. Dharma was the cardinal factor which guided everybody and the day to day work was being carried by Dharma alone. Dharma protected the interests of the whole society. Natural life was happy–as given in the Mahabharat:

न वै राज्यं न राजा*सीन्न च दण्डो न दाण्डिकः
धर्मणैव प्रजाः सर्वा रक्षन्ति स्म परस्परम् (*Shanti Parva*, 59:14)

Later on the society was vitiated and there was deterioration in the execution of Dharma. People became panicky and there was vacuum in the absence of any superior authority to command. People started neglecting the Vedas.Then they approached the Prajapati, the Creator, for remedy. He then created a work with 1,00,000 sections.

Brahma: The Creator

ततो*ध्याय सहस्त्रणां ष्टातं चक्रे स्वबु)जम्
यत्र धर्मस्तथैवार्थः कामष्ठचैवाभिवाल्र्णतः। (*Shanti Parva*, 59:29)

The creator named this work as Dandaniti, a guiding

force for the whole of humanity. This would lead to happiness and prosperity for the entire world.

दण्डेन सहिता ह्येज़ा लोक रक्षण कारिका।निग्रहानुग्रहरता लोकाननुचरिज़्यति।।
दण्डेन नीयते चेदं दण्डं नयति वा पुनः।दण्डनीतिरिति ख्याता त्रैल्लोकानभिवर्तते।।

(*Shanti Parva*,59:77-78)

Shiva, Visalaksha, Umapati being called by many names accepted the works of the Prajapati, the creator and reduced it taking the life span of people into consideration and called it Vaisalaksha. It was further reduced to 5000 by Indra who called it Bahudantak which was further reduced by Brahaspati and Usana to 3000 and 1000 respectively. The Mahabharat says as: Shankar: Vaisalaksh: 10,000

तत्स्तां भगवान् नीलत पूर्वजग्राह ष्टांकरः।बहुरूपो विष्ठाालाक्षः ष्ठिावः स्थाणुरूमापतिः।।
प्रजानामा युज़ो]ासं विज्ञाय भगवांछिव:।संचिक्षेप ततः ष्टास्त्रं महास्त्रं ब्रह्मणा ख्रतम्।।
वैष्ठाालाक्षनिति प्रोद्रं तदिन्द्रः प्रत्यपद्यत। दष्ठााध्याय सहस्त्रणि सुब्रह्मण्यो महातपाः।।
भगवानपि तच्छास्त्रं संचिक्षेप पुरंदरः।सहस्त्रैः पंचभिस्तात यदुद्रं बाहुदन्तकम।।

(*Shanti Parva*, 59:80-3)

Vahudantak was further reduced to 3000 sections by Brahaspati - which was later called by Varhasyapatya

अध्यायानां सहस्त्रैस्तु त्रिभिरेव वष्टहस्पतिः
संक्षिष्वेरो व्रध्या वार्हस्पत्यं तदुच्यते।।(*Shanti Parva*, 59:84)

Sukracharya (Usana) reduced the Barhaspatya from 3000 to 1000 sections.

अध्यायानां सहस्त्रेण काव्यः संक्षेपम व्रवीत्।
तच्छास्त्रमिति प्रज्ञोयोगाचार्यो महायष्ठाः(*Shanti Parva*, 59 : 85)

On creation of the Nitishastra with 1000 sections by the Sukracharya, the Brahma was further approached by the Devas, to name a person to see that Nitishastra is executed well. The creator Brahma then created Manas Putra: Virja.

Virja took Sanyas and did not like to accept the kingship on the earth. Virja had a son Kirtiman but he also adopted

Moksha Path- Kardarm was the son of Kirtiman and he also got himself engaged in great Tapsya. Anagna was the son of Kardarm and he became a great administrator/King and Dandaniti expert. Atibal was the son of Ananga and he got a great kingdom to rule. But he was a prey in the clutches of Indriya and the Kingdom was not managed well. King Ben was the son of Sunitha, the Manas Kanya of Mrityu. King Ben was killed by the rishis' Mantraputra–Kushas as he was cruel to his subjects. King Ben was crude and he tortured good people, rishis and his subjects. The Rishis through mental power and by मंथन मंत्रेचार from the right thigh of Ben created 'Nikhida. He is the creator of people residing in the Vindhya called Nikhada. Ben (1) Nikhida through right thigh (2) Prithu: through right hand.

Again the Rishis through *mantrocharana* by chanting mantras and by *manthan*, churning the right hand of king Ben created another man Prithu. He was well versed in the Dandaniti and he was ready to follow the D*andaniti* in the interests of all people. Sukracharya became the Priest. Maharsi Garg became the Jyotishi; astrologer of the kingship. Many Rishis residing on the banks of the river Saraswati became his ministers. It is said that king Prithu was the direct 8th decedent of Lord Vishnu. The line of succession was: Vishnu, Virja, Kirtiman, Kandarm, Anang, Atibal, Ben, Nikhidh, Prithu.

The following Rishis are known as authorities of Dharmashastra: Brahaspati, Visalaksha, Sukracharya, Indra, Prachetas Manu, Bharadwaj and Goursheera.

एतत् ते राजधर्माणां नवनीतं युधिज़्ठिर। वष्टहस्पतिल्ह भगवान् न्या"यं धर्मं प्रष्ठांसति।
विज़ालाक्षष्ठच भगवान् काव्यष्ठचैव महातपा:।सहस्त्रक्षो महेन्द्रष्ठच तथा प्राचेतसो मनु:।।
भरद्वाजष्ठच भगवांस्तथा गौरष्ठिरामुनि:।राजष्ठास्त्र प्रणेतारो ब्रह्मण्या ब्रह्म वादिन:।।

(*Shanti Parva*,58; 1-3).

A well known scholar, Salatore remarks, "Kautiliya clearly states, at the beginning, and at the end of his books that his work was a compendium of all the Arthshastras, which in view of acquisitions and maintenance of the earth, have been exposed by ancient teachers" (Salatore, 35).

पष्टथिव्या लाभे पालेन च यावन्त्यर्थष्ठास्त्रणि पूर्वाचार्यैः।
प्रस्थापितानि प्रायष्ठास्तानि संहत्यैक मिदमर्थ ष्टास्त्रं ख्रतम्।।

(*Kautiliya Arthasastra*, 1)

धर्ममर्थं च कामं च प्रवर्तयति पाति च। अधर्मानर्थ विद्वेज़ानिदं ष्टास्त्रं निहन्ति च।।
येन ष्टास्त्रं च ष्टास्त्रं च नन्दराजगता च भूः।अमर्ष्ठोणो ृतान्याज़ु तेन ष्टास्त्रमिदं ख्रतम्।।
ख्रज़्टवा विप्रतिपलत बहुधा ष्टास्त्रेज़ु भाज़्यकारणाम् स्वमेव विज़्णु गुप्तष्ठचकार सूत्रं
च भाज़्यं च।। (*Kautiliya Arthasastra*, 1,1-3)

Salatore further remarks, "It must be confessed that there is nothing to indicate the source upon which Kautiliya based his succession lists. Neither his own work nor that of any other thinker helps us in this matter. We have to fall back upon a hypothetical explanation that Kautiliya seems to have had four distinct categories of teachers in his mind– the first comprising three teachers, second– seven, the third again seven, and the fourth- two (Kautilya's unnamed teacher and himself)".

First *Shreni*: 1. Manu, the law giver (1900-1800 BC), 2.Brihaspati (1700-1500 BC) and, 3. Usana (Sukracharya, 1700-1500 BC)

Second *Shreni*: 1. Bharadwaja (1500-1200 BC), 2. Vishalaksha (1500-1200 BC), 3. Parasara (1500-1200 BC), 4. Pisuna fi'kqu–(Narad, 1200-400 BC), 5. Kaunapadanta (Bhisma, 1200-400 BC),6.Vatavyadhi (Udava, 1200-400 BC) and, 7.Bahudantiputra (Indra, 1200-400 BC).

Third *Shreni*: 1. Katyana (1200-400 BC), 2. Kanika Bhardwaja (1200-400 BC), 3.Charayana (Carayana, 1200-400 BC), 4. Ghotamukha (1200-400 BC), 5.Kinjalka(1200-400 BC), 6. Pisuna's son (1200-400 BC) and, 7. Ambhiyas(1200-400 BC).

Fourth *Shreni*: 1. The unnamed teacher (400-320 BC) and 2. Kautilya (400-320 BC).

The total number of Rajadharma School would be nineteen and in brihat form (adding names from Manu to Kautiliya) it would be twenty-four. These are mentioned in Mahabharata: *Goursira, Mahendra, Kavya, Manu Pracheta* and *Sambara* (Salatore, 39).

Following are the rishis mentioned in Mahabharata who form the school of Dharmashastra (*Shanti Parva,* 47:5-12):

Vyas, Asit, Narad, Vasistha, Deosthan, Kaushik (Vishwamitra), Vatsyay, Harit, Asmak, Lomas, Sumantu, Dattatreya, Jaimini, Vrihaspati, Pail, Sukra, Sandilya, Chyavana, Deval, Maitreya, Sanatkumar, Kratoo, Kapil, Daksh, Valmiki, Parasar, Tumbaroo, Mareech, Kuru, Kasya, Maundalya, Gautam, Parasuram, Galavya Muni, Trinbindu, Dhaumya, Vayu, Bivand, Pippalad, Dhraum, Sambart, Krishnu Bhautik, Pulah, Angira, Kutch, Mandavya, Kasyap, Pulastya.

Education and Branches of Vidya

An individual well-versed in a subject should teach students. Our ancient scholars have laid down the rule that *Vidwan* must teach and propagate the subject in which he is proficient. It is futile to keep one's learning to oneself. One must become a teacher and transmit one's learning to future generations.

Just as there are four stages in a man's life Brahmacharya, Grhasthya, Vanprastha, Sannyas: there are four stages in teaching also. These are called Adhiti, Bodh, Acharana and Pracharana.

Adhiti means to learn: a man must first learn a subject thoroughly. Next he must try for bodh, that is, he must try to gain insight into, and proficiency in what he has learned. The third is acharana. It is acharana with which there is trouble. *Acharana* means weaving into our life the knowledge we have gained in a subject. In other words, translating our knowledge into practical life– living in accordance with what we have learned. The qualifications of a *vidwan* are not complete with the three– adhiti, bodh and acharana. The fourth and the final qualification is *pracharana.* It means taking care to see that what we have learned is not wasted but imparted at least to a few. Propagating learning is Pracharana.

Pujya Saraswati comments that Sriharsha has spoken about this poetic elegance. He is the author of Naisadham, the story of Nala. Nala was the king of Nisada, hence the name of the work Naisadham. It is poetical work much appreciated by the learned. There is a saying, नैसाधम विद्वद औज़धम्। (Naisadham is medicine for learned people). In the passage describing how Nala learns the Chaturdasa Vidyas, the four stages are mentioned. The poet makes a pun on the word Chaturdasa.

अधिति-बोध-चरण-प्रचरणेर दष्ठाचतुर्भह प्रणयण्णुपधिभिह।
चतुर्दष्ठातम् क्रतभभ कुतः स्वयम् वेदमि विद्यासु चतुर्दष्ठार्भम्।।

(Naisadham 1-4; Saraswati,184)

The word Chaturdasha yields two meanings: one meaning is fourteen. Dasha is ten; chaturdasha is four plus ten –fourteen. The four Vedas, the six angas, four upangas– together fourteen Vidyas. Another meaning of chaturdasha– four dashas or four stages. The poet has played on the idea that after learning the chaturdasha vidya–Nala translated them into four stages of adhiti, bodh, acharana and pracharan.

The fourteen 'abodes' of knowledge are the four Vedas, the six angas or limbs of the Vedas: Mimamsa, Nyaya, Puranas and Dharmashastra.

The fourteen Dharma-pramanas (authorities of Dharma) are called the *Chaturdasha-vidya.* The well-known poetic work Naisadham mentions that Nala was conversant with these fourteen branches of learning. The poet Sriharsha plays on the word chaturdasha: he says that Nala accorded chaturdasha to the chaturdasha vidya, meaning he gave the fourteen branches of learning four dashas: reading, understanding what is read, living according to the teaching contained in what is read, and making others also live in accordance with them. All religious knowledge is encompassed by these fourteen branches of learning. चतुर्दष्ठातम् क्रतभम् कुतः स्वयम् न वेदमि विद्यासु चतुर्दष्ठास्वपि (Naisadham, 1.4)

Pujya Saraswati mentions that there are yet four vidyas. If we add these to the fourteen, we shall have eighteen vidyas–astadasha vidya which are all inclusive. Of them, fourteen are directly concerned with Dharma. The remaining four Ayurveda, Arthveda, Dhanurveda and Gandharvaveda– do not directly deal with Dharma. They are not Dharmasthanas (abodes of Dharma) but they qualify to be vidyasthanas (abodes of knowledge). The first fourteen are both Dharmasthanas and vidyasthanas (abodes of Dharma as well as abodes of knowledge/ learning) (Saraswati, 132).

The Dharmasthans and vidyasthans are together commonly known as the shastras. The word 'shastra' means an order or commandment. We speak of a royal 'shaasan' meaning a royal 'edict'. There is Anushasan Parva in the Mahabharata. Works on shastras incorporate the ordinances that are calculated to keep us disciplined and ensure that we tread the right path.

While all the fourteen shastras are basic and authoritative texts, the *vedas* are their *crown.* Just as Buddhism, Zoroastrianism, Christianity and Islam have the Tripitaka, the Zend-Avesta, the Bible and the Quoran respectively as their scriptures, we have the Vedas as our prime scriptures.

Of the fourteen branches of learning, the first four (the four Vedas) form the basis for subsequent ten. Together they constitute the complete corpus of shastras on which our religion is founded.

I. Four Vedas, Six Angas, Mimansa (directly connected with Dharma, Nyaya, Purana and Dharma Shashtra (total 14).

II. Ayurveda (Life Science or medicine); Arthashashtra (Political and Economy), Dhanurveda (military Science) and Gandharva Veda (music). Together they are four.

Abodes of Knowledge (Vidyasthanas)

These are eighteen in number and are also called *Ashtadasha Vidya*: Veda (04: Rig Veda, Yajur Veda, Sama Veda, Atharva Veda), Vedang (06: Jyotish, Nirukta, Siksha, Vyakaran, Kalpa, Chhanda), Mimamsa, Nyaya, Purana, Dharmshastra Ayurveda Arthveda Dhanur Veda and Gandharva Veda. The last four are also known as Upa Vedas. Mimansa, Nyaya, Purana and Dharmashastra are together known as Upanga.

Abodes of Dharma (Dharmasthanas)

These are altogether fourteen and known as *Chaturdasha Vidya*: Veda (4), Vedanga (6), and Upanga (4: Mimansa, Nyaya, Puran, Dharmasastra).

What we know by the collective corpus of Sashtra is consisted of both Dharmasthanas as well as Vidyasthanas.

Vedas

Sanskrit is the language of the Gods. The Gods created Devavani. In this language stand the ancient scriptures of Vedic and Puranic religion. The Pre-vedic literature is the most ancient record of any people of the world and forms the source of the earliest history of the Indo-Aryan race, nay, mankind as a whole.

The Vedas take us back to the times for which we have no written records. The words of the Veda constitute a world by itself and throw crucial light over the historical development of the Indian mind. The literature of the Vedas is termed Shruti, meaning what has been heard, that is, what is not the work of man.

Vedas are eternal (nitya), beginningless (anadi) and not made by man (apauruseya); they were destroyed in the deluge at the end of the Last Kalpa, and that at the beginning of the present Kalpa commencing with the Krita-Yuga of the present Mahayuga, the Rishis Brhaddevata enumerates *women seers* of the hymns through tapas reproduced in substance if not in form the ante-diluvian Vedas which they carried in their memory by favour of God.

औरत महात्मा योगी। गोघा घाज़ा ब्विपारा पालेज़ाम्मातष्टकलज़का।।
ब्रह्मजाया जुहूर्नाम अगस्त्य खसा दितिः। इन्द्राणी चेन्द्रमाता च रारमा रोम
ष्टोर्वष्ठी। लोपा मुद्रा च नद्यष्ठच यमी नारी च ष्टाश्वती। श्री लर्क्षा सार्पराज्ञी वाक्
श्र)। मेधा च दक्षिणा। रात्रि सूर्या च सावित्रे ब्रह्म वादिन्य म्ररिताः।।

This is another expression of the historical view of modern scholars like Tilak. They state that the Vedic or Aryan religion can be proved to be inter-glacial, but its ultimate origin is still lost in geological antiquity, that the Aryan religion and culture were destroyed during the last glacial period that invaded the Arctic home and that the Vedic hymns were sung in the post-glacial times by poets, who inherited the knowledge or contents therein of an unbroken tradition from their ante-diluvium fore-fathers.

The glory of the Vedas is that they are a collection of mantras that at once notable as much for the energising character of their sound as for the lofty truths they proclaim. A medicine though, bitter, does the body good, while some types of food, though delicious, do harm. The Vedas serve a two-fold purpose: while they have the mantra power to do immense good to each one of us and to the world, they also contain teachings embodying great metaphysical truths.

Here it must be emphasised that on the doctrinal level, the Vedas deal both with worldly life and the inner life of the self. They teach us how to conduct ourselves in such a manner as to create Atmic well-being. Their concern is not with the liberation of the individual alone; they speak about the ideals of social life and about the duties of the public. How the Brahman ought to lead his life and how the king must rule his subjects and what ideals women should follow:

an answer to these questions are stated in the form of laws which are to be found in these scriptures.

The Vedas indeed constitute the apex of our law books. The idea that the Vedas are eternal does not fit into the mental outlook of western Indologists. They claim-impartiality and conducting research in a scientific manner. Notwithstanding these, they are not prepared to accord an elevated status to this text. Sankaracharya charges that many research scholars have also found themselves unable to accept the view that the Vedas are eternal (Saraswati, 152).

Modern historians have adopted chiefly two methods to determine the date of the Vedas: the first is based on the astronomical references in the scripture, and the second on the morphology of the language in the same. But they have not come to any definite conclusion either. Tilak has assigned the date 6000 B.C. to the Vedas. According to some others it is 3000 B.C. to 1500 B.C.

The Guru Sankaracharya further blames the historians of their partiality. There is no difference of opinion among historians about the dates of the scriptures of other religions. They agree that the Buddhist Tripitaka was written during the time of Ashoka but that the teachings of Buddha included in it belong to an earlier time. There is similar unanimity of view that the New Testament is 2000 years old. And all agree that the Quoran was composed 1300 years ago. In the case of the Vedas alone that historians have not arrived at a decisive date. The date of the Vedas, fixed at 6000 B.C. or so, is based on an astronomical conjunction mentioned in them. But again the doubts have arisen whether such an astronomical conjunction would not have occurred earlier. Sankaracharya is of the opinion that the sages had a vision that could penetrate through the eons. So such calculations will not hold in the case of the Vedas which the great sages brought together with their trans-sensual powers of perception. Thus we find that the internal astronomical evidence found in the Vedas and made much use of by modern researches does not help in fixing their date.

The second method is the linguistic one. Here we have to consider not only the language but also the script. Brahmi is the source of all the script in use today in most parts of the country. Devanagri and Tamil scripts may seem totally unrelated, but the fact is otherwise. From the edicts and inscriptions we can find out with some precision the period taken for each alteration in the script. It is in this manner that the dates of some edicts have been determined. The Vedas have never been inscribed on stone anywhere. So there is no question of our fixing this date on the basis of any of the scripts.

Scholars have tried to fix the date of the Vedas by examining the characters of the sound of the words. 'Every two hundred years the sound of a word undergoes such and such a change', observes one authority on linguistics. "A Vedic sound, in the form we know it today, is the result of a number of mutations. If it has gone ten mutations, it means that the Vedas are 2000 years old, or if thirty, they are 6000 years old, which would mean that our scriptures did not exist before 4000 B.C. We hear such view frequently" (Saraswati, 153).

The Vedas have been preserved with the utmost care with a firm belief that the mantras will be efficacious only if the syllable is chanted with precision (so far as its sound and textual correctness are concerned). It was for this purpose that a separate caste (reciters of vedas) is assigned with the mission of caring for them. Research conducted without realising this truth will not serve any purpose (Saraswati, 155fn).

Lokmanya B.G. Tilak discusses the date of the Vedas in his book, *The Orion*. In his preface to this work, Tilak says, "... as I was reading the Bhagwad Gita, it occurred to me that we might derive important conclusion from the statement of Krishna, that he was Margsira of the months". He further says that he has endeavoured to show... that the tradition recorded in the Rigveda unmistakably points to a period not later than 4000 B.C. when the vernal equinox was in Orion (Orion is the Greek name of Margsira).

As mentioned earlier, Vedas are eternal because it comes from the heart of the Prajapati, the Creator. People knew it through shruti. Hence it is called shruti. We must not distrust the belief that the Vedas are not the work of mere mortals. Followers of other religions too ascribe a divine origin to their scriptures. Jesus says that he merely repeats the words of God and according to the Muslims, the Prophet speaks the words of Allah. What we call 'Apauruseya' is a revealed text in this case. The word of Lord has come through the agency of great men to constitute religious texts.

Whatever our field of work, we must be dedicated to it with one-pointed-ness of mind for its truths to be revealed. They say that such truths come to us in a flash. Thus Vedas are not the works of mortals; they are revealed themselves to the seers in their heart-space (Hrdayakasa), seers who were inwardly pure (seers as men possessing pure inner organ).

It is said that originally there was only one Veda. It was divided into four by Vedavyas-Krishna Dwaipayan Vedavyas.

Trayee is also the name of the Veda. That means previously there were only the three Vedas: Rigveda, Yajurveda and Samaveda. The fourth Atharvaveda is the latest. स्त्रिया मष्टक्सामयजुबी इति वेदास्त्र्यस्त्र्यी। (*Amarkosa*, 1.6.3).

There are four main Ritwiz in Yagya–one for each Veda who sits in the four directions in performing Yagya in order. They are Hota, Adwaryu, Uddwata and Brahma. Ritwiz of Rigveda is called Hota. Ritwiz of Yajurveda is called Adwaryu. Ritwiz of Samaveda is called Uddwata. Ritwiz of Atharvaveda is called Brahma.

Veda has six parts:(i) Mantra Samhita (Chand, Rishi, Devata and Viniyoga), (ii) Brahman Granth, (iii) Aranyaka, (iv) Sutra Grantha, (v) Pratisakhya and (vi) Anukramani.

अनन्ता: भ* वेदा: The Vedas are unending. The seers have revealed to us only a small part of them but it is sufficient for our welfare in this world and the next. We are not going to create many universes like Brahma that we should know all the Vedas. We need to know only as many as are necessary to ensure our good in this world" (Saraswati, 192). He further says that in each of the four Vedas, there are different 'Pathas' and Pathabhedas. The same musical composition or *raga* is sung in different panis (Pani is a school or style of music).

Modern indologists are of the view that the Rigveda came first, that the Yajurveda came later and so on but, according to our Shastras, all the Vedas are eternal. All the Vedas are associated with the sacrifice that came to mankind with creation itself.

The Rig Veda

The Rig Veda is all in the form of poetry. What came to be called *Sloka* in later times is the *rk* of the Vedas. '*Rk*' means a *Stotra,* a hymn. The *RigVeda Samhita* is made up entirely of hymns in praise of various deities. Each *rk* is a *mantra* and a number of *rk*s in praise of a deity constitute a *Sukta.*

The Rig Veda has 10,170 rks and 1,028 suktas. It is divided into 10 *mandalas* or 8 astakas. It begins with a *Sukta* to *Agni* and concludes with a *Sukta* to the same *Agni.* For this reason some believe that the Vedas must be described as the scriptures of fire worship, a view with which we would be in agreement if *Agni* were believed to be the light of the *Atma* (the light of knowledge of the reality). The concluding *Sukta* of the Rigveda contains a hymn that is a prayer for amity among all nations, a true international anthem. It goes,

"May Mankind be of one mind, may it have a common goal, may all hearts be united in love. And, with the mind and the goal being one, may all of us live in happiness."

सं गेच्छधवं सं वेधध्वंसं वो मनां सि जानतां।
द्वेवा भागं यथा पूर्वे संजानाना उपासेते
समानो मंच: समिति: समानी सेमा नं मने: सह चित्तर्मेज़ां।
समानं मंचेमभि मंत्रेभे व: समानेने वो हविज़ो जुहोभि।।3।।
समानी व आर्कूति: सभाना ह्रदयानि व:।
समान मेस्तु वो मनो यथो व: सुसहासेति।।4
सोम वेदोऽस्मि (*Rigveda*,10,191:2-4)

The glory of the Rig Veda is that it is replete with hymns to all deities. Scholars are of the opinion that, besides, it contains teachings for our life. The wedding rites are based on that part of this Veda which pertains to the marriage of the daughter of the Sun God. There are also passages of dramatic character like the dialogue between Pururvas and Urvasi. The hymns to Ushas, the goddess of dawn, and similar mantras are considered to be of high poetic beauty. Since the Rigveda is placed first among the four Vedas, it must naturally have an exalted position over the *matrix* of the work (Karma) of the Yajurveda and the songs of the Samaveda.

The Yajur Veda

The 'Yajus' is derived from the word, 'Yaj' meaning "to worship". Yajna is also from the same root. Just as *rk* means a hymn, Yajus means the worship associated with sacrifice. The chief purpose of the Yajurveda is the practical application of the Rigvedic hymns in the religious work called Yagna or sacrifice. The Yajurveda describes in prose the actual conduct of the rites. If the Rigveda serves the purpose of adoring the deities verbally the Yajurveda serves the same purpose through rites.

The Yajurveda is different from the other Vedas in that it may be said to be divided into two Vedas which are considerably different from one another): the Sukla Yajurveda and the Krishna Yajurveda (white or black Yajurveda). Sukla Yajurveda is also called Vajasaneya. Vajasaneya is one of the names of the Sun God. It was the Sun God who taught this to the sage Yagyavalkya.

Yajurveda systematises the Karmayoga, the path of work. The Taittriya Samhita of the Krishna Yajurveda deals with sacrifices like darsa purnamas, Somayag, Vajapeya, Rajasuya, Aswamegha etc. Yajurveda also has a number of hymnic mantras of a high order which is not found in the Rigveda.

Among the followers of the four Vedas *Yajurvedins* predominate. The majority in the north India (Brahmins) belong to the *Sukla Yajurveda*, while most people in the south India belong to the *Krishna* Yajurveda.

The Sama Veda

'Sama' denotes that which bring equipoise or tranquility to the mind. There are four well-known ways of dealing with an opponent or rival: Sama, Daana, Bheda, and Danda. The first method is that of conciliation, making an enemy a friend through affection. The Sama Veda enables us to be friend with the divine forces and even the Parmatma. Many of the Mantras of the Rigveda are intoned with a cadence in the Sama Veda; thus we have Samagana while the rks are chanted with the tonal differences of Uddata, anudatta and Svarita, the Samans are intoned musically according to certain rules. Our music, based on the seven notes has its origin in Sama Veda. All deities are pleased with Samagana. We become recipients of their grace not only through the offerings made in the sacrificial fire but through the intonation of the Samans by the Udgata. Samagana is particularly important to Soma sacrifices, in which the essence of the Soma plant is offered as oblation.

Though the Samans are indeed Rigvedic mantras, they are specially capable of pleasing the deities and creating the Atmic uplift because, they are intoned musically. This is what gives distinction to the Sama Veda. Srikrishna Paramatma says in the Gita, सोम वेदोऽस्मि (Of Vedas I am the Sama Veda).

वेदानां सामवेदोऽस्मि देवानामास्मि वासव:
इन्द्रियाणां मनष्ठचास्मि भूतानास्मि चेतना।।22।। *(Bhagawat Geeta, 10:22)*

Chandrasekharendra Swami further elaborates that the lord is everything, including good as well as bad. Even so, as he speaks to Arjun about the things in which his divine quality specially shines forth, he mentions the Sama Veda among them (Saraswati, 195). In the Lalita-Sahasranam (The one thousand names of the Goddess Lalita, Amba has the name of Samagan priya (One who delights in Samagan); she is not called Rigveda Priya or Yajurveda Priya. Shyama Shastri [1762-1827: One of the foremost Vaggeyakaras of carnatic music: a vaggeyakara (literally, Song-maker) is one who not only creates the text of a song but also determines its musical form and content] refers to the Goddess Minakshi as Samagan-Vinodin in one of his compositions. In the Sivastotram (Siva astothra-satam), the 108 names of Siva, Siva is worshipped thus.

The Tevaram extols Siva as one who keeps chanting the Chandoga Saman (छंदोग-समनोद्वम् वयम्). Appayya Diksita has sought to establish that Iswara or Siva, Amba and Vishnu are Ratna-Trayi (the three gems) occupying the highest plane. And all three have a special relationship with the *Samaveda.*

The Atharva Veda

'Atharvan' means a Purohit, a priest. There was a sage with this name too. That which was revealed by the seer Atharvan is the Atharva Veda. It contains mantras with which one wards off misfortunes and disasters and brings about the destruction of one's enemies. The Atharva Veda is a mixture of prose and poetry. The mantras of other Vedas also serve the same purpose as those of the Atharva Veda. But what is special about the latter is that it has references to deities not mentioned in the others and has mantras addressed to fierce spirits known as mantrikam (Magical rites). It is to be noted that the Atharva Veda also contains mantras that speak of lofty truths. It has the Prithivi-Sukta the hymn to earth, which glorifies this planet with all its creatures.

The Atharva Veda is noteworthy for the fact that the Brahma, the supervisor of sacrifices, is its representative. But we must remember that of the ten important Upanishads three belong to this Veda–Prasanna, Mundaka and Mandukya. It is believed that those who seek liberation need nothing to realise their goal other than the Mandukya Upanishad.

Guru Swami further goes to remark that we learn from stone inscriptions that the Atharva Veda had a following until some centuries ago. Information about Vedic schools is provided by such inscriptions found near Perani, not far from Tindivanam, at Ennayiram and a place near Walajabad, in the neighbourhood of Kanchipuram. Even during the reign of the later Cholas the Atharva Veda was learned in Tamil speaking areas.

There are eighteen divisions among the Brahmins of Orissa. One of them is made up of Atharvanikas, that is, Atharvaveddins. Even today, Atharvaveddins can be seen, though their number is small in parts of Gujarat like Saurastra and in Kosala (U.P.).

Owing to the efforts made by the Paramguru and Sri Jayendra Saraswati Swami, the study of the Atharva Veda has been revived in the South. Students from Tamil Nadu have been sent for this purpose to Sinor in Gujarat.

Swamiji remarks, Gayatri is the mantra of mantras and it is believed to be the essence of the three Vedas–which means that the Atharva Veda is excluded here. According to one view, before one starts learning the Atharva Veda, a brahmachari must go through a second upanayan ceremony. Generally, the Gayatri imparted to a child at the Brahmopadesha ceremony is called Tripada Gayatri–it is so called because it has three padas or three feet. Each foot encompasses the essential spirit of one Veda. The Atharva Veda has a separate Gayatri and if people belonging to other

Vedas want to learn this Veda they have to go through a Second Upanayan to receive instructions in it. For the followers of the first three Vedas, however, there is only one Gayatri and those belonging to any one of them can learn the other two Vedas without another Upanayan."

Anantah Vai Vedah, the Vedas themselves proclaim so (The Vedas are endless). We cannot claim that all the Vedas have been revealed to the seers. Only about a thousand sakhas or recessions belonging to the four Vedas have been revealed to them.

Brahma the Creator, alone knows the Vedas in their entirety. Before the present Brahma, there was a great deluge, and preceding it, there was another Brahma. And similarly before them too there must have been another Brahma. But through all these vast vistas of time, through successive deluges, the vibrations caused by the Paramatma's breath have existed in space; the vibrations urged the first Brahma to do the work of creation. These are indestructible. Brahma who appears after each great deluge performs his function of creation with it (Saraswati, 160). Chandrasekharendra Saraswati further elaborates that Brahma created this world with the sound of the Vedas and this sound is not destroyed even during a great deluge. By chanting these sounds he brought the entire world into existence. Brahma could create this universe with the sound of the Vedas because of his power of concentration. To bring the desired result, these sounds or mantras are to be chanted without any tonal error whatsoever.

During the time of creation, the spiritual reality or Nirgun Brahma (the unconditional Brahma or Brahma without attributes) is revealed to perform manifold functions. From the Nirgun Brahman comes a flow of energy to perform such functions. Brahma came into being as a part of this flow. Since he was all tapas, all concentration, he could grasp all the Vedas with his extra-ordinary power. The classification into the four Vedas and one thousand or so rescessions was a later development. As Brahman came into being, his heart was filled with all Vedic sound. The Vedas showed him the way to perform his function of creation. He recognised that the sound of the Vedas pervaded everywhere. Only some mantras have revealed themselves to the sages and these constitute the Vedas that have become our heritage.

At the time of chanting a mantra we usually mention the rishi associated with it, its chhandas or metre and the name of the deity invoked. The sages learned the mantras with the power of concentration acquired through austerity. They were bestowed with celestial ears, so they could hear the mantras in space. Only those who have attained the state of undifferentiated oneness of all can perceive them. It is in this way that the seers become aware of the mantras and made them known to the world. It must be remembered that they did not create them. They brought us immeasurable blessings by making the mantras known to us. We cannot adore the seers sufficiently for their gift of the mantras which are beyond the grasp of our ears. That is why before chanting a mantra we offer prayers of the concerned rishi.

Our forefathers devised a number of methods to preserve the unwritten Vedas in their original form, to safeguard their tonal and verbal purity. They laid down the rules to make sure that not a syllable was changed in chanting, not a swara was altered. In this way they ensured that the full benefits were derived from intoning the mantras. They fixed the time taken to enunciate each syllable of a word, and called this unit of time or time interval 'matra'. A remarkable method was devised to make sure that words and syllables are not altered. According to this the words of a mantra are stung together in different patterns like vakya, pada, krama jata, mala, sikha, rekha, danda, ratha, ghana etc.

Some Vedic scholars are called 'Ghanapathins' which means those who have learnt the chanting of the scripture upto the advanced stage called 'ghana'. 'Pathin' means one who has learnt the 'paath'. When we listen to a 'ghanapathin' chanting the ghana, we notice that he intones a few words of a mantra in different ways, back and forth. The sonority, natural to vedic chanting is enhanced in 'ghana'. Similarly, other methods of chanting like Krama, Jata, Shiksha and Mala are divine too.

In 'Vakyapatha and Samhitapatha' the mantras are chanted in the original order with out any special pattern adopted. In the Vakyapatha, some words of mantras are joined together in what is called 'sandhi'. In 'Padapatha', each word in a mantra is clearly separated from the next. It comes next to Samhitapatha and after it is Kramapatha. In this the first word of a mantra is joined to the second, second to the third, the third to the fourth, and so on until we come to the final word.

In Jatapatha, the first word of the mantra is chanted with the second, then the order is reversed–the second is chanted with the first. Then again, the first word is chanted with the second, then the second with the third, the third with the second and again the second with the third, and so on. In this way, the entire mantra is chanted going back and forth. In the Sikhapatha, the pattern consists of three words of a mantra, instead of two of the Jata.

Ghanapatha is more difficult than these. There are four types of this method. Here also the words of a mantra are chanted back and fourth and there is a system of permutation and combination in the chanting. To explain all of it would be like conducting a class in Arithmetic.

The sound of the Vedas guards the world against all ills. Our forefathers devised these methods of chanting to protect the sound of our scriptures against change and distortion.

Samhita patha and Padapatha are called Prakriti patha (Natural way of chanting) since the words are recited only once and in their natural order. The other methods belong to the 'Vikrit patha' (artificial way of chanting) category. In Krama, though the words do not go in the strict natural order of one-two-three, there is no reversal of the words–

the first after the second, the second after the third and so on. So we cannot describe it fully as Vikrit patha. Leaving out Krama, there are eight Vikrit patterns and they are recounted in verse to be easily remembered.

जटा माला ष्ठिाखा, रेखा, ध्वज, दण्डो रथो धनहं।
इन्यस्तु विक्रतुयत प्रोक्तह, क्रम पूर्व महर्ज्रिभि:।।

All these different methods of chanting are meant to ensure the tonal and verbal purity of the Vedas for all time. In Pada the words in the natural order, in Krama two words together, in Jata the words going back and forth. The words tally in all these methods of chanting and there is the assurance that the original form will not be altered. The benefits to be derived from the different ways of chanting are given in this verse:

समहिता प्रथमेतोण यत् फलम् प्रोचयते बुद्धययह:।
पठेतु द्विगुणम् विधत् क्रमे तु चे चतुर्गनम।
वर्ण क्रमे सतगुणम् जतयन्तु सदर्णकम।।

Considering that our ancestors took so much care to make sure that the sound of the Vedas did not undergo the slightest change, it is futile for modern researchers to try to establish the date of our scripture by finding out how the sounds of its words have changed.

Shakhas (Branches)

The Rishis as per their conveniences allotted the mantras to their disciples. The Rishis in allocating the mantras to their disciples adopted different methods: on the basis of Gods, topics etc. Thus, there was no uniformity in distributing the mantras of each Veda to their respective disciples. Naturally that led to different branches (shakhas) of each Veda.

The Rigveda has 21 shakhas among which Sakal shakha is available. The Yajurveda has 109 shakhas which are divided in two parts: Shukla (white or bright) and Krishna (black or dark). Shukla Yajurveda has fifteen branches and Krishna Yajurveda has ninety-four. Out of fifteen of Sukla Yajurveda only two are available (Kanva and Madhyandin)- Out of ninety-four Krishna Yajurveda, only Taittariya Kath, Kapisthal, Swetaswar are available.

The Black (Krishna) Yajurveda is called Taittariya. The name comes, it is said that the pupils of this school of priests were transformed into partridges अतिक्रुध तैतरीय; in order to pick up the Yajus disgorged by one of their companions who was wroth with his teacher. The legend originated in the nature of the Black Yajus, which is a motley undigested jumble of different pieces, represented in the story by the variegated appearance of the partridges.

Another of the principal school of Black Yajus is supposed to owe its name Khandikiyas to the same fact that the Black Yajus is made up of Khandas- fragments. The white is, on the other hand, so called, either because the mantras and Brahmans are so clearly distinguished from one another, or because the Mantra has been cleaned and separated from the Brahman, and thus the whole made more lucid and intelligible as contrasted with the Black in which the verses and Brahman proper are mixed together and consequently less intelligible. The Kathak is the only work of the Brahman order mentioned by name by the great Sanskrit writers belonging to this school of black Yajus.

The Samaveda has 1000 shakhas but only Kaumuthi (Kauthuma), Jaiminiya, Ranayaniya are available. The Atharvaveda has also 50 shakhas but only Paippallad and Sonkya are available. In this way we find that the total shakhas are 21 + 109 + 1000 + 50 = 1180.

People in the distant past had remarkable abilities and possessed great yogic and intellectual power. So they could gain mastery of many vedic recensions. As for the great sages it was a matter of Vedas revealing themselves in a flash. Others with their unusual abilities were able to master not only the Vedas but also other branches of learning. The Vedas in their infinitude being are like the expanse of an endless ocean, no one has been able to master all of them. Even so, in the remote past there were individuals conversant with a large number of shakhas.

In later times, men began to lose their divine yogic power. At the beginning of the age of Kali it became very weak indeed. The life span of man began to get shorter and his health and intelligence declined. In the Krita-Yuga man lived so long as his skeleton lasted. Even if his blood dried up and his flesh was destroyed he survived until his bones collapsed. They were called Asti-gata-praanas. In Treta, people were Mamsa-gata-Praanas (lived so long as their flesh lasted and did not perish even when the blood dried up). In Dwapara, people became rudhir-gata-praanas (lived until till their blood dried up). In this Kali age, we are merely anna-gata-praanas (live so long as the food lasts). We have little capacity to perform rituals and Puja. But we are capable of chanting names of the Lord Krishna, Ram and so on. It is time that by uttering the names of the Lord we will be liberated. Even so we must not allow the Vedas to become extinct. They were bequeathed to us from the time of creation.

Vyasa: Composition and Compositor

When Sri Krishna departed from this world darkness enveloped the world. He was the radiance of knowledge for the world, the light of compassion when he departed much injury was done to gyan and darkness descended into the world. Kali, who is the evil incarnate, acceded to authority. All this is the sport of the Paramatma, the sport that is inscrutable. Sri Krishna came as a burst of light, but later, he created a state in which the fear of darkness arose everywhere. Then, urged by his compassion, he decided that the world must not go waste. He thought that it could be saved by administering an antidote against the venom of Kali. This antidote was the Vedas. It would be enough if precautions were taken to make sure that the Kali Maa did not devour them–the world would be saved. In the darkness surrounding everything they would serve the purpose of lamp lighting the path of mankind.

In the age of Kali, they would not shine with the same effulgence as in the previous ages. But the Lord resolved that they must atleast burn with minimum of lustre to be of benefit to mankind and this he ensured through Ved Vyas, who was partially his incarnation.

The sage who was to carry out Bhagwan Krishna's resolve was not then called Ved Vyas. His name too was Krishna, and since he was born in an island, he had the appellation Dwaipayan (Islander), Badarayana is another name of lord Krishna. Krishna Dwaipayan knew all the 1180 shakhas (recension) of the Vedas revealed to the world by the various sages. They were mingled together in one great stream. Being gifted, our ancestors could memorise all of them. For the benefit of weaker people like us, Vyasa divided them into four Vedas and sub divided each into shakhas. Vyasa accomplished the task of dividing Vedas easily because he was a great Yogi with vision and because he had the power gained from austerities.

The Rigveda shakhas contain hymns to invoke the various deities; the Yajurvedic shakhas deal with the conduct of sacrifices; the Samaveda shakhas contain songs to please the deities, and the Atharvaveda shakhas, besides dealing with sacrifices, contain mantras recited to avert calamities and destroy enemies.

Considering that people in the age of Kali would be inferior to the forefathers, Krishna Dvaipayan thought that it should be sufficient for them to learn one shakha of any of the four vedas. It was the Lord that put this idea into his head. Vyasa assigned the Rigveda shakhas to Paila, Yajurveda shakhas to Vaismpayan, Samaveda to Jaimini and the Atharvaveda to Sumantu.

Krishna Dvaipayan came to be called Veda Vyasa for having divided the Vedas into four and then having sub divided them into 1180 shakhas (recession). Vyasa literally means an essay or a composition, classifying objects is also known as 'Vyasa'.

According to Krishna Dvaipayan arrangement, though it is obligatory for a person to learn one recension, it does not mean that there is a ban on learning more. The intention is that at least one shakha must be studied. Even after Vyasa's time there have been examples of Panditas mastering more than one shakha from the four Vedas.

In the past there must have been individuals who knew more than one Veda. Jnanasambandhar calls himself Nanmarai Jnana Sambandhar, since he was suckled by Amba herself it must have been easy for him to master the four Vedas. During these 5000 years and more since Veda Vyasa is supposed to have divided the Vedas, many shakhas have been lost. Out of 1180 we are in the unfortunate position of having only six or seven.

The Rigveda has 21 shakhas with one extant shaka called Sakala Sakha or The Aitareya Shakha since Aitreya Upanishad occurs in it. It is assigned to Paila. The Yajurveda: The Sukla Yajurveda has 15 shakhas with only two extant shakas called Kanva Sakha having followers in Maharashtra; and Madhayandina Shakha having followers in North India.It is assigned to Vaisampayan.

The Krishna Yajurveda has 94 shakhas with Taitatriya having large following in the south (details of Maitrayani Kath, Kapistal and swetaswar are not available). It is assigned to Jaimini.

The Samaveda has 1000 shakhas of which only three are extant called Kauthuma: more following in South than Talavakra shakha which has also followers in the south where as Ramayaniya has followers in Maharashtra. It is assigned to Jaimini.

The Atharvaveda has50 shakhas of whichonly two are extant called Saunaka Paippalladi (details are not available). It isassigned to Sumantu.Thus, the total shakhas available out of 1180 are – 1 + 3 + 3 + 2 = 9.

Brahmana Granth

Brahmanas are texts comprising knowledge of the sacred hymns, traditions and customs.They profess to teach the performance of the sacrifices, yagya and Vedic rites. These are commentaries on Vedas.The Brahmana lays down the various rites–Karma–to be performed and explains the procedure for the same. It interprets the words of the mantras in the samhita, how they are to be understood in the conduct of sacrifices.The Brahmans constitute a guide for the conduct of Yagyas.

The difficulty of giving an exhaustive definition of a Brahmana has been felt by the Brahmanas themselves. Sayana, beutifully captures this tension of defining Brahmanas in this following passage. In his introduction to the Rigveda and in his introduction to Aitreya Brahmana, he says that 'a Brahmana is two-fold containing either commandments (vidhi) or additional explanation (arthavad) (Max Muller, 342)'. For Apastambha too 'Brahamanas are commandments for sacrifices; all the rest consist of additional explanations' (Max Muller, 342).

Sayana further questions this distinction between Vedas and the Brahmanas and asks, "how can it be said that the Veda consists of the mantra and the Brahmana consists of the essential qualities when neither of the one nor of the other part can be satisfactorily defined? For if it is said that a mantra alludes to those things which are commanded, this definition would not be comprehensive of all mantras, because there are some which are themselves commandments ... Again, if it is said that a mantra is what makes one think (makes man to think), this definition would include the Brahmanas also.

Other definitions have been given, that a mantra ends with the word: 'thou art', or that it ends with the first person plural: but none of these definitions can be considered as exhaustive. The only means, then by which a mantra can be distinguished from a Brahamana lies in their general sacrificial appellation, which holds the most different things under the one common name of mantras. There are some recording the performance of sacrifices; some contain praises, some end with the word the (*tva*), some are invocations, some are directions, some contain deliberations, some contain complaints, some are questions, some are answers etc. All these attributes are so heterogeneous, that none of them can be used for a definition. Knowing, however, that the Veda consists only of two parts, we may say that whatever does not come under the name of mantra is Brahmana, whether it contains reason, explanation, censure, reccommendation, doubt, commandment, relation, old story, or particular determination. None of these subjects belongs to the Brahmanas exclusively, but they occur more or less frequently in the mantra also, and could therefore not be used as the definition of the Brahmana. The same objection applies to all other definitions which have been attempted. Some have said, that the frequent occurrences of the particle *iti* (thus) constitute a Brahmana; others that a Brahmana closes with a world *Ityah* (Thus he said); others that a Brahmana contains stories, and etc. but all this would apply with equal force to some of the mantras. The only division, therefore, of the Veda that holds good consists in comprehending one part under the old traditional appellation of mantra, and considering all the rest as Brahamana.

But it might be objected Sayana continues, "that for instance in the chapter on the Brahmayagya, other parts of the Veda are mentioned, besides the Brahmana and mantras, under the title of Itihas (epic stories) Puranas (cosmic stories), Kalpas (ceremonial rules), Gathas (songs), Narasansi (heroic poems). This however, would be the same mistake, as if we should place a Brahm coordinate with a Brahman who is a mendicant. For all these titles, like Itihas etc. apply only to subdivisions of the Brahmana. Thus, passages from the Brahmanas, like 'The Gods and the Asuras were fighting', etc. would be called Itihas; other passages like 'In the beginning there was nothing' would be called Puranas; therefore, we may safely say, that the Vedas consist of two parts only, of mantras and Brahmanas" (Max Muller, 343). According to Madhusudan the Brahmanas consist of three parts: commadments, additional explanations and the Vedant doctrine. For him a commandment may consist either in a simple definition (the obligation to Agni is given in eight cups) or it may include the aim (he who wishes for life in heaven may perform sacrifice in the new and full moon) or it may provide detail means by which the sacrifice is performed or it may contain all this together (Max Muller, 344-345).

Like Samhitas, Brahmanas were adopted by different Charanas of the same Veda and in most cases are different rescensions of one and the same original. There was originally but one body of Brahmanas for each of the three Vedas; for the Rigveda, the Brahmana of Bahvrichas, for the Samaveda, the Brahmana of Chhandogas, for the Yajurveda in its two forms of Brahmanas of the Taittiriyas, and the Shatpath Brahmana. These works were not written in metre, like the Samhitas, and were therefore more exposed to alteration in the shruti tradition (Ibid, 345).

Most of the existing Brahmanas are collective works. The Brahmana of the Taittiriya both in Apastambhiya and the Aitreiya shakhas contains portions bearing the name of Katha. These portions were the property of the followers. The component parts are frequently called Brahmanas instead of chapters or sections. The same applies to the Aranyakas and Upanishads. In some cases, these smaller Brahmanas are quoted by their special titles not frequently by the name of the Charana by which they were adopted but by the name of the Charana in which their original collection took place. Thus even when Aetareya Brahmana was adopted by Ashvalayanas, it is not popularly known by the latter name. Maitreyi Brahman is the title given to that portion of the Brihadaranyaka that contains the famous dialogue between Yagyavalkya and Maitreyi.

For the Brahmana of Chandogas the principal collection is called Praudha or Panchvinsha Brahmana (consisting of twenty-five sections). Shadvinsha Brahmana was later added to this collection along with Adbhuta Brahmana. It is however interesting to note that Brahmanas of Chandogas are often numbered as eight. Shatpath Brahmana reveals quite clearly the gradual accumulation of various theological and ceremonial tracts that form the core of this new corpus of literature.

The following available Brahmana Granths are assigned to each Veda:

Rigveda: Aitareya Brahmana (5000 slokas; to this belongs Aitareya Aranyaka in five books or Upanishadas), Sankhyana Brahmana or Kaushitaki Brahmana.

Yajurveda: It has two branches - Krishna and Shukla.

(a) Krishna (Black or Dark):Taitiriya Brahmana and Madhyavarti Brahmana of Taittiriya Samhita;

(b) Shukla (White or Bright): Vajasney Sanhita and Shatpath Brahmana (i. Kanva shakha with 17 chapters and (ii) Madhyardin with 14 chapters.

Samaveda: (i) Tandaya Brahmana or Maha or Praudha or Panch Vinsha (ii) Kharvinsya Brahman or the Sadravinsa Brahmana, Adbhutadhyaya Brahmana; (iii) Sambidhan Brahmana (iv) Arkheya Brahman; (v) Mantra Brahmana or Chhandogya Brahmana; (vi) Dvaitadhyaya Brahmana; (vii) Jaimini Brahmana or Talvakaran Brahmana; (viii) Jaimini Upanishad Brahmana or Satyayan Upanishad Brahmana; (ix) Vansa Brahmana; (x) Sanhitopnishad Brahmana; (xi) The Ballavi Brahmana (lost).

Atharvaveda has only one Brahmana which is Gopath Brahmana.

5.
The Aranyakas and the Upanishadas

The word 'Aranyaka' is derived from 'Aranya' means forest. Neither in the Samhita nor in the Brahmana is one urged to go and live in a forest. Vedic rites are to be performed by the house holder living in a village. But after his mind is rendered pure through such rites, he goes to a forest as a recluse to engage himself in meditation. It is to qualify for this stage of Vanprasthas, to become inwardly pure and mellow that Vedic practices like sacrifices are to be followed. For Max Muller, Aranyakas are the intermediary link between the Sutra literature and the Brahmanas (Max Muller, 313).

The Aranyakas prepare one for one's stage in life as an anchorite. They expound the concepts inherent in the mantras of the Samhitas and the rites detailed in the Brahmanas. In other words, they explain the hidden meaning of the Vedas, their metaphysical passages. Indeed, they throw light on the esoteric message of our scripture. For the Aranyakas, more important than the performance of the sacrifices is awareness of their inner meaning and significance. The Aranyakas incorporate the metaphorical passages representing the metaphysical inquiries conducted by the inmates of forest hermitages.

As Sayan tells us the Aranyakas had to be read in the forests and were primarily intended for the Vanaprasthas. This is why these are aptly named as the 'Treatises of the Forests'. Thus, these were addressing non-materialistic concerns for those who after having performed all the duties of a student and a householder, retire from the worldly affairs to the forest to end their days in the contemplation of the deity. Arunikopanishad tells us that the Sannyasin, the man who no longer recites the mantras, and no longer performs sacrifices, is bound to read, out of all the Vedas only the Aranyaka or the Upanishads. In several instances the Aranyakas form part of the Brahmanas, and they are thus made to share the authority of Smriti. It has been observed, that part of an Aranyaka was ascribed to a human author, Asvalayana. Another part is quoted by Sayana in his commentary on the Rigveda as being a sutra work of Saunaka's. There are good proofs to acknowledge certain differences between the Brahmanas and the Aranyakas. Comparing the two Max Muller argues that Aranyakas presuppose Brahmanas as is clear from the Brihdaranyaka. Here, we have the story of Janaka promising a huge prize to the wisest Brahman on the occassion of a sacrifice. If we compare this description as it comes before us from the third Adhyaya of the Brihdaranyaka with the same story from the Satpath Brahmana (XI.4.6), we find almost the repetition of all the details. However, in the case of Brihdaranyaka, the story comes with additional details particularly with respect to the philosophical disputes that took place between Yajnavalakya and other Brahmans at this event.

The Aranyakas are immensely valued for their philosophy. The philosophical parts more popularly known as Upanishads are probably the most extensively read portion of Vedic literature. These provide the foundational base on which various systems of philosophy in India rest. Thus not only Vedantists but philosophers of the Sankhya, the Vaiseshika, the Nyaya and the Yoga all seek justifications and legitimacy by going back to the Upanishads. Not merely philosophers but various sects that have existed across the sub-continent and across the centuries in India also derive legitimacy and life blood from Upanishadas. Max Muller says that in the Upanishads there is enough space and freedom and breadth of thought that it is not difficult to find in them some authority for almost anyshade of philosophical opinion.This is also the main reason for the evrgrowing number of Upanishads as it is relatively easier to compose new texts and link them with the existing corpus and justify philosophical tenets.

The Upanishads were originally parts of the Aranyakas and Brahmanas. Only in the case of Vajasneyi Samhita we find an Upanishad as a part of a samhita. The Vajasaneyi Samhita is comprised of the Isha Upanishad forming the 40th book, and the Siva Sankalpa, forming part of the 34th book. For Max Muller, Vajasneyi Samhita is a composition of later years. In later times, the Upanishads obtained a more independent position and though they still professed to belong more particularly to one or the other of the four Vedas, that relationship became quite lax and changeable.

The true etymological meaning of the word Upanishad had been forgotten in India. Upanishad lietrally means sitting near or sitting at the feet of someone in order to listen or in order to meditate and worship. It says, *Namasa it upa sidata* or approach him with praise (Rig Veda, 9, 11, 6). We also find, *Vayah Suparnah Upa Sedur Indram priyamedhah rishayah nadhamanah* which translates as 'The poets with good thoughts have approached Indra at the beginning, like birds with beautiful wings' (Rig Veda,10.73.11). However, instead of this original meaning, in later years, Upanishad acquired a mystic charm and is generally explained by Rahasya or Guhya Adesh and mystery. An artificial etymology is given, according to which Upanishad would mean 'destruction of passion or ignorance by means of divine revelation'.

Pujya Saraswati remarks that if the Samhita is the tree, the Brahmana is the flower, and the Aranyaka is the fruit (i.e., in its unripe stage), the Upanishads are the mellow fruit–the final fruit or Phala. The Upanishads paves the way for realising the non-difference between the Jiwatman (individual self) and the Paramatma. The main objective of the Upanishad is to motivate people towards an inquiry in the ultimate reality and the attainment of the stage where one becomes wise enough and mature enough to sever oneself from all Karma. It is on this basis that the Vedas are divided into the Karmakanda and the Gyanakanda, the part dealing with work and the part dealing with knowledge (enlightenment). The two are also spoken of as the Purva Mimansa and the Uttara Mimansa respectively.

The Vedas find their final expression in the Upanishads. Indeed, the Upanishads are called Vedanta. They form the final part of the Vedas in two ways. In each recension, we have first Samhita, then the Brahmana, which is followed by the Aranyaka, the Upanishads coming at the close of the Aranyaka. The Upanishads throw light on the meaning and purpose of the Vedas and represent the end of the scripture in more than one sense : while the text forms the concluding part of the Vedas, their meaning represents the ultimate truth of the same. The Upanishads are the Shikhar, the summit, of our philosophical system.

In the Upanishad, we find that the question of the means of knowledge is definitively raised. The Vedas are not always recognised as the sources of complete knowledge (though in some instances they are).

Shwetaketu, despite much Vedic learning, cannot solve the question of transmigration, Narada admits to Sanat Kumar his incompetence to understand the Atma. The Taittiriya Upanishad expressly reduces the knowledge of the Vedas to an inferior position by assigning them to the stage of the mind-made Atma which has to be surmounted before reaching the final truth. But these views were gradually and naturally supplemented by another Veda: hence the term Vedant which first occurs in the Shwetashwatar Upanishad and denotes the Upanishads as the end of the Veda in which its deepest secret is disclosed. There are more than 250 Upanishads. Shankar Bhagavatpada selected ten for his comments: ईशा-केन- कठ-प्रश्न-मुण्डक, माण्डूक्य, तैत्तिरीय, ऐतरेय च छान्दोग्यम्–वष्टहदारण्यकम् दष्ठा।

Besides these ten, there are *Shwetaswatar, Kaushitiki* and *Nrisingh Tapani.* Thus, altogether we have thirteen.

Native tradition derives the term Upanishad, from roots which yield as its sense either that which destroys innate ignorance, or that which leads to the Brahman. It is more important to note that from an early period the stress is laid on the secret character of the instructions contained in these works: the rule is that they are the highest mysteries and that this doctrine should not be imparted to any pupil, other than a son, who has not already studied with the teacher for a year and who does not intend himself to become a teacher. The same view is enforced by facts recounted in the texts. When the deepest part of the discussion arrives, the two concerned go apart and talk of the new doctrine of action as the source of human fate.

Therefore, when we seek for an origin of the term which will not defy the laws of etymology, it is necessary to find something which will accord, with this essential nature of secrecy. The word is derived obviously from the prefixes up-ni and -sad, sit; and the only natural meaning is a session, a sitting down near some person, who naturally is assumed to be the teacher. This is in accord with the mode of teaching followed in India, which as we have seen involved the sitting of the pupil and the teacher facing each other, while the latter repeated the less on to be learned by the former. The lessons of the teacher to his pupil were not public in the ordinary sense of the word: to be practicable they naturally required quiet, but the ritual texts show us more than that: they bear witness that certain texts of special importance were to be taught to the people in the forest, and not in the normal place, the abode of the teacher. What is in accord with this admirable fact that the Upanishads form part of, or are attached (in the case of the most important and the oldest of these works) to texts which tradition gives the name of Aranyaka. The name clearly must have been derived from the fact that the discussion contained in these works were studied in the forest; the alternative view is that the Aranyakas were specially intended for study by the Vanaprasthas, men who, after serving their apprenticeship as Brahmana students and having fulfilled their duties as house-holder would retire to the forests to study. This is clearly a more advanced conception than that attained in early Upanishads.

Aranyakas

1. Aitareya Aranyaka
2. Taittiriya Aranyaka
3. Jaimini Aranyaka Brahamana
4. Sankha Yana Aranyaka.

It may be worth mentioning that Kausitaki Upanishad is part of the Sankhayan Aranyaka (Keith, II: 499).

Upanishads

As stated earlier, Upanishads are ever growing in numbers and we have different numbers for them. A collection of Atharvan Upanishad varies from 34 to 52. Another calculation suggests the total number of Upanishads as 108. A Collection at the time of Dara Shukoh consisted of 50 Upanishads and translated into Persian. We can however conclude that there are 220 Upanishads available (*Kalyana Upanishada Anka*). Following are the important among these:

1. Aitareya Upanishad
2. Brahadaranyaka Upanishad
3. Chandogya Upanishad
4. Taittiriya Upanishad
5. Kausitaki Upanishad
6. Kena Upanishad or Talvatara Upanishad
7. Jaminiya Upanishad
8. Katha Upanishad
9. Isha Upanishad/Vajasneya Upanishad
10. Swetaswatara Upanishad

11. Mundaka Upanishad
12. Mahanarayan Upanishad (Part of Taitiriya Aranyanka)
13. Prasna Upanishad
14. Maitrayaniya Upanishad
15. Mandukya Upanishad

Sutra Grantha

The Sutra period is of peculiar importance to the history of Indian Literature as it forms the connecting link between the Vedic Sanskrit and the later Sanskrit. While several works written in Sutra are clubbed as post-Vedic or modern Sanskrit literature, we also find other examples which were though written in continuous Anushtubh Slokas or more frequently inter-mixed with Trishtubh and other verses are the outcome of the Vedic Age itself; and this trespasses in a certain degree upon the frontiers of the later Sanskrit.

It is difficult to explain the peculiarities of the style of the Sutra literature to anyone who has not worked his way through the sutras themselves. It is impossible to give anything like a literal translation of these works, as they are written in the most artificial, elaborate and enigmatic form. Sutra means string; and all the works written in this style, on the subjects are nothing but one uninterrupted string of short sentences, twisted together into the most concise form. Brevity is the style of composition and it is a proverbial saying among the Pandits that an 'author rejoiceth in the economising of half a short vowel as much as in the birth of a son'. Every doctrine thus propounded whether grammar, metre, law or philosophy, is reduced to a mere skeleton. All the important points and joints of a system are laid open with the greatest precision and clarity, but there is nothing in these works like connection or development of ideas.

Literary works, belonging to the preceding periods, the Brahmanas as well as the mantras are considered by Indian theologians as forming the Shruti or divine revelation, in contrast to the Sutras and all the rest of the literature. The sutras although based on the Shruti and therefore in some instances are called Shrauta Sutra, are avowedly composed by human authors.

What is called Smriti includes not only Sutras but also Slokas such as the laws of Manu, Yagyavalkya, Parasara, which sometimes are called the Smritis, but the text of Sutras have mostly been superseded by the metrical paraphrase.

Scholars have divided ancient Sanskrit works into three groups- the vedic Samhitas (Rig, Yajur, Sama and Atharva), the Brahmanas and Sutras. The first of two is referred as Veda or Shruti but Sutras are not Veda. However, many of these are closely linked with the Veda and also include mantras. Sutras on the other hand form a corpus that is also known as Kalpa (one of the six auxiliary lores or angas of the Veda).

Kalpa Sutra

According to Kane the word Kalpa is used in two ways: the comprehensive way in which the aphoristic works on vedic ritual, domestic ceremonies, law, government and administration of justice all are included; the other meaning includes only those aphoristic works that are concerned with vedic sacrifices and similar matters.

In this second sense of the term, Kalpa is the Shastra that involves one in 'work'. A man learns to chant the Vedas, studies Siksha, Vyakaran, Nirukti and Jyotishya. He has to apply these sutras to the rites he is enjoined to perform. He has to wash away his sins, the sins earned by acting according to his whims. This he does by doing good work. For this he must know the appropriate mantras and how to enunciate them correctly, understanding their meaning. Also certain materials are needed along with a house that is architecturally suited to the conduct of the rituals. The fruits yielded by these must be offered to Iswara. Kalpa concerns itself with these matters.

If taken in a comprehensive manner, Kalpa corpus can be divided into three classes or groups: *Shrauta Sutra, Grihya Sutra* and *Dharma Sutra.*

In the south there exists what is called 'Andpillai Prayoga', 'Andpillai' belonged to Tiruppanantel and was named after the deity Ganesh (Pillayai) Tira Vidaiwra rudur (Tanja district). It is according to his method that Shrauta works are performed. The Shrauta sacrifices are sacraments of large scale not conducted in the home but in a Yagyashala. Rites that are not so big are 'Grihya' and performed at home. Since big sacrifices have become rare the Grihya Sutras have gained greater importance. Besides, alien shastras, alien practices, are becoming more and more popular.

Following is the list of Kalpa Sutras associated with their respective Vedas:

Shrauta Sutras deal with solemn vedic sacrifices mentioned or discussed in Vedas and Brahmanas. These are also referred as pertaining to *Karmakanda.*

Rig Veda: Aswalayana and Sankhyayana.

Yajur Veda:

a. KrishnaYajurveda:Apastambas,Hiranyakesiya/ Satyashada,Baudhayan,Bharadwaj,Vaikhanasa,Vadhul, Manava and Varah.

b. Shukla Yajurveda: Katyayan/ Parasar.

Sama Veda: Masak,Latyayan, Drasyayan and Khadir.

Atharva Veda: Vaitan.

Grihya Sutras detail domestic ceremonies like Upanayana, marriage, daily and periodic rites and the use mantras for them mostly from one shakha of the Vedas.

Rig Veda: Aswalayana, Sankhyayana and Kausitaki

Yajur Veda: a. Krishna Yajurveda: Baudhayan, Bharadwaja, ApastambaHiranyakesi, Manava, Vaikhanasa, Kathak, Varah and Agnivesha.

b. Shukla Yajurveda: Paraskara (Katiya) and Baijapa.

Sama Veda: Gohila, Khadira, Jaiminiya and Drahyayana.

Atharva Veda: Kausika

Both Shrauta and Grihya Sutras engage with forty samsakaras to be formed from conception to death. Here, it may worth keeping in mind that a samsakara is that which refines the performer. I would also like to mention that the total number of Shrauta and Grihya Sutras belonging to Krishna Yajurveda are too large and only important ones are mentioned here.

Dharma Sutras unlike Grihya Sutras rarely describe the rituals related to domestic life. Wider in scope and ambition, Dharma Sutras primarily deal with the rules of conduct, law and custom. What we understand by the English term 'law', is derived from them. The Dharmashastra is based on them. They are also the basis of moral and legal Shastras of Manu and others. However, these are closely connected with the Grihya Sutras in subject and topic. According to Kane, 'the authors of the (older) Dharma Sutras do not claim to be inspired seers or superhuman beings. While the other Smritis such as those of Manu and Yajnavalkya are ascribed to Gods like Brhma. Gautama Dharma Sutra is regarded as the oldest surviving Dharma Sutra. Some of the other significant Dharma Sutras include: Apastarmba, Vasistha, Hiranyakesi, Vishnu, Harita, Sankha-Likhita and Manava.

Sulaba Sutras are of two types: *Samanya* and *Vishishta.* These are composed by Katyayana, Baudhayana and Hiranyakeshi. These seers are for all the four Vedas.

Pratishakhya

It is related to grammatical norms for the recitation of Vedas. However, many of them are extinct. The rules of Pratisakhyas were not intended for written literature and they are there only to serve as a guide giving instructions on how to learn the Vedas by heart and to repeat it as part of the daily devotion. Among Pratisakhyas, Katyayana's

Pratishakhya shows a considerable advancement in grammatical technicalities. Some of Katyayana's Sutras are found to be repeated in Panini's grammar. This might seem strange but it is said that not all the Sutras (now incorporated in his grammar) came from Panini himself, and it is most likely that Katyayana in writing his supplementary notes to Panini, simply repeated some of his Pratishakhya Sutra and that, at a later time, Vartika became part of the Panini's text.

Pratishakhya belonging to the Atharvaveda is known as *Shaunakiya Chaturdhyayika.* A small treatise has been found containing the Taittariya Pratishakhya and this might be called the Pratishakhya of Samaveda. However, according to Max Muller it was badly written and so unintelligible that without a commentary little use can be made of it. It is called Sama Tantra and it evidently treats the same subjects which normally occur in the Pratishakhyas. Its authenticity is supported by Charanvyuha, where a Sama Tantra is mentioned, but without any particulars.

Max Muller has also remarked that in the Rig Veda the rules of our Pratishakhyas are not uniformly observed and the same is the case with other Vedas. As Shaunak was himself a member of the Sakal, we may quote his Pratishakhya as the Sakal Pratishakhya. But strictly speaking it could only be called one of Sakal Pratisakhyas, preserved by the pupils of Shaunaka, who soon after found themselves into a new Charan under the name of Shaunakiyas. Tribhasyaratna is said to be the substance of the works of three celebrated sages Atreya, Mahish and Vararuchi. The Pratishakhya ascribed to the Katyayana shows a considerable advancement in grammatical technicalities. It is said that Panini's rules are intended for a language which was no longer the pure Sanskrit of the Veda. Katyayana's Pratishakhya seems to belong to a period when there existed but one recognised literature, that of the Rishis.

Max Muller has noted that he had not found any Pratishakhya for the SamaVeda. He however discovered a very small treatise that contains the Taittiriya Pratishakhya and this might be named as the Pratishakhya of the Sama Veda. This was found to be badly written and was quite unintelligible. Without a commentary, very little use can be made of it. It is called Sama Tantra and evidently treats the same subjects that usually occur in the Pratishakhya. Its authenticity is supported by Charanvyuha where a Sama Tantra is mentioned but without any further details (Max Muller, 143).

The following list (which is from *The History of Sanskrit Literature* by Max Muller) gives the name of the principal authorities quoted in these four above Pratishakhyas (Max Muller, 1959:142-3):

1. Agnivesh (Taittiriya Pratishakhya),
2. Agnivesh Yayan (Taittiriya Pratishakhya),
3. Agrayana (Nirukta),
4. Atreya (Taittiriya),
5. Anyatareya (Sakal Chaturadhyayika),
6. Apisali (Pnini),
7. Ahvarakas (Taittiriya),
8. Ukhya (Taittiriya),
9. Uttamottariyas (Taittiriya),
10. Udichhyas (Panini),
11. Audumbaryana (Nirukta),
12. Aupamanyava (Nirukta),
13. Aupasivi (Katyayana Pratishakhya),
14. Aurnavabha (Nirukta),
15. Khandamayana (Taittiriya),
16. Kanva (Katyayana),
17. Kathakya (Nirukta),
18. Kasyapa (Katyayana),
19. Kaundinya (Taittiriya Pratishakhya),

20. Kautsa (Nirukta),
21. Kauhaliputra (Taittiriya Pratishakhya),
22. Kraushtuki (Nirukta),
23. Gargya (Sakal Pratisakhya, Katyayana, Panini, Nirukta),
24. Galva (Nirukta, Panini),
25. Gautama (Taittiriya),
26. Charmasiras (Nirukta),
27. Chakravarmana (Panini),
28. Jatukarnya (Katyayana),
29. Taitiki (Nirukta),
30. Taittiryakas (Taittiriya),
31. Dalbhasya (Katyayana),
32. Panchalas (Sakal),
33. Paushkarsaridi (Taittiriya, Panini),
34. Prachyas (Sakal, Panini),
35. Plakshi (Taittiriya),
36. Plakshayana (Taittiriya),
37. Babharvya (Sakal),
38. Bharadwaja (Taittiriya, Panini),
39. Mandukey (Mandukya, Padakrit, Sakal),
40. Masakiya (Taittiriya),
41. Mimansakas (Taittiriya),
42. Yaksa (Sakal),
43. Vatabhikara (Taittiriya),
44. Vatsapara (Taittiriya),
45. Vatsya (Chaturadhyayika),
46. Varshyani (Nirukta),
47. Valmiki (Taittiriya),
48. Vedamitra (Sakal),
49. Vyali (Sakal),
50. Satabalaskha Mandgalya (Nirukta),

51. Sakatayana (Sakal, Katyayana, Chaturadhyayika, Nirukta, Panini),
52. Sakapuni (Nirukta),
53. Sakala- Padakrit (Sakal),
54. Sakala (Sakala Pratishakhya),
55. Sakalya (Sakal, Katyayana, Panini),
56. Sakalya Pitri (sakal),
57. Sankhyayan (Taittiriya),
58. Saityayana (Taittiriya),
59. Saunaka (Sakal, Katyayana, Chaturadhyayika),
60. Sankritya (Taittiriya),
61. Senaka (Panini),
62. Sthaulasthivi (Nirukta),
63. Sphotayana (Panini),
64. Harita (Taittiriya)

6.
The Vedangas

Among the basic texts of Hinduism, the six angas or limbs of the Vedas are next in importance to the Vedas themselves. The Veda Purusha has six limbs or parts–mouth, nose, eyes, ears, hands and feet. These are called 'sadang'.

The name does not imply the existence of six distinct books or treatises intimately connected with their sacred writings, but merely the admission of six subjects the study of which was necessary either for the reading, the understanding or proper sacrificial employment of the Veda. Manu calls the Vedangas by the name of Pravachanas. Commonly, the word Pravachana is meant the Brahmana, and it is called so because it is proclaimed. There is a passage in the Prasathanabheda which says 'for each Veda there are several shakhas the difference of which arises from different Pravachanas' प्रस्थानभेद एवं प्रवचन भेदात्यति वेदं भिन्ना यूयस्य: ष्टाखा:। Here Pravachana means Brahmana because the difference of Brahamana shakhas does arise from Brahmanas peculiar to each. It is possible, however, that Madhusudan used Pravachana in the sense of pronunciation, the difference in pronunciation is the chief cause of the samhita-shakhas. Pravachana is used in the Kathopanishad (ii, 23) in the sense of 'reading'. And indeed, instead of looking for the Vedangas in those small and barren tracts which are now known by this name, it is in the Brahmanas, and Sutras that we have to look for the Vedanga doctrines in their original and authentic form. The short Vedangas which are generally added to the manuscripts of the Veda, and which by several scholars were mistaken for the real Vedangas, represent only the last unsuccessful attempts to bring the complicated and unitelligible doctrines of former sages into an easy and popular form, and to preserve at the same time the names which had been sanctioned by antiquity.

A very clear and rational statement as to the character of the Vedangas in early times is given in the Brihadaranyak Upanishad and its commentary. According to them, the different doctrines of Vedangas are to be considered as integral part of the Brahmanas in the same manner as the Puranas and the Itihas. These were to be taken in the sense of epic of Puranic stories, incorporated in the Brahmanas, as illustrations of ceremonial questions.

Max Muller says that it is more difficult to determine where and when the Vedangas were first mentioned as six. In the Mundaka Upanishad the number of the Vedangas is given as six, but in a line which is not unlikely to be interpolated. Yaska quotes only the Vedangas, but not the six Vedangas, where we meet with the well-known verses memorialis, containing the titles of the six vedangas: ष्टिाक्षा कल्पो व्याकरणं निरूक्तो छन्दो जयोतिज़ं।। (Max Muller, 111). Apastamba, who occassionally quotes slokas in his sutras, does not seem to have known this verse. His words are षंडगो वेद: कल्पो व्याकरणं ज्योतिज़ं निरूक्तं ष्टिाक्षा (ibid,111). What follows in the only manuscript known to Max Muller was eaten away by worms; but then comes the word छन्दों, विचिते which was the title of a metrical treatise and is quoted as much before Pingala in the Sabda-Kalpa-druma. तस्य ग्रन्था: छन्दो विचित पिंगल छंदोमंजरी श्रुत बोधादय: सन्ति। One of the Parishisthas of the Sama Veda begins with the words अथातष्टच्छंदसां विचयं व्याख्यास्याम:। The Parishisthas, however, are of later period than Apastamba and Pingala; for the author of Parishistha declares that he made use of Pingala's work. ब्राह्मणातंस्मि नष्ठचौव पिंगलाच्य महात्मन:। निदानाहुकथ ष्टास्त्रच्छ छंदसां ज्ञानमुद्यतं।। The title Nanksfofpfr refers, therefore, most likely to the Nidana-sutra, which also begins with

अथातष्ठछंदसां विचयं। In the commentary on the Sakala-Pratishakhya, at the end of the 14th Book, the Vedangas are enumerated as follows: व्याख्यास्यामः। कल्पो व्याकरणं निरूतं ष्ठिाक्षा छंदोविचिति ज्योर्तिज़ामयनं।.

The same number occurs in Manu. There is a passage in the Chhandogya Upanishad where a mention of the six Vedangas might be expected, at the beginning of the 9th Prapathak. The number six however, does not occur there, although Vedangas doctrines are clearly implied under some what unusual names. Narada, having solicited instruction from Sanat Kumara and being inerrogated by him as to the extent of his previous knowledge, says, 'I have learnt the Rig Veda, the Yajur Veda, the Sama Veda, the Atharva Veda (which is the 4th), the Itihas and the Puranas which are the Vth (Grammar) or the Veda of Vedas, the obsequies of the Manus *Pitrayan*, the art of computation *Rashi*, the knowledge of omens *devam*, the revolution of periods *nidhi*, commentary *mahakaladi nidhishashtram*, the intention of speech (or art of reasoning, बाकोवालियं) the maxim of ethics ,dk;ua, the divine science (or construction of scriptures) nsofoka], commentary or *Nirukta* the sciences appendant on holy writ (or accentuation, prosody and religious rites), ब्रह्मविद्यां, the adjuration of spirits भूत विद्यां, commentary भूततंत्र, the art of soldier क्षत्र विद्यां, commentary धनुर्वेद, the science of astronomy नक्षत्र विद्यां, the charming of serpents सर्पविद्या, the science of demi-gods (or music and mechanical art), गारूढ़ Garuda: all this I have studied; yet do I know the text, and have no knowledge of the soul.

The earliest mention of the number six with reference to the Vedangas seem to be contained in one of the Brahmanas of the Samaveda. But there again, though the number six is given, titles of the several Vedangas are not mentioned. It is said there of Svaha स्वाहा, that her body consists of the four Vedas and that her limbs are the six

Angas, or members of the Veda. चत्वारोऽस्यै वेदा: ष्टारीरंज्ञाडंगान्यंगानि। औज़धि वन्सपयो लोभानि। The four Vedas are her body; the six Angas her limbs; herbs and trees her hair). It is possible, however, that more ancient Brahmanas allude to the number six; at all events we see that it was sanctioned for the Vedangas before the end of the Brahman period. These six limbs are

Mouth: Vyakaran

Nose: Shiksha: rules for correct pronunciation of Vedic mantras. (Phonetics: Pronunciation)

Eye: Jyotis (Astronomy: Astrology)

Ear: Nirukta (Lexicon, Elymology: Explanation of words or difficult words occurring in the Vedas

Hand: Kalpa (Manual of rituals) Ceremonial: Details of religious ceremonies.

Foot: Chhand (Prosody metre).

Shiksha: The Nose

Enunciation of the mantras is most important to the Vedas. Shiksha is the science that deals with the character of the Vedic syllables–it determines their true nature. The science of the sounds of human speech is called Phonetics and it is more important to the Vedic language than to any other tongue. The reason is that even if there is a slight change in how one vocalises a syllable the efficacy of the mantra will be affected.

Shiksha deals with varnah, uccaran, svara, matra, bala, sama and santan (इत्युक्त: ष्टािक्षा ध्यायति). The sound of each mantra is determined with utmost accuracy. How different sounds have their source in different parts of the body and how they are vocalised and all such details which are of scientific and practical importance are dealt with in this Ang. Sayana says, ष्टािक्ष्यंते वेदना योप दिज़्यते स्वर वर्णादयां यता सा ष्टािक्षा। सैंपा ष्टािक्षा।

There is a beautiful verse by Panini in Paniniya Siksha which tells us how careful we must be in pronouncing Vedic syllables:

भ्याघ्री यथा हरेत पुत्राण दमस्त्राभ्यम् न च पिड्येत
भितपतनाभेदभ्यम् तद्वद वर्ण प्रयोजयेत।

The Vedic syllables must be pronounced with clarity. The character of their sound should not be distorted even a bit. But no force should be used in vocalising the syllables. There should be no damage done– no erosion of the sound– and no violence should be suggested in the pronunciation. How does a tigress carry its cubs? Tigress and cats carry their young ones by holding them firmly with their teeth, yet in doing so they do not hurt the little ones. The Vedic hymns must be chanted in the same way, the syllables enunciated gently and yet distinctly (Saraswati, 286).

Chhanda: Legs

The Rig Veda and the Sama Veda are entirely poetical in form. The Yajur Veda consists of both prose and poetry. The Atharva Veda consists of mixture of prose and poetry. It is because poetry forms their major parts that the Vedas are called chhandas. Poetry also has its measurement expressed in feet and number of syllables. The shastra that deals with such measurement is chhandas and the texts on which it is chiefly based is chhanda sutra by Pingala. People who have received initiation into a mantra touch their heads with their hands, mentioning the name of the sage associated with the mantra, touch their nose mentioning the chhandas and touch their heart mentioning the deity involved. All vedic mantras in verse are chhandas. Non-Vedic poetry is in the form of sloka. The term chhandas also refers to poetic metre (Prosody). There are many types of vritta (metre) in poetry. Slokas are of course vrittas. There is a metre called 'Anustubh' in which the Ramayana and the Puranas are composed. There are rules governing the number of feet in each stanza and the number of syllables in each foot. The following books are available that deliberate on chhanda:

Gargya Prokta Upanidan Sutra (Samaveda), *Pingala Nag Prokta Chhandah Sutra* (*Chandovichit*), *Venkat Madhavakrit Chandonukramani, Jaideva Chanda Sutra, Halajudh Briti, Chando Manjari, Vritta Ratnakar, Shruta Bodha* and *Janashree Chhando Bichiti.*

Vyakarana–Mouth

This branch of literature is represented by Panini Vyakarana. There are two separate treatises or grammatical subjects, which belong to a period anterior to Panini. The sutras are the Unadi: Sutras of Santancharya. However, as Panini mentions Sutras of Santancharya, and gives general rules with regard to them they must have existed before him.

There are a number of works on Sanskrit grammar. The most widely used and important is the one by the great sage Panini. There is a gloss– a vartika on his Vyakaran sutra by Vararuchi. It is also known as Astadhyayi. Pantanjali has written a bhashya or commentary on Panini's Sutra. Some other important works are *Vyakarana Bhashya* (Panini), Vararuchi's *Vyakarana Sutra* and Patanjali's treaty on Panini's grammer, *Sutra of Santanacharya, Unadi Sutra,* Commentry of Katyayana on Vartik-Panini grammar, *Saraswata* Grammar, *Hemchandra* Grammar, *Prakrit Prakasha, Prakrit* Grammar, *Kalapvya* Grammar, *Mugdh Bodh* Grammar.

Nirukta–Ear

Nirukta serves the purpose of a vedic dictionary or Kosha. Nirukta which deals with the origin of words, their roots, that is, with the etymology, is the ear of the Vedapurusha. It explains the meaning of rare words in the Vedas and how or why they are used in a particular context.

Nirukta is represented by the name of Yaska's Nirukta, Kashyapa, Sakpuni. Nirukta consists of three parts. The first part is the Nirghantuka, second Naigama and third Daivata.

Radhakant has quoted in his Shabda Kalpdruma the definition of Nirukta which occurs as one of the Karikas in Kashikaritti:

वर्ण गमो वर्ण विपर्ययष्ठच्य द्वौ चाप तै वर्ण विकार नाष्ठौ।
धतौ स्त दर्ष्ठाति ष्ठायेन योग स्त दुच्यते पंच विध निरूक्तं।।

(Max Muller, 156)

The Nirukta, together with the Pratishakhyas and Panini's grammar supply the most interesting and important information about the growth of grammatical science in India. Valuable materials preserved in these works is useful for tracing the origin of one of the most ancient branches of philosophy: the Grammar.

There are only two nations in the whole history of the world which have conceived independently (without any suggestions from others) the two sciences of logic and grammar. They are India and Greece.

Jyotish– Eye

Jyotish is the science of celestial bodies and consists of three skandhas or sections. So it is called स्कन्ध त्रयत्मकम. Sages like Garga, Narada and Prasara have written treatises on this subject.

The sun God, in disguise, taught this science to Maya, the carpenter of the Asuras. The work incorporating his teachings is called Surja Siddhant. Besides Varahmihir, Arya Bhatt and Bhaskaracharya have written treatises on this science. Recently Sundareshwara Shrautin wrote works on this subject called Siddhanta-Kaustubham.

Kalpa – Hand

In order to make the understanding of the prescribed ceremonies easier, Baudhayana composed the Kalpa. The Brahamanas are endless and difficult to understand, therefore the old masters have adopted the Kalpa-sutras according to different shakhas. These Kalpa-sutras have the advantage of being clear, short, complete, and correct.

Kalpa is the Shastra that involves one in work. A man learns to chant the vedas, shiksha, Vyakaran, chhandas, Nirukta and Jyotish. What does he do next? He has to apply these sastras to the rites he is enjoined to perform. Kalpa is needed to do so.

Itihas Purana

The Puranas are the magnifying glass of the Vedas. The principles and rules of Dharma that are dealt with in the Vedas are enlarged and elaborated upon in the form of stories. A subject briefly touched upon may not make a deep impression on the mind. If the same were told as an absorbing story it would at once make an impact on the mind of the listener or reader.

The Vedas urge us to speak the truth- Satyam Vada. How one becomes exalted by remaining truthful at all costs is illustrated by the story of Harischandra. Dharmam chara (follow Dharma, live a life of Dharma) is a Vedic injunction consisting of just two words. The importance of the pursuit of Dharma is explained through the long story of Dharmaputra in the Mahabharat. मातष्ट देवो भव पितष्ट देवो भव (Be one to whom the mother is a God– Be one to whom the father is a God): these two admonishments are enlarged through the magnifying glass in the story of Sri Ram. Such dharmic virtues as humility, patience, compassion, chastity, which are the subjects of Vedic ordinances, are illustrated through the noble examples of men belonging to ancient times, women of hallowed reputation. By reading these stories or listening to them we form a deep attachment to the virtues and qualities exemplified by them.

In several parts of Brahmanas and Aranyakyas, when an account is given of the literature, known to the ancient Indian, we meet with the names of Gatha, Narasansi, Itihas and Akhyana (songs, legends, epic poems, and stories) as parts of the vedic literature.

ब्राह्मण नीति हासन्पुराणानि कल्पान् गाथा नाराष्ठांसो।इतिहासः पुराणं विद्या उपनिज़द् लोकाः सूत्राराय नु व्याख्यानानि व्याख्यानानि॥(*Taittiriya Aranyakas*)

The Puranas are also history as the saying goes, इतिहास पुराणाभ्यां वेदं समुपवष्टहयेत् A Vyas composed the Puranas in 400,000 granthas. A Granth is a stanza consisting of 32 syllables. Of these Skanda Purana alone accounts for 100,000. It is perhaps the world's biggest literary work. The remaining 17 Puranas add upto 300,000 granthas. Apart from them, Vyas composed the Mahabharat in nearly 100,000 granthas.

Each Puran is devoted to a particular deity: There are Saiva, Vaisanava and Shakta Puranas :

Brahma Puran	:	Brahma
Padma Puran	:	Padma
Narada Puran	:	Narada
Markandeya Puran	:	Vaisnava
Vishnu Puran	:	Vaisnava
Siva Puran	:	Saiva
Bhagwat Puran	:	Aagneya
Agni Puran	:	Aagneya
Bhabishya Puran	:	
Brahma Vaivarta Puran	:	
Ling Puran	:	
Varah Puran	:	Varah.
Vayu Puran	:	Vayu
Skanda Mahapuran	:	
Vaman Puran	:	Vaman
Kurma Puran	:	Kurma
Matsya Puran	:	Matsya
Garuda Puran	:	Garud
Brahmand Puran	:	Brahmand

Parashara was the original author of Vishnu Puran.But Vyas wrote it in the present form. Parashara was the father of Vyasa. It may be a point of interest here that Vishnu

Sahasranama and the Shiva Sahasranama are part of Mahabharat. The Pradosha-Strotra is in the Skanda Puran.

In the Puranas themselves it is mentioned that these were narrated by Siva to Parvati or to Vishnu. It is also said that Vishnu taught them to Narada and some other sages.

Thus the stories told by the Gods were later passed on from one sage to another sage or to a King. In the end the Puranas were narrated by Vyasa to Suta, and by Suta to the Sages in Naimisharanya.

It was from a high seat offered by the sages at Naimisharanya that Suta taught the Puranas. Suta was the disciple of Vyasa.

Upa-Puranas

Along with Puranas, we have a number of Upa-Puranas. These include Vinayak Puran, Kalki Puran, Tula Puran, Magha Puran, Vaisakha Puran, Upamarga, Bhaktavilas, Adi, Narsingh Samb, Nandi, Aditya, Soma. The Kurma Puran shows the following names:

1. Adya Sanatkumarokta
2. Narsinha
3. Skanda
4. ShivaDharma
5. Durvasasokta (sage Durvasas)
6. Nardiya
7. Kapila
8. Vamana(Sage–Parashara)
9. Usanasirita (declared by sage Usana)
10. Brahmanda
11. Varuna
12. Kalika
13. Maheshwara
14. Samba
15. Saura
16. Marich

17. Parashokta
18. Bhargav

The Brahadharanya Puran clearly intimates its knowledge of many other Upa-Puranas besides these Eighteen and gives the following 18 names of the Upa-Puranas:

1. Adi Puran	10. Brahmanda
2. Aditya	11. Vishnu Dharmottara
3. Brahammdradiya	12. ShivaDharma
4. Nandiya	13. Vishnu Dharma
5. Nandiswara	14. Vamana
6. Brahanma dighwara	15. Varuna
7. Sansa	16. Narsinha
8. Kriya-yoga-sar	17. Bhagavat
9. Kalika	18. Bhadharana

The Ekamra Puran gives the following Upa- Puranas:

Brihannara Suiha, Brihadvaisnav, Garuda, Brahmanaradiya, Naidiya, Prabhascka, Devi, Kalika, Akhetaha, Brahnnadi, Litavati, Ekamara,Ekapada, Laghubhagavats, Mretyunjaya, Angira Sake, Nandikeshwara and *Sambe.*

Smriti

Smriti includes not only Sutras, but also slokass, such as Laws of Manu, Yajnyavalkya and Parashara. Most of these are founded on Sutra. Smritis have no claim to an independent authority but derives their authority from their intimate connection with Shruti–which means recollection. Kumarila remarks, "Recollection is knowledge, the object of which is some previous knowledge; and if Manu and other authors of Smriti had not originally been in possession of an authoritative knowledge, it would be impossible to appeal to their recollection as an authority.

Shruti and Smriti are the authorities: धर्म जिज्ञासमानानं प्रमाणं परमं श्रुति:। Yagyavalkya says: *"Puran Nyaya Mimansah Dharmasastrang Mishrita. Vedah Sthanani Vidyanam Dharmsya Cho Chaturdasah"* (*Yajurveda Smriti*: 1.7).

The word Smriti means memory or recollection of what was previously cognised; and the smriti works are the recorded recollection of those great sages who had deeply studied the Vedas and mastered their precepts - their injunctions as well as their prohibitions. The Vedas are Apaurusheya, not man-made, and are therefore self-authoritative, needing no external support. The Smriti on the other hand are man-made: Yet they are authoritative, and because they come from men with profound knowedge of the Vedas.

In the phrase, 'Smriti sile ca tatvidam', meaning the recollection and conduct of those who are conversant with those, the Vedas, the significance of the tatvidam is that the validity of the Smriti depends on the conformity of their ideas to the Vedic precepts.

The Smritis must be looked upon as an authority for today and tomorrow and for all time because they are founded on the Vedas. There are more than 100 Smrits now. But the following have greater importance:

1. Manu Smriti
2. Yagyavalkya Smriti
3. Atri Smriti
4. Vishnu Smriti
5. Harit Smriti
6. Ausnas
7. Angiras
8. Yama
9. Apastamb
10. Sambarat
11. Katyayanas
12. Brahaspati
13. Parashara
14. Vyas
15. Sankh
16. Likhit
17. Daksh
18. Gautam
19. Shatapata
20. Vasista
21. Prajapati

Philosophy

The science of literature which deals with creation to death is philosophy. दष्टष्यते यथार्तया वस्तु पदार्थज्ञानमिति दर्ष्ठानम। Its main branches are: (1) Vaisesika (2) Sankhya (3) Yoga (4)

Nyaya (5) Purva Mimansa and (6) Uttara Mimansa.

Mimansa

Mimansa means esteemed or sacred inquiry, an exposition. Mimansa is an exegesis of the Veda. Nirukta explains the meaning of the words of the Vedas, also the etymology in the fashion of a dictionary, Mimansa goes further to find out the significance of the mantras, their intent. It also gives its decisions on these points.

Of the fourteen branches of learning Chaturdasha Vidya, after the four Vedas, and the Sadanga, we have the four upangas of the Vedas remaining. These are Mimamsa, Nyaya, Puranas and Dharmashastra.

माम is the root of the word Mimamsa; 'son' is the Pratyaya. Mimamsa means "esteemed or sacred inquiry", an exposition. Mimamsa is the exegesis of the Vedas. Nirukta explains the meaning of the words of the Vedas, also their etymology in the fashion of a dictionary. Mimamsa goes further, to find out the significance of the mantras, their intent. It also gives its decision on these points.

Pujya Saraswati mentions, "The Vedas constitute the Law of Ishwara. Since they are eternal and endless the law is also eternal. All of us are the subjects of the monarch called Ishwara. He has engaged many officials, authorities like Indra, Vayu, Varuna, Agni, Yama, Ishana, Kubera, Nirrti and others to take care of this world. They need a law to protect the creatures of all the fourteen worlds. How should we, the subjects of Ishwara, conduct ourselves according to this law, how are the officials appointed by Ishwara to rule over this domain? We may find out the answer to these questions by examining the Vedas. There are judges who deliberate on the laws of this world and resolve doubts concerning them with the help of the lawyers. If the Vedas are the law that determines how Dharma is to be practised, it is Jaimini who interprets the meaning of this law. His interpretation is Mimansa" (Saraswati, 381-383).

Uttara Mimansa, that is, the Brahamana Sutra as well as Upnishads, constitutes Brahmvidya or Vedant. It is the foundation of the three important philosophical systems–Advait (non-dualison or monism) Vishishtadvaita (qualified non-dualism or qualified monism) and Dwaita (Dualism). Every system has its sutras Bhashya and Vartika. The Purvamimansa sutra is by Jaimini Maharshi, its bhashya by Sabare Swami and its Vartika is by Kumarila Bhatta.

There are Judges who deliberate on the laws of this world and resolve doubts concerning them with the help of the lawyers. If the Vedas are the law that determines how Dharma is to be practised, it is Jaimini who interprets the meaning of this law. His interpretation is Mimansa (Saraswati, 382). Both Sankhyas and Mimansakas belong to the Vedic system. Sankhyas believe that Ishwara is not the karta or author of the Jagat (universe). Ishwara is pure knowledge.

According to Sankhya, the atma is pure and is the basis of all, detached from everything. The author of the Sankhya Sutra is Kapil Maharsi. Notable works are Ishwara Krishna's Sankhya-Karika and commentary by Vijyanabhikshu on Sankhya Sutra. Sankhya respects the authority of law.

Nyaya is called Tarkasastra and its author is Gautama. Its main purpose is to establish by reasoning that the creator of this world is Parmeshwara. It seeks to prove the existence of Iswara through inference. Reasoning thus has a major place in Nyaya.

Sri Saraswati has elaborated the meaning of Nyaya, "Logic or reasoning is of course indispensable to any study. The Vedas make a statement and Mimamsa determines its meaning. Though we have faith in the Vedas, doubts arise in scriptural passages. If these doubts are cleared through reasoning the message of the Vedas will be affirmed. All logical reasoning must be accepted only if it is firmly rooted in authority. Also, arguments must not stem from the urge to be merely contradictory (Saraswati, 411).

When Sankara was about to depart from this world his disciples requested him for a brief upadesha. It was then that he imparted his succinct teaching in the form of five stanzas which go by the name of *upadesa Panchaka* or *Sopan panchak.*

Upadesh Panchaka or Sopana Panchak

दस्तारकह सुरभि रम्यतम्,
श्रुतिमतसर्तको नुसिधियतम्

It means that one must give up the habit of captious arguments and that in dealing with a question one must employ proper reasoning duly respecting the views of the Vedas. Without reason to guide us, it is like roaming aimlessly in the forest. But the reason must be founded on authority. Nyaya finds the meaning of Vedic passage in this manner.

Kanad too created a Nyaya Shastra. It is called Vaisheshika.The name Vaisheshika is derived from the fact that it inquires into such particularities. There is a good deal of science in this Nyaya Shastra. Atmic matters like the individual self, the cosmos, Ishwara, Moksha or liberation are examined. Both Nyaya and Vaisheshika conduct enquiries based on anuman.

The Nyaya inquiring into truth is through the four pramanas of knowledge: Pratyaksha, Anuman, Upamana and Shabda. Pratyaksa is direct perception; anuman is inference; upamana is inference by analogy or comparison; and Shabda is the pronouncement by a reliable authority like the Vedas.

They are called Trik based on Shiva Sutra. Besides, the following books are important: Spandasarbhasya, Shiva Drishti, Paratrishika, Trivritti, Ishwara Pratyabhigya Karika, Sidha Trayi, Shiva Strotravali, Tantra Lok.

The fourteen worlds, Atala, Vitala, Nitala or Paatala, Sutala, Talatala, Mahatala, Rasatala, Bhuloka, Bhubharloka, Swaraloka, Maharloka, Janaloka, Tapoloka, Satyaloka constitute an immensely vast kingdom. It has an emperor and all living beings are his subjects. The kingdom as well as its rulers is eternal and it has its own laws. If the kingdom and King/Emperor are eternal, the law also must be so. This law is constituted by the Veda. Though this kingdom, the cosmos is called Anadi, it is dissolved and created again and again. The only eternal entities are the Parameshwara and his law, the Vedas.

Nibandha

The earliest period of Dharma Shastra literature may be about 700 AD supposedly the time of great Kumarila Bhatta. There were a number of Vedic Dharma Shastras including the Mahabharata and the Puranas. These were very popular throughout the country and they had been declared authorities. But the supreme task before the society was then to turn out regular codes of law from a synthetic study of these dicta. The scholastic system of the Mimansa with its thousand rules of interpretation: was developed by the classical works of Savra Swami Kumarila and Prabhakar. The logic of this literature attracted the best intellects of the country to take up the above task with avidity. For more than a thousand years, they engaged themselves in writing glosses on the important texts, comprehensive digests, manuals on special topics of law, and various other books, all of which pass by the name of Nibandha.

However, scholars differed honestly in their interpretations and it gave rise, with local popularity and sanction, to many different schools and sub-schools of law with a healthy rivarly among them, all of which happend from the very start of the Nibandha literature.

Prof. D.C. Bhattacharya has very clearly mentioned in details about the nibandha (Bhattacharya, 364). Almost as binding as the modern high court rulings, every book in the area of law derived its authority from the fact that the author was looked upon as an Apta (an ideal person) who had attained the highest moral and intellectual standard. For the ultimate sanction of the Veda to be stamped on every law book, he must be a man of religion too in the best sense of the term.

Main books on Nibandhas are commentaries on Manu–Yagyavalkya: Vishwarupa, Medhatithi, Kalyan Bhatta or Gautam, Manu and Narada, Saraswati Vilas Vishwaroopa on Mitakshara, Balakrida Kulluka Bhatta or Manu, Govindaraja or Manu. There are various schools of Nibandha writers i.e., Mithila School, Kamroop School and Bengal school of Nibandhakaras. Bhavadeva Bhatta (Dashkarma Paddhati and Tautatita-Mata-Tilaka), Jimutvahan (Dharmratna) and Bharat Chandra Shiromani (Asauchasara) belong to Bengal School of Nibandha.

Mithila School of Nibandha

Mithila produced by far the largest number of works on Dharma (1200-1500) in the whole of India, thanks to the patronage of the Karnat and Brahman kings. Sridatta Upadhyaya wrote seven treatises on daily rites. He is cited by Chandeshwara. His frequent reference to the Gaudas should be noted. Harinatha Upadhyaya wrote Smritisara in two parts. Chandeshwara Eight Ocean– Ratnakar; Kritya Ratnakar, Dana Ratnakar, Vyavahar, Sudhi Ratnakar, Puja Ratnakar, Vivad Ratnakar, Grihastha Ratnakar, Rajniti Ratnakar. Vardhama Upadhyaya son of Gangesh wrote Smriti Paribhasa, Shraddha Pradip Chintamani- Vachaspati Mishra wrote ten works on Nyaya, thirty works on Shruti (Vivad Chintamani), Dwait Nirnaya, Vyavahar Chintamani (shared with Gangesh the supreme title 'Param Guru' (The Greatest Teacher), only twice used in the vast literature of Mithila).

On *Vivada* important names are Graheshwara Mishra (achara), Ganeshwara Mishra (Shradha Teertha) and Bhava Sharma. Other names on Nibandha include Padmanabh Datta (Sanskrit Grammar), Rudradhar/Shankar Mishra (works are lost), Vidyapati (Ganga Vakyavali: ascribed to queen Visvasdevi), Danvakyavali (ascribed to queen Djirmati), Durga Bhakti–Tarangini (ascribed to Narasimhadeva), Mishru Mishra (Vivad Chandra)

Vardhaman Mishra (Danda-Viveka), Devanath (Smriti-Kaumudi).

Kamroop School

Important scholars of this schhol are Damodar Mohan Mishra (Ganga Jala), Pitambara Siddhantavagisa (Daya Kaumudi), Jagadguru Bhattacharya (Suddhi Kaumudi and Vijavahar Kaumudi) and Sambhunatha Siddhantvagisa (Akala Bhaskar).

Banaras School of Law

This school is also known for acting as the meeting ground of scholars from all corners of the country. Important figures of the school are Bhakta Lakshmidhar (Kritya Kalpataru) and Kashinath Vidyaniwas Bhattacharya (Saccharita Mimansa).

South India School of Law

This is also known as *Dakshinatya Nibandhas* and it is almost extinct.

Uttakal or Orissa School of Law

Notable contributors of this school are Vidyakar Vajapayan (Nityachara Paddhati), Narsinha Vajapaya (Nityachara Pradipa), Divyasinha Mahipati (Kalpa deep, Shraddha deep), Gadadha (Achar Sar) and Murari Mishra (Prayaschita Manohar).

Madras School of Law

The names of significant contributors of this school are Madhavacharya (greatest scholoar of the South who wrote Parashara Madhanya or Parashara Samhita and Kala Madhava), Hemadari (Chaturvarga Chintamani), Devana Bhatta (Smriti Chandrika) and Ramachandra Acharya (Prakriya Kaumudi).

In short, the following Nibandhakaras are considered important in the matters of Law: Jimutvahan–Daya Bhag,

Kal Viveka, Vyavahar Matrika; Shoolpani– Smriti Viveka; Raghunandan– Smriti Tatva 28 parts; Aniruddha– Harlata; Asauchvivaran] Pitridayata; Ballal Sen –Aachar Sagar, Pratishta Sagar, Adhut Sagar, Dan Sagar; Sri Datta Upadhyaya–Acharadarsa, Samaya Pradeep, Shradh Kala; Chandeshwar–Smriti Ratnakar, 'Eight Oceans' Eight Ratnakar; Vachaspati Mishra– Vivad Chintamani, Devanna Bhatta–Smriti Chandrika; Hemadri– Chaturbarg Chintamani; Madhavacharya–Kalamadhav and Seven others; Narayan Bhatta– Triasthalisethu, Antyesti Padhati, Prayag Ratnakar; Nand Pandit– Shradh Kalpalata; Kamalakar Bhatta– Niranay Sindhu; Neelakanth Bhatta– Bhagwant Bhaskar; Mitra Mishra–Virmitrodaya; Lakshmidhar–Kritya Kalpataru; Jagannath– Vivadaranav; Tarka Panchanan– Dharmsindhu; Kashinath Upadhyaya.

There were commentaries on important Vedic granthas. Prominent among these are: Shankaracharya– Advaita Vad; Sri Ramanujacharya– Vishishta Dwaitvad; Sri Nimbaracharya– Dwaitadwaitvad; Sri Ballavacharya– Sudhadwaitvad; Sri Madhawacharya– Dwaitvad Sanpreday, Gaurida Sampradaya.

Aagam or Tantra

The custom or tradition followed from the Vedas to the Nibandhakars Granthas or Nibandha Granthas are called 'Nigam', opposite to 'Nigam' is called 'Agam'.

Satwik Granthas are called Tantra or Agam. Rajas called Yamel, Tamas is called Damar. Since inception men have been of Rajas and Tamas temperament. All Sur-Asur-Daitya-Danava must have certain bases. For them Granthas of both Rajas–Tamas nature were written. Bamagam is the main subject for Asuras.

There are 64 Granthas in Saktagam. However, none is available so far. Yet, following are considered as foundational for the *Tantra mat*: Kaulopanishad, Arunaupanishad, Adwaitbhabaupnishad, Kalikopnishad, Bhabopnishad, Bajhapanishad, Tripuropnishad, Taropanishad.

Following are for the *Mitra Marg*: Chandrak, Jyotsyanabeti, Kala Nidhi, Kularnava, Bhubneshwari, Barhayaspatya, Durvasa.

The following are available for *Samayachar*: Subhagam Panchak consists of Samhita of Vasistha, Sanak, Sukra, Sanandan and Sanatakumar.

More than 100 books are for the Sakta Tantra but following are important: Kularanava, Kulachuramani, Tantra Raj, Sakti Sangam Sastra, Kali Vilas, Gyanarapan, Namkeshwar, Maha Nirvan, Rudrayemal, Tripura Rahasya, Daksnimurti Samhita.

Vaishnawagam

Panchshastra–Two works related to Vaisnavagam.

Vaikhanas Agam: Only the following Samhitas are available in the Panchashastra:

Abibardhanya Samhita,

Ishwara Samhita,

Kapinjal Samhita,

Jayakhya Samhita,

Parasar Samhita,

Padhna Tantra,

Brahadryay Samhita,

Bharadwaj Samhita,

Lakshmi Tantra,

Vishnu Tilak,

Sri Prasna Samhita,

Vishnu Samhita and

Saswat Samhita.

Shaivagam

From the mouth of Lord Shiva 28 Tantras came out– There are 208 Tantra and Uptantras and out of 208 only 64 are important. But no work is available. The following works are important:

Shivacharya–Pasupat Sutra, Nareshwar Pariksha, Tatwa Sangrah,Tatwa Traya, Bhog Karika, Moksh Karika, Parmoksh Niras Karika, Shruti Sukti Mala, Chaturveda–Tatparya Sangraha, Tatwa Prakasika, Sut Samhita, Nadakarika, Ratna Traya.

Sidhant Sikhamani is the only authentic book on Veer Saiva. There are 92 works in Pratbhiyagyan Marg. Out of 92, three are important: Sindhant Tantra; Namak Tantra; Malini Tantra.

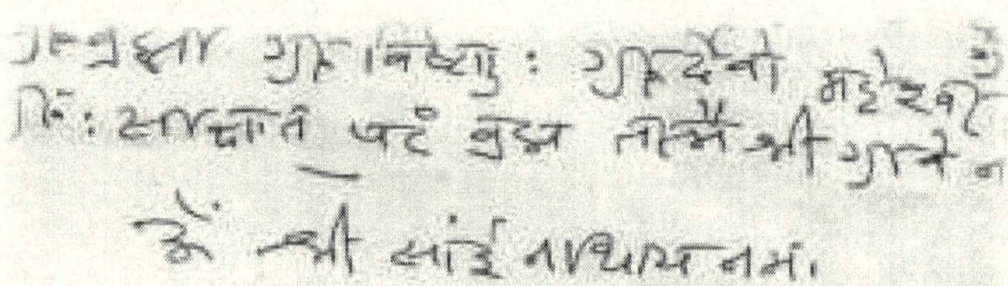

PART – TWO

ANCIENT LAW SEERS AND THEIR WORKS

गुरुर्ब्रह्मा गुरुर्विष्णुः गुरुर्देवो महेश्वरः
गुरुः साक्षात् परं ब्रह्म तस्मै श्री गुरवे नमः
ॐ श्री साईं नाथाय नमः।

7.
Dharma: The Principle For Governance

Introduction

The two great epics of the Hindus are the Ramayana and the Mahabharata. There is certainly a diversity of opinion among oriental scholars as to the probable dates of these compositions; but all are in agreement that these were composed in ancient period and therefore present a picture of society and government as they existed in ancient India. The Mahabharata contains many stories, accounts of primitive Aryan society and ancient history, which are not only foreign to but also older than the main theme of the epic. The Mahabharata is therefore very rightly regarded as a compilation of ancient Aryan rhapsodies, cleverly grouped round the central theme (Das, 346).

The gradual evolution and development of modern institutions (social, religious and political) has long since found a favourite subject of research and speculation with philosophers and antiquarians. For instance, among these thousand and one questions, it is often asked, what was the beginning of different forms of government in the world? People naturally feel eager to go to the root of a thing in order to be able to lay hands on the fundamental principles working under it. The necessity of this becomes all the greater and more urgent in view of many accretions that form themselves in course of time and gather around the fundamental principle, thereby, obliterating it completely from one's view and obstructing its free play and working. But if it is once got hold of, and rightly understood, the accretions that gather around it can easily be shaken off like those on the places of an electric battery. An omission to take this step either through ignorance, negligence or interested motives has been the fruitful source of a world evil and has from time to time, led to serious political upheavals, upsetting the existing order of things and producing chaos, disorders, and great human misery. This is in accordance with the well-known law of nature, which always helps the moral order of the universe to assert itself, whenever it is in danger of being choked to death or reduced to inactivity. The best government in the world, is therefore, that which always keeps the fundamental principle in view, and maintains its free working at all costs, by shaking off the foreign accretions that gather around it.

Now, what is the fundamental principle of government? To be able to answer this question, we must first understand whether kings were born or made in ancient times. In tribes led by chief, the head used to be elected as such by the common suffrage of the community men, on account, of his valour and ability to lead them from one hunting ground to another, and protect them from the invasion of rival neighbouring tribes. In this sense, the chief who was the king of later times in embryo, might be said to have been made by the tribesman (Das, 347). But he might also be said, in a special sense to have been born, in as much as the valour and ability which went to make up his leadership were also born with him. But he was certainly not born, in the accepted sense of the word which implies hereditary right to be king or leader (by reason of his mere birth, irrespective of personal fitness). In the early stages of human civilization, however, personal fitness alone decided the choice of the people in the selection of a chief; and as history repeats itself, we find the same principle working in a developed form in modern republican or democratic forms of government. The fundamental principle of government appears to be an inherent right of the people to govern themselves under the direction and guidance of a leader whom the people choose on account of his personal fitness and who is invested with certain powers by the people themselves with a view to enable him to carry on the work with which he is interested. The rights, privileges and powers of the leader or king are made up of the rights, privileges and powers of the people themselves willingly parted with in his favour in return for security and protection of the life, liberty and property, where the leader is left too much to himself without any healthy control from the representatives of the people, his tendency is invariably to usurp and arrogate to himself all the rights, privileges and powers of the people, and play the autocrat or tyrant. Thus, unless checked, it leads to the thorough demoralization and degradation of the people. But the moral order of the universe reasserts itself in the long run by means of violent upheavals, social and political, as have taken place in many countries in the recent past- and readjust the balance of power as between the king and the people. Autocratical, bureaucratical and oligarchial forms of government are unnatural, demoralizing and unsuitable to the progress and advancement of mankind; and they contain seeds of destruction in themselves, which germinate and fructify in course of time. The best form of government is democratical whether we find it in pure democracy or limited monarchy.

It is a mistake to suppose that Hindus have been accustomed, from time immemorial, to an autocratical form of government and that the popular element never existed as a distinct force in the country. It was not absolute monarchy but limited monarchy that existed and flourished in ancient India. But before this limited monarchy firmly established, many revolutions and political upheavals had taken place in order to readjust the balance of power, between the king and the people. The following extract from the Mahabharata will illustrate the meaning:

"Bhisma said, 'Listen attentively, O Thou foremost of the virtuous', how monarchy was first created in the Satya Yuga. At first, there was neither king nor kingdom, punishment, nor object of punishment on this earth. Men used to protect themselves and one another following the just principles of religion. They went on in this fashion for sometime; but afterwards they found it difficult to protect themselves or one another, in as much as infatuation got hold of their minds. This led to the subversion of wisdom and of the moral order; and people become avaricious, subject to evil passion, addicted to worldliness, and devoid of all sense of right and wrong ... Men having then strayed out of the path, the Vedas and religion become (almost) extinct".

It is said that the sacrifices and the Yagnas, having been discontinued, the Gods became greatly alarmed. They repaired in a body to Prajapati, the creator, and represented to him the deplorable condition to which the human race had been reduced. Where upon the Prajapati wrote out a work consisting of 100,000 chapters on social and political ethics for the special benefit of mankind, and handed it over to the Gods. Siva took it and compressed it into 10,000 chapters and called it by the name of *Vaisalaksha.* Indra compressed it again into 5000 chapters and called it by name of *Vahudanka.* Vrihaspati further reduced the number of chapter to 3000, and Sukracharya, still further reduced it to 1000, with a view to enable men to read the whole of it, in course of this short life-time. Then the Gods went to Vishnu, who at their request, created a *Manasputra, Viraj* by name, to be the head of mankind. He was followed by a succession of kings who ruled over the Earth, with more or less righteousness and justice. Then came *Vena,* who on account of his tyranny, profligacy and immoral way, was killed by the maharshies, or the great sages devoted to the worship of Brahma, the Supreme Being. They, then, set on the throne his son, *Prithu,* who became an ideal king and ruled over the earth, with great wisdom and justice (*Shanti Parva,* 59).

The above account taken from the Mahabharata shows that before the monarchial form of government was established, a democratic form of government had existed among the ancient Indo-Aryans, which, however, in course of time, had degenerated into anarchy. Whatever the form of government it is, it has always been found that there should be a competent leader or chief, who could command the confidence of men, by governing them strictly according to the principle of equity, justice, and the law, and holding the balance of power even between himself and the ruled. Whenever this balance was sought to be disturbed by the chief, the people or their representatives availed themselves of the first opportunity to readjust it, by overthrowing him, as was done in the case of Vena by the sages in ancient India.

There is another very important passage in the Mahabharata, which goes to show how the king was created by the ancient Indo-Aryans on the principles of 'give and take', and how the people willingly submitted to be guided by him in return for their protection and safeguard of their interests, and maintenance peace and order in the country. It will also illustrate the principle underlying the right of taxation on the part of the king, and how that right was voluntarily given over to him by the people themselves. The following is the translated passage:

In the days of Yore, when the earth become devoid of a king, the people began to devour one another. At that time, some virtuous people met together and made an agreement among themselves to the effect that they would banish all such men as were harsh tongued of angry disposition, adulterous and voluptuous, and addicted to the habit of stealing and misappropriating another's property. Securing the confidence of the people they lived (peacefully) for sometimes; but in the long-run, with a heavy heart, they had to approach Brahma (the creator) whom they addressed thus: 'Lord, we are being annihilated for want of a king. Grant us, therefore, a king. We all will adore him, and he will protect us (in return)'. Hearing this prayer of the people, Brahma asked Manu to take up the duty of protecting them; but Manu declined (the honour), saying, 'I am always afraid of committing a wrong and sinful act. It is a very difficult task to govern a kingdom, and particularly to keep people on path of virtue and righteousness.' Then the people addressed themselves to Manu, saying, Lord, do not thou be afraid of anything. Sin will never, touch thee. We will fill up thy treasury (royal) by contributing into it heads of cattle, a fiftieth share of gold (money) and a tenth share of grain ...Those, who are capable of bearing arms and riding, will follow thee, as the Gods follow Indra. Thus thou wilt will be as powerful as Kuber himself, and be able to protect us with ease. Thou wilt also be entitled to a fourth share of the spiritual benefit which we may be able to acquire under thy protection. Protect us, therefore, oh Lord, like Indra, the chief the Gods, and sally forth, like the burning sun, to conquer our foes. May their pride be humbled by thee, and many Dharma protect us for ever. The people thus saying, the powerful Manu, who was sprung from a noble race, issued forth (from his castle), in a blaze of glory, followed by innumerable armed men with a view to take up the duty of protecting the people (*Shanti Parva*, 67).

The above account of willing submission of the people to a king tallies, in substance, with Carlyle's account of wild armed men raising their strongest aloft on the buckler-throw and with changing armour and hearts, saying solemnly, 'Be thou our acknowledge strongest'. Both the accounts furnish us with an unmistakable clue to the fundamental principle underlying government, a deviation and departure from which has more than anything else, retarded the progress of mankind.

It has already been stated in the Mahabharata that an elaborate political and social constitution drawn up by Prajapati, and subsequently much reduced in bulk and matter, and considerably simplified by the Gods, with a view to bring it within the reach of the knowledge of ordinary mortals, had been in existence before the monarchial form of government was firmly established in the country. This constitution among other things, laid down the duties of the king, and the manner in which he was to qualify himself for his high office. The king, had (in his boyhood and youth) to pass through a course of special training and rigorous discipline under the guidance of learned sages who always took care to instill into his mind the principle of good governance. The good of the people formed, as it were, the central point of his many sided activities, and he was taught from his infancy to act and behave in such a way as to win popular praise, and secure popular contentment. The very word, Raja connotes the idea of pleasing the minds of the people by acts of good governance ('rajah prakriti ranjanat'). There is no equivalent word in Sanskrit for autocrat, despotism and tyrant. Autocracy, despotism, tyranny were antagonistic to the genius of Indo-aryans, and they never took kindly to our soil. The king was, no doubt, the supreme personage in the state, but his mere word was not law. His powers were defined and circumsrcribed by the constitution, which was in the keeping of the holy sages, who always guided his counsels, and restrained him from vagaries and eccentricities. It would be interesting to read in this connection some extracts from the Mahabharata, showing the constitution and function of the various councils which helped the king in work of the governance.

But before we make the extracts, we must refer to a belief which was generally current among the old Indo-Aryans and which exists partially, even to this day, among their descendants– I mean the belief in the efficacy of sacrifices and Yagnas performed in honour of, and for the propitiation of the Gods, presiding over various spheres of our solar system. It has been always found that there should be a competent government. Notwithstanding the government, sacrifices and yagnas, if properly performed, were regarded as very effacious in producing plenty of rains, an abundant harvest, and consequent happiness and prosperity of the people. The ancient shastras highly eulogise the performance of sacrifices and Yagnas, and every house holder was enjoined to perform the five sacrifices everyday (Das, 349) That having been the current belief among the Indo-Aryans, it should not be a matter of surprise at all, if the performance of the sacrifices was regarded by them as supremely important, and essentially necessary for the well-being of individuals as well as of the state. The king, as head of the state, had to perform large and difficult sacrifices, for which he had to engage the services of the best men available. These men were not only highly pious and spiritual, but also very large-hearted, as they generally, belonged to the order of the sages or rishies who had renounced the self and the world for the good of mankind. The purohit or the royal priest who was often also guru or spiritual preceptor of the king, was selected from this holy order, and came first in the order. Then came the ritwiks or the performers of sacrifices in each of the six seasons, who were also drawn from the same order. The royal priest besides presiding at sacrifices, and serving as spiritual guide to the king, also acted as his Prime Minister; some of the ritwiks also often acted as mantris or ministers. The indispensability of the purohita will appear from the following passages quoted from the Mahabharata:

"The purohita should be nominated and worshipped first, and the king installed on the throne, afterwards" (*Shanti Parva*, 73).

राज्ञा पुरोहित: कार्यो भवेद् विद्वान् बहुश्रुत:।उभौ समीक्ष्य धर्मार्थाव पुमे यावन्तरम्।। धर्मात्मा मन्त्रविद येज़ां राज्ञां राजन् पुरोहित:।राजा चौवं गुणो येज़ां कुष्ठालं तेज़ु सर्वष्ठा:।।1.2।।

Then again, "The prosperity and protection of kingdoms depend entirely on the king and the royal priest" (*Shanti Parva*, 74).

योगक्षेमो हि राज्ट्रस्य राजन्यायत्त उच्यते।
योगक्षेमो हि राज्ञो हि समायत्त: पुरोहिते।।1।।

Next to the ritwiks, in order, come the mantris, i.e. ministers or councillors whose number was never less than three. They were selected from the best men of the country, and their duty mainly consisted in advising the king on all important matters, relating to the well-being of the state, in addition it also assumed a diplomatic character. One performed the office of the Home Minister, another of Foreign Minister, while the third had control of the Intelligence department and so forth. They were also the custodians of what are known as state secrets. On all important matters of state, the king first sought their counsel. Then it was placed before the guru or spiritual preceptor, together with the personal opinion of the king. The guru carefully weighed all that opinions, one by one, and came to a decision, which again was placed before the council and acted upon accordingly to the votes of the majority (*Shanti Parva*, 83; Das, 350). तेष्ठां त्रयाणां विविधं विमर्ज़ख्र तं मन्त्रमार्गे प्रणयेद् सत्त:।।53-54।। Next in order, come the council of the amatyas or those ministers who always remained with the king to advise and guide him in all matters, important or otherwise, and execute the royal command. This council was truly representative of the people, in as much as the members, whose number was not less than thirty three were drawn from all classes (identical with the principal castes). The following extracts of the Mahabharata is helpful in explaining this point:

Bhisma, addressing Yudhisthira, said, "You should appoint four holy Brahmanas as amatyas who are well versed in the Vedas and have returned home from the abode of their preceptors after finishing their studies, (shatakas), eight powerful kshatriyas who can weild arms, twenty one Vaisyas, possessing vast riches, three sudras, distinguished by humility and purity of characters and one suta (charioteer), well versed in the puranas and possessing eight virtues. All the amatyas should be fifty years of age, modest, intelligent, impartial, just and devoid of seven disqualifications, viz., avarice, fondness for hurting etc. You will promulgate an order by consulting only eight of these thirty three amatyas, viz., four brahamanas, three kshatriyas and the suta (*Shanti Parva,* 85):

चतुरो ब्राह्मणान् वैधान्स्त्र मन्त्रं राजोपधारयेत॥7-11॥

The statement shows that the king in Ancient India were not of aristocratic nature and there was limited monarchy, established on a firm footing and people were adequately represented in the government. Besides these councils, there were of course, the courtiers who daily attended the royal courts and helped the king in his daily deliberations. These men were selected from the best and noblest families, for their sterling virtues. Bhisma advised Yudhisthira to appoint as courtiers men who were 'modest, truthful, characterised by straight forwardness and a control over their minds and passions and a possession of eloquence (*Shanti Parva,* 83).

He also advised him to appoint to all high and important posts men who were "well-tried, sprung from noble families, averse to bribe-taking, unprofligate, faithful, versed in the Vedas, devoid of pride, modest, intelligent, possessed of purity, spirited, patient, forgiving devoted to the king, efficient, grave, sincere, of few words, possessed of knowledge as to what to do and what not to do, capable of understanding hints, compassionate, capable of acting according to time and circumstance, and devoted to duty". The officers, who were incharge of the revenues of the state, should also be of the above qualifications.

The following abstract of the Mahabharata will illustrate how the government in the country and the provinces functioned in Ancient India: The king should appoint some one as the head of one village, some one as head of ten villages, some one as head of twenty villages, some one as head of hundred villages and some one as head of thousand villages. Their principal care should be protection of the people. The Lord of one village should communicate to the Lord of ten villages, and he should communicate to the Lord of twenty villages, and he to the Lord of one hundred villages, the fault and failings of the people living within their respective jurisdiction. Thus every Lord shall communicate, to his immediate superior the faults and failings of the people. The Lord of a village has a right to all things produced in it. He shall pay revenue to the Lord of ten villages and the Lord of ten villages to the Lord of twenty villages and so on. The Lord of a hundred villages shall enjoy all the products of a thickly populated large village. But this village shall remain under the control of the Lord who is his immediate superior. The Lord of a thousand villages shall be entitled to possess a country-town, full of riches and grain. The king should appoint a vigilant and wise minister to superintend the military arrangements and other affairs of the Lords of villages and a governor-general to superintend all the affairs of the country-towns. As the stars are placed high above the planets, so should the governor-general be placed high above all the courtiers and they shall keep an eye on their work and their whereabouts.

नगरे नगरे वा स्यादेक: सर्वार्थ चिन्तक:
उच्चौ: स्थाने घोररूपो नक्षत्राणामिव ग्रह:
भवेत् स तान् परिक्रायेत् सर्वानेव सभासद:।।11।। (*Shanti Parva*, 87)

From the above account, it will appear that there was a healthy and sound system of both centralization and decentralization in ancient India. This was also a case with the process of taxation and revenue collection: The king 'ought to fix the rules and rates of taxation after carefully considering the conditions of sale and purchase of goods on the part of the merchants, the margin of the profits, the condition of the roads and ways over which goods are conveyed, and the expenditure which they incur for the maintenance'... Rules of taxation should be framed in such a way as to enable both the king and the Tax-payers to enjoy the fruits of their labour'. The parallels are drawn with a calf who by drinking milk from the udder of a cow, becomes strong, and able to carry burdens, but if it fails to carry burdens it means it is not getting sufficient supply of milk. So do the people, by becoming rich as a consequence of the levy of moderate taxes by the king, become capable of inaugurating many a useful work. But if they are robbed of all their gains by the king, they cannot accomplish any good. So the king should never levy immoderate taxes.

मष्टतो वत्सो जातवला: पीड़ां सहति भारत
न कर्म कुरुते वत्सो भष्टष्ठां दुग्धो युधिज़्ठिर।
--परिरक्षन् स्वयं नष्टप:।।21-22।। (*Shanti Parva*, 87)

In necessity the king should never recourse to force to raise the requisite capital; but with a persuasive language promise to return back the money once the task is fulfilled (*Shanti Parva*, 87).

इयमापत्समुत्चन्ना परचक्रभ्यं महन् इदमात्वधायैव राज़्ट्र मिच्छन्ति वाधितुम।।27-28।।

In another excellent passage illustrating the principle on which rates of taxes should be levied a simile is drawn from the nature of animal kingdom:

As the bee collects honey from flowers, without hurting the plant, as men draw out milk from the udder of a cow, without cutting it off, or starving the calf, as a leech insensibly draws blood from the body, as a tigress catches hold of the neck of her cub, with her teeth without hurting it, and as mouse nibbles off flesh from the feet of a sleeping man, without being discovered, so should the king imperceptibly collect his revenues, without oppressing or annihilating his people मधुदोहं दुहेद राज़्ट्रं भ्रमण एव पादपम। च पीड्येत।।4-5।। (*Shanti Parva*, 87). Thus, it can be safely argued that the rule of governance was closely tied with the moral order of the nature, and together these two constituted as Dharma.

Paitamah Tantra

The first book on the basic principles of law not only for the Bharat but for the entire manavas is called *Paitamah Tantra.*The Paitamah Tantra is the cardinal authority vested with the guiding features for human kind in social, political, religious aspects of human civilization (Kane, 301). The first work on law (Dharma, Artha, Kama) not only for India but for the entire world of manavas consists of 100,000 chapters. It is called Paitamah Tantra. Unfortunately, the book is not available. We have failed to keep such valuable authority. This has been only referred by authors/ sages/ seers in their original works or in various commentaries. Naturally, versions vary from commentators-Nibandhakars and Smritikaras as the issue of certain problems arising out among the authors. However, nobody can deny the fact that the book carries the supreme authority on the earth related to the foundations of law guiding one's life in the society. The Prajapati is credited for composing this original work on Dharma for the *Manavas.*

In the Mahabharata we are told how the supreme being composed a hundred thousand slokas on Dharma, how Manu Swayambhuva promulgated these Dharmas and how Ushanas and Brahaspati composed Shastras based on the works of Manu Swayambhuva (Kane, 309):

ऋष्ठीनुवाच तान्सर्वानदष्टष्ठय: पुरुज़ोत्तम:।
कृतं ष्टातसहस्तं हि ष्टलोकानामिदमुत्तमम्।।
लोकतन्त्रस्य कृत्स्म यस्माद्दाऽम: प्रवर्तते।............................

....
भुवेज़ु धर्मेज़ु ष्टास्त्रे चौष्ठानसे कृते।
वष्टहस्पतिमते चौव लोकेज़ु प्रतिचारिते।।(*Mahabharat*, 336:38-46)

In another place the account is slightly different and Manu does not figure therein. Shanti Parva describes how the original work of Brahma on the three: Dharma, Artha and Kama, in 100000 chapters *Paitamah Tantra* was successively reduced to 10000, 5000, 3000 and 1000 chapters respectively by Visalaksha, Indra, Bahudantak Brahaspati and Kavya Ushana (*Shanti Parva,* 59:80-85).

The prose introduction to the Narada Smriti says that Manu composed in 100,000 slokas, 1080 chapters and 24 Prakarnas a Dharmshastra and imparted it to Narad, who abridged it into 12000 verses and taught it to Markandeya, who in his term compressed it into 8000 slokas and passed it on to Sumati Bhargava who again reduced it to 4000 slokas. The Narada Smriti तत्रायमाध: ष्टलोक:। आसदिदं तमोभूतं न प्राज्ञायत किंचन। तत: स्वयं भूर्भगवान्प्राद्र रासिच्चतुर्मुख:।। (Manu 1.5; Kamal Seel in his comment on ष्टान्तरक्षित तत्वसंग्रह in mid. 8th century A.D.; सुरेष्ठवर वष्टहदारण्यक भाज़्य वार्तिक Kane, 309). Manu then gives the first verse of that work which is a combination of the Extant Manu 1.5-6 and says that Vyavahar was the 9th Prakarana out of 24 in the original work of Manu. It will be noticed how this version differs from that of the Mahabharata wherein Narad is altogether ignored. The extant Manusmriti 1.32-33 narrates how from Brahma sprang Viraj, who produced Manu, from whom were born the sages including Bhrigu and Narad, and how Brahma taught the shastra to Manu, who in his term imparted it to ten sages (1.58), how some great sages approached Manu and sought instruction in the Dharma of the Varnas and the intermediate caste, and how Manu told them that his pupil Bhrigu would impart the shastra to them (1.59-60). This appearance is kept throughout the work. The sages interrupt Bhrigu's discourse in several places. Manu is said to be omniscient and Manu is mentioned by name dozens of times in the work with the "Manuraha (IX. 158, X 78 etc.), or Manur-abrvavith" or Manoranushasanam" (VIII. 139, 279. IX 239 etc.) that the introductory words in the Narada Smriti are not spurious or a later addition follows from the remarks of Medhatithi that according to the Narada Smriti, Prajapati composed a work of 100,000 slokas which was abridged by Manu and others (Kane, 309).

According to the Bhavishya Puran as quoted in Hemadri, the Sanskar Mayukh and other works, there were four versions of the Swayambhuva Shastra composed by Bhrigu, Narada, Brahaspati and Angiras (भार्गवीया नारदीया च वार्हस्पत्यौरिस्यापि । स्वायंभुवस्य ष्टास्त्रय चतस्त्र: संहिता मता:।। चतुर्वर्ग, दानखण्ड, p.528; *Sanskar Mayukh* p.2) So early a writer as Vishwarupa cites verses from Manu Smriti as those of Swayambhu (comment on Yagyavalkya II. 73,74,83,85 where Manu 8.68.70-71, 380 and 105-106 are respectively quoted as Swayambhu, while quotations from Bhrigu cited by Vishwarupa (Yagyavalkya, 1.185 and 252) are not found in the Manu Smriti. In the same way most of the verses quoted from Bhrigu by Apararka are not found in Manu Smriti, one verse, which Aprarka quotes from Bhrigu (on Yog. II, 96) speaks of the views contained therein as that of Manu (Apraraka cited by Kane, vol.1:310).

येजु पापेजु दिव्यानि प्रतिष्ठुद्धानि यत्न:। कारयेत्सज्जनै स्तानि नाभि ष्टास्तं त्यजेन्मनु: ।।

One can simply imagine the vastness and usefulness of the book which carries 100,000 chapters and deals with Trayi, Anawikshki and Varta (trade-commerce) and the Dandniti. What Manu has referred in his Manu Smriti is maintained in the Paitamah Tantra.

त्रैविधेभ्य: स्त्रयीं विद्या दण्डनीतिं च ष्टाष्ठवतीम् ।
आन्वीक्षिकीं चात्मविद्यां वार्तारम्भांष्ठच लोकत: ।। (Manu, 7:43)

He should learn the three fold knowledge (of the Vedas) from those who possess knowledge of the three (Vedas) and the eternal (art) of polity, logic, and knowledge of self; but business from the people (Manu: 7: 43). Dandniti is rather the science of subjugation (punishment) of friends or foes. They say danda is from Daman (restraint): Medhtithi.

By the Brahaspatya (Medhatithi treatises of Brahaspati mentioned in the epic), Medhatithi unites from the people with all three (art of polity, logic and knowledge of self), 'learn these from anyone who knows them' (Hopkins p. 153).

Rajaniti is described as the nectar of the ocean of the Arthashastra, Dharmashastras deal with all aspects of society and, therefore they deal with Rajadharma also. Danda came to mean the power of control and punishment. It conveys the power of the king or supreme ruler called Dandadhar or Dandadhara to dispense justice and to punish wrong doers.

Mahabharata repeats the topic of one lakh verses on the whole of 'Lokatantra' and that Manu, Usanas and Brahaspati will propound the shastra and spread it in the world. A special name 'Varta' was given to the three, agriculture, rearing cattle, trade and commerce (Vanijya) including various arts (*Mahabharata,* 68: 35).

वार्ता मूलो अयं लोकस्त्रय्या वै धार्यते सदा।
तत् सर्व वर्तते सम्यग् यदा रक्षति भूमिपः।।

The Ramayan says, "Vartayam Swmsritastata Lokoyam Sukham-eddhate."

This world when it resorts to Varta prospers happily. Kautiliya makes it clear that Arthshastra and Varta were distinct and yet Varta was subject of study for the king; it was one of the three forms of Rajavidya (Kautiliya - 1.1.1).

दण्डनीति रेका विद्येत्यौष्ठानसाः।
तस्यां हि सर्व विद्यारम्भाः प्रतिवधा इति (Kautiliya - 1.1.4)

On Anavikhiki, Kautiliya remarks:

सांङ्खयं योगो लोकोयतं चेत्यान्वीक्षकी। धर्माधर्मो त्रय्याम थनिथौ वार्तायां नयापनयौ दण्डनीत्याम। वलावले चौतासां हेतु भिरन्वीक्षमाणान्वीक्षकी लोकस्योपकरोतिः व्यसनेऽभ्युदये च बुद्धिम व्यवस्थापयतिः प्रज्ञा वानय क्रिया वैष्ठारधं च करोति।।
(*Arthasastra* 1.1.6).

This subject leads to prosperity and all Dharmas are based on this aspect of knowledge. We have all sorts of descriptions in the Paitamah Tantra– which is evident from the reference above.

The state was not a loose assemblage of parts, each having its own interests and moving at its own will; it was characterised by an organic unity. The king, the ministry, the territory, the resources the forests, the military forces and the allies constitute the seven continents of the state.

(i) Swami– King (ii) Amatyas– Minister constituted the central government, (iii) Purohit– important function, (iv) Rastra– Territory, (v) Durga– Fort, (vi) Bala– Force and (vii) Kosha– Treasury. The seven constituents of the state are regarded as the limbs of the body politics. All limbs are very important– Manu also gives his views on this as follows:

तेज़ु तेज़ु तु कृत्येज़ु तत्तदष्टगं विष्ठिाज़्यते ।
येन यत्साध्यते कर्म तस्मिंस्तच्छ्रेज़्ढ मुच्यते।। (Manu, IX.297)

Kamandaka, Arthshastra of Kautilya and Manu smriti mention the seven important wings or limbs and this follows the Paitamah Tantra.

परस्परोपकारीदं सप्तांग राज्यमुच्यते। (Kamandaka - IV.1)
स्वाम्य मालजनपद दुर्ग कोज़दण्ड मित्राणि प्रकृतय:।
आदिवर्जा: प्रकृतय: सप्तैता: स्वगुणोदया:।
उता: प्रत्यंग भूतास्ता: प्रकृता: राज्यसंपद: (*Arth.*, VI.1)
सप्तास्येह राजस्य विज़्टब्धस्य त्रिदण्डवत्
अन्योन्यगुण वैष्ठोज़्यान्न किंचिदतिरिच्यते।।(Manu- 9.296.1; Altekar, 27)

Also mentioned are the characteristics of mantri, purohit and amatyas and the people who carry forward their appointments "steps have been suggested to safeguard their securities: for that spies have been retained. Besides that, elaborate provisions were made for the spy: his appointment, selection, procedures and the jurisdiction for individual as well as for the king, the high officials and the state (territory)". Kautilya has discussed the similar provision in his Arthashastra तेज़ां वाध्यं चारं छत्रभष्ठार व्यजनपादुका सनयान वाहनोपग्राहिण स्तीक्षणा विधुः। तं सत्रिणः संस्था स्वर्पयेज़ुः (*Kautiliya Arthashastra,* 7: 11.4/2). Protection of the Rajaputra has been described in the Paitamah Tantra that there is no threat for the existence of the kingship from the insiders. Kautilya has also elaborately thrown light on this topic. रक्षितो राजा राज्यं रक्षत्यासन्नेभ्यः परेभ्यक्ष। पूर्व दारेभ्यः पुत्रेभ्य। (*Kautiliya: Arthashastra,* 12 : 16.1). Kautilya gives emphasis on the spies and has devoted a great length on this. In the Paitamah Tantra it is presumed more space was given and details of the types of spies and their important roles for the benefit of the state were discussed. Kautilya also gives due weightage on this point:

प्रजितार्थ मानाभ्यां राजा राजोपमीविनाम्।
जानीयुः ष्टौचभित्यतोः पंच संस्था प्रकीर्तिताः।। (*Arthashastra,* 6.10.3)

Kautilya has also devoted in length when he deliberated on the issue of conflict. Four primary cases are noted for the growth of friends, treasury, for the decline of enemy and enemy's friends and for the decline of the treasury of enemy. त्वं चाहं मित्र लभावहे इत्येवमादिः समसन्धिः। त्वं मित्रम् इत्येवर्मादर्विज़मसंधि :। तयोर्विष्ठोज़लाभार्दातसन्धिः।। (*Arthasastra,* 115.9.2). To meet such ends, three types of victories (Dharma, artha and asura vijaya) are prescribed.

Vaishalaksha Tantra: Bhagwan Shankar

The Paitamah Tantra (composition of Prajapati) of 100,000 chapters, was read by Shankar and he compressed it to 10,000 chapters. Bhagwan Shankar who is also called by the name Vaisalakha gave it the name of Vaisalakh Tantra. Indra abridged the Vaisalakha Tantra of 10,000 chapters to 5,000 chapters and called it by the name of Vahudantak Granth. Very few references have been found (that too very indirectly) about this book. Hence it is being discussed only on the basis of scanty references available here and there.

Vishwarupacharya popularly known as Sureshwaracharya has written a commentary on Yagyavalkya Smriti being called Valkrira.

Bahudantak Granth of 5,000 chapters composed by Indra was abridged by Brahaspati into 3,000 chapters and was called by the name, Brahaspatya Tantra. The work of Brahaspati (3,000 chapters) was further abridged by Sukracharya-Ushana by 1,000 chapters.

After many years of Valkrira, Vigyaneshwar Bhattaraka, who wrote a commentary on Yagyavalkya Smriti being called Mitakshara has mentioned the name of Vishwarupacharya and his commentary Valkrira in Achaaradhyaya, where the name of Visalaksha has been found in references.

Bahudhantak Granth

The Visalaksha Granth abridged Granth of Paitamah Tantra was further compressed by Indra with 5000 chapters. Unfortunately we are not in a position to tell whether this book is available at present or not. No references have yet been made to others on the details of the Bahudantak Grantha by Indra.

Brihaspatya Tantra

The Bahudantaka Granth abridged by Indra was further compressed by Brihaspati son of Maharsi Angira with 3000 chapters and this abridged Granth of Brahaspati is now called Brihaspatya Tantra.

The fragments of Brihaspatya Tantra are among the most precious relics of the early legal literature of India. Apart from the intrinsic value and interests, as containing a full exposition of the whole range of the Hindu Law, their close connection with the code of Manu gives them a special claim to consideration and renders them a valuable link in the chain of evidence by which the date of the most authoritative code of ancient India has been approximately determined (Jolly, 271).

That Brihaspati was an ancient teacher of Arthashastra follows from Kautiliya, where Brihaspatyas are cited six times. In the Mahabharata (*Shanti Parva*, 59. 80-85), Brihaspati is said to have compressed into 3000 chapters the work on Dharma, Artha and Kama composed by Brahma. The Mahabharata, Vanaparva (32.61) speaks of Brihaspati-Niti. The Mahabharata several times cites verses (gatha or slokas) that are said to have been sung by Brihaspati (*Shanti Parva* 23: 15, 56. 38-39, 57-6.7; also *Shanti Parva*, 58.13-16, 69: 23-24 (Kane, I: 287).

Brihaspati also wrote a sutra work on Vyavahara and other topics of Dharma which follows from a quotation contained in Vishwarupa and Haradatta (Kane, I:289). Viswarupa also quotes a few verses from Brihaspati on Vyavahara and Prayaschita and in one place at least indicates that the verse he attributes to Brihaspati occurred in the same work in which a prose passage quoted by him occurred. From this it follows that the Sutra works of Brihaspati on Dharma contained verses also in Vishwarupa's time. Whether the two works on Arthashastra and Dharma were composed by the same Brihaspati is a valid doubt that cannot be denied. It looks probable that they were composed by different authors. Yagyavalkya (1. 4-5) mentions Brihaspati among the expounders of Dharma. He is probably referring to the sutra work on Dharma disclosed by quotation from Vishwarupa.

700 verses on Vyavahar and a few hundred more on achara and prayaschita are cited from Brihaspati in the Mitakshara and other commentaries and Nibandhas. That seems to have been composed independently. The legal texts attributed to Brihaspati are so numerous as to make up an entire law book which contains a full exposition of forensic law hardly inferior in size to Narada Smriti.

Vishwarupacharya in his commentary as Yagyavalkya in Balkrira on the slok No. 307 & 323 of Acharadhyay of Yagyavalkya has mentioned many sutras of the book Varghaspatyatantra. References are available in the Balkrira characteristics of Senapati/Doot Mantri and that of Uprik (It is like a supervisor). References of the sutra of the Varghaspatya Tantra are also available on the main function of the king in the early hour of the day. Before dawn in the morning, the king on getting up should finish the Vedic rituals and daily worship of the God and after that he should go through the accounts of the state. Kautilya has also made references of the Vrihaspatya Tantra in his Arthashastra: पक्षौ कक्षावुरस्यं प्रतिग्रहः ईति वार्हस्पत्यः। (158-159: 6 : 1).

P.V. Kane has elaborately discussed Brihaspati. He says that the complete Smriti of Brihaspati on law has not yet been discovered. It will be, when discovered, a very precious monument of ancient India exhibiting the high water mark of Indian acumen in strictly legal principles and definition (Kane, I, I: 484). Fahrar collected together 84 verses ascribed to Brihaspati in the legal treatises of Apararka and others with German translation of notes and Jolly collected about 711 verses of Brihaspati on law and translated them in volume 33 of the *Sacred Book of the East.*

Brihaspati was probably the first jurist to make a clear distinction between civil and criminal justice:

तदाह वष्टहस्पतिः। द्विपदो व्यवहारष्ठच धनहिंसा समुद्वः।
द्विसप्तधार्थ मूलञ्च हिंसामूल श्रनुर्विधः(*Vyawahar-Matrika*, 277)

In Smriti Chandrika too we have पारुज्ये हे वधस्चौव परस्त्री संग्रहस्तथा हिंसोद्भवानि चत्वारि पदान्याह वष्टहस्पतिः। Yet, we are not sure whether these references in the Kane's Dharmashastra on Brihaspati are related to his famous book Brihaspatya.

Shukracharya (Ushana): Aaushanas Tantra

Shukracharya is an ancient sage in the Rig veda. Usanas wrote a work on politics to be deployed in several circumstances. Kautilya quotes this seven times. It is almost certainly referring to a work on the administration of justice. Importance of the man can be understood from the fact that the Mahabharata has referred to this work in the Shanti Parva (37):

वष्टहस्पति पुरोगाँस्तु देवर्ज़ीनसष्ठकृत् प्रभुः। तोज़यित्वोपचारेण राजनीति मधीतवान्।। उसना वेद यच्छास्त्रं यच्च देवगुरुर्द्विजः।तच्च सर्व सवैयाख्यं प्राप्तवान् कुरुसत्तमः।।

It is said that Bhisma learnt politics from Brihaspati and Ushana. Many important ideas and principles are discussed in the Shukraniti as ukfyda द्विविधं ज्ञेयं वष्टहत् क्षुद्रविभेदतः। (*Shukra* 4:7).

Shukracharya's two famous slokas are:

उद्यम्य ष्टास्त्रमायान्तमपि वेदान्तगं रणे।निगृहीयात् स्वधर्मेण धर्मापेक्षी नराधिपः।। विनष्ठयमानं धर्मे हि योऽभिरक्षेत् स धर्मवित। न तेनधर्महा स स्यान्मन्युस्तन्मन्यु मष्टच्छति(*Shanti Parva* 56:29-30 and *Shukraniti Sar.* I: 124: 125)

Shukracharya has mentioned that the works of the king. This has also been referred by Manu but these are not the same which Shukracharya has referred to:

- to collect taxes from the subjects;
- to make salary of the employees in time;
- to instruct Amatyas on different works;
- not to allow to do such works from the Amatyas and subjects which harms them;
- to distribute the works;
- to decide the doubtful works in a particular sector;
- to make punishment as per rules and
- to take steps for the maintenance of work smoothly, specially keeping an eye on those who are engaged in bad works.

Manu, Medathiti and Mahabharata mention the authority of Shukracharya (Ushana) (Manu, 7.154; Vanaprashtha Parva, 285.6-7 & Vana Parva, 284.31). Importance of Ushana/ Shukracharya in the field of Rajaniti can be ascertained from the fact that it deals with the duties of princes (chapter I), the functions of the crown, prince and other state officers (chapter II), general rules of morality (chapter III), characteristics of friends, treasure, art and science, social custom and institution, king's functions, fortresses and the army (chapter IV) along with the supplementary and miscellaneous entries (chapterV).

Shukracharya in the beginning of the book says, "Shukracharya, the off spring of Bhrigu questioned with respectful decorum by Purvadevas or Asuras, his disciples, gave them a discourse on the essence of morals in the logical order.

For the good of man, Brahama created Lord, had spoken that treatises on morals which contained 100 lakh, i.e., 10 million slokas. By a process of selection, the essence of that Niti Shastra, which was an extensive argumentative thesis has been complied in an abridged form by Vasistha and others like Shukracharya for the increase of prosperity of rulers of the earth and of others whose life is of short span.

Thus it can be easily said that the book is described as having its origin in a lecture by a professor to his disciples. Brihaspati's disciples are the devas, Shukra delivers the Nitisar- the essence or compendium, not the whole treatises. The other reading is Nitishastra which makes Shukra, the author of the whole thing.

There is an indication that Shukra was only one of the many acharyas who undertook to compile a synoptical edition of the vast work of Brahma. The abridgement was called for by the fact that art is long and life is short.

Manu: Manusmriti

Manu Smriti occupies specially high and unique position in Dharmashastra literature. The word Dharma is a word of a very wide connotation and means not only duties enforceable in-court of law but duties and obligations of all kinds–legal, social, religious, ethical, political and all others - from morning to night, from birth to death, including rites and ceremonies both pre-natal and post natal. It is with this wide sense of Dharma, that Dharmashastra literature is concerned.

Manu Smriti itself mentions for characteristics or sources of Dharma– Shruti, Smriti, Sadachar and that which appeals to one's own conscience– the last being known in modern jurisprudence as equity, justice and good conscience. Out of these four, the Shruti is the Veda, the revealed word. Manu Smriti does not claim to be the directly revealed word of God but the introductory part of its first adhyaya states that the contents of the book were revealed by Manu the father of mankind, to the sages who had assembled, not directly by his own discourse to them but through another sage Bhrigu. Manu communicated the contents to Bhrigu and the latter told the assembled sages in presence of Manu himself.

तपस्तप्त्वा सष्टजधं तु सर्ववयं पुरुज्ञो विराट्।
तं माँ वित्तास्य सर्वएव स्त्राज़्टरं द्विजोकमा:।।33।।
अहं प्रजा: सिसष्टश्रुस्तु तपस्तप्त्वा सुदष्टष्ठचरम्।
प्रतीन्प्रजानाममसष्टजं महज़ध्नादितो दष्ठा।।34।।
मरीचि म॥यगिंरसो प्रलस्त्यं प्रलहं ऋतुम्।
प्रचेतसं वसिज़्ठं ज भष्टगुं नारदमेव च।।35।।
एते मनूंस्नु सप्तान्यानसष्टजन्भूरि तेजस:।
देवान्देव निकायांष्ठच महज़ध्ष्ठचामितौजस:।।36।।(*Manu Smriti*: 1: 33-36).

Manu Smriti has 12 Adhyayas and 2694 verses. It has moulded the lives of millions in India for endless generations and when Indians emigrated beyond India, influence of Manu Smriti spread over to those countries also. The Burmese Dhammatas (*Dhammatats*) are based on Manu Smriti and it was the foundation of Burmese Law. It has been used as an authority in the island of Bali. According to Brihaspati Smriti, this singularly high and authoritative position of Manu Smriti is due to the fact that it correctly represents the sense of the Veda. The content of Manu Smriti includes origin of the universe, sources of law; stages of life and religious duties; morality of the brahman house holder; duties of women, kings and of different castes; civil and criminal law; the mixed castes and classes– procedure in time of need; penance, expiation and the exposition of philosophical principles– acquisition of final happiness.

There are commentaries on Manu Smriti by Medhatithi, Sarrajuarayana, Kulluka, Raghavanand, Nandan, Ramchanda, Manirama, Govindraja, Bharuchi.

Bharadwaja Niti

Bharadwaja happens to be the son of Brihaspati, the famous writer of Vrihaspatya Nitishastra (Tantra). The Bharadwaja Niti forms a branch of Vajaspatya Tantra. Bharadwaja is a famous profounder of the Nitishastra. There is a Shrauta Sutra and Grihya Sutra attributed to Bharadwaja. That Bharadwaja was an ancient writer of Arthashastra follows from Kautilya, where the views of Bharadwaja are cited seven times and Kanika Bharadwaja once. It appears from quotation in Vishwarupa and other early commentators that a Sutra work on Dharma attributed to Bharadwaja was in existence. On Yagyavalkya (1.15) Vishwarupa quotes a prose passage from Bharadwaja prohibiting the learning of *malechcha* tongue and calling upon the preceptor to teach his pupil pure words, observance of Sandhya and kindling of fire (Kane,vol. I, part I: 291).

तथा च भारद्वाजः--न म्लेच्छभाज़ ष्िाक्षेत।
म्लेच्छो ह वा एज़ यद्पराब्द इति विज्ञायते।
तस्माच्छिज़्यमुपनीय साधु ष्टाब्दान् ज़िक्षयेत् सन्ध्योपासाना ग्रीध्रनानि।

References have been made in the M.B. Rajadharmanushasan Parva about Bharadwaja, the profounder of the Nitishastra (Rajadharmanushasan Parva: 58: 2-4). Similarly, references about the principles enunciated by the Rishi Bharadwaja mentioned in the Mahabharata are also available in the Manu Smriti (Manu: 7: 101-102).

Sambar Niti

Brihaspati was the Teacher of the Devas, where as Shukracharya, the teacher of the Asuras. The Niti given by the Lord Brihaspati was popular among the Devas and the Niti given by the Shukracharya in his Aaushanas Tantra was popular and prevalent with the Asuras. References are available for Sambar who was a *mayavi.* Sambar gave his law for those who play hide and seek and keep the enemy in lurch. He warns that enemy should not be allowed to move freely, neither they be pardoned without getting them defeated in the war. In the Mahabharata we find

मन्यते कर्शयित्वा तु क्षमा साध्वीति शाम्बरः,
असंतप्तं तु यद् दारू प्रत्येति प्रकृतिं पुनः।। (*Shanti Parva* 102:31)

The Sambar Niti says that the enemy should be pardoned of his crime after enemy is weakened only then such enemy would be bound by the victorious persons.

Further it is said by the Sambar Niti that one should not depart from treasury, army, friends who are always helpful. Mahabharat says, कोष्ठां दण्डं वलं मित्रं यदन्यदपि संचितम् न कुवध्तान्तरं राज़्ट्रे राजा परिगतः क्षुधा।। (*Shanti Parva*, 130: 32).

Sambar further says that wealth should be preserved. Without wealth the life of one is almost a hell (Udhyoga Parva, 72:22). The Sambar Niti considers poverty the worst part of one's life.The Mahabharata repeats the same in the Udhyoga Parva (134:12). Many authorities of the Nitishastra, however, have criticised the views of Sambar.

Matang Niti

The Mahabharata mentions the name of Matang as a thinker. He propounds a niti - that is why his name has been taken as the thinker and propounder of the Rajaniti. Bhagwan Matang says that nobody should surrender- one should labour hard and try for victory.

उद्यच्छेदेव न नमेहुद्यमो हेव पौरूज़म्
अप्यपर्वाणि मन्येत न नमेदिह कर्हिचित।।19।।
इति मातैं वचन परीप्सन्ति हितेप्सवः
धर्माय चौव प्रणमेद् ब्राह्मेणभ्यष्ठच मद्विधः।।20।।

(Udhyoga Parva,127: 19: 20)

Kalakbrikshya Niti

Kalakbrikshiya Muni has given his niti to the king, kshemdarsi of Kaushal. The king used to carry out the administration with the help of his ministers–but all the ministers were dishonest and they used to procure wealth from the kingdom for the gratification of their desires. Naturally the administration was deterioting day by day.

The Kalakbrikshiya Muni kept a crow–through that art he entered the palace of the king and narrated the misdeeds of the ministers to the king which were later on proved. The king was advised to remove such dishonest persons one by one failing which if all are removed at a time, they would join together and could try to get the king ousted. Hence, it was the niti of Kalakbrikshiya to keep dishonest persons one by one out and to weaken the enemy so that there be no obstruction to run the kingdom with honest persons (Shanti Parva: 70: 69: 70 and 82: 5).

Kanik Niti

Kanik was a shrewd minister of the king Dhritirashtra. He is called a diplomatic minister. With the growing strength of the Pandavas, Dhritirastra was very suspicious whether Pandavas would occupy the throne of the kingdom whereas he himself wanted Duryodhan and Dusshasan. He therefore was planning to scuttle the growing power of the Pandavas and to keep them out of the scene.

Kanik as he was clever and a great manipulator for such planning was called by the king Dhritirashtra and he was instructed to plan such a way that Pandavas might be out of scene. Kanik's suggestions to the king are his nitis. It is explained in the Mahabharata Adiparva:

तत आहूय मन्त्रज्ञं राजष्ठास्त्रार्थ विसमम्
कनिकं मन्त्रिणां श्रेज़्ठं धष्टतरोज़्ट्रोऽब्रवीद् वचः।।2।। (*Adiparva*,139: 2)

This clearly shows that Kanik was a great authority on economy and polity and he was called by the king Dhritirashtra to manage the problem he was facing due to the popularity of Pandavas.

उत्सिक्ताः पाण्डवा नित्यं तेभ्योऽसूये द्विजोतमा। तत्रमे निष्ठिचत तमं संधिविग्रहकारणम्।।
ख्रकणिक त्वं ममाचक्ष्व करिज़्ये वचनं तव।।3।। (*Adiparva*: 139: 3)

The Kanik Niti is very harsh and does not allow concessions to enemy even if the enemy is weak and is ready to surrender. His emphasis is more on Danda than on pity. (*Adiparva*: 139: 6.7). In his Niti, Kanak has very cunningly given the way and means by which the enemies could be tamed.Kanik also tries through his niti to placate the enemy if the king feels that his army is not in a position to match the enemy, the procedure for softness be adopted towards the enemy and efforts be made to have compromise with the enemy through good-soft spoken words. It is gathered that Kanik might have been influenced by Manu - because Manu expresses the similar view as that of Kanik (Manu, 7: 171-172).

Bidulanushashan

Bidula was the widow Maharani of Saubir kingdom. She was well versed in the Rajaniti shastra and had the courage to defend her kingdom when his son Sanjay got defeated in a war with the kingdom of Sindhu Raja; she bucked up his son with courage to procure the lost kingdom like his father. However, she also blamed his son as weak, impotent, timid and unable to survive in the state.

The Mahabharata in Udyog Parva has dealt in greater length in four chapters the courage of the widow which also shows her maturity in the field of politics, law and administration.

It is a matter of pity that the name of the courageous widow/Maharani Bidula is unknown to us, whereas many writers have named this great widow as the embodiment of courage and shrewdness in politics, war and law. Bidula is being cited as an example by Krishna in the Mahabharata :

कुन्त्युवाचःअत्राप्यदाहरन्ती भामितिहासं पुरातनम्।
विदुलायाष्ठच संवादं पुत्रस्य च परंतप।।1 (*Udyoga Parva*, 133: 1)

This example has been cited by Krishna in presence of Yudhishtir, so that Yudhishtir may rise to the occasion for getting themselves ready to fight the wicked Duryodhan/ Dusshasan for the injustice caused to the Pandavas by the Kaurvas.

Bidula encouraged her son Sanjay even by telling him that he was not her son– as he was very timid/devoid of energy and was the very embodiment of impotence - such people are ashamed of the family, society and nation. Bidula also blamed him of lack of enthusiasm and vigour, might and potentialities to fight. The dialogue between the mother–Bidula and the son– Sanjay is thought provoking and becomes the torch bearer principles for politics, war, and law. This was a booster to Yudhisthir for inclination towards the preparation for war with the Kaurvas. She expects her son to rise to the occasion when she remarks:

निदर्ष्ठानान्युपायांष्ठच बहून्यदर्ष्ठाणानि च
अनुदर्ष्ठित रूचोऽसि परयामि कुरु पौरूज्ञम।।32।।(*Udhyog Parva*, 135: 32)

Bidula further guides his son to take help and cooperation from those kings who are enemies of the Sindhu Kingdom by manipulation, by taking cooperation from enemy's enemy and by consolidating with them one should fight the enemy. This is nothing but politics and the art of war. This is the *niti*:

पुरुज्ञार्थमभि प्रेतं समाहर्तमिहार्हसि
क्रधाँल्लुब्धान् परिक्षीणानवलिप्तान् विभानिता-
स्पर्धिनष्ठचौव ये केचित तान् युक्त उपधारय
एतेन त्वं प्रकारेण महतो मेत्स्य से गणा-
महावेग इवोद्‌भूतो मातरिष्ठवा बलाहका-

तेज़ाम्प्रप्रदायी स्या: कल्योत्यायी त्रियवद:
ते त्वां प्रियं करिष्ठयन्ति पुरोधास्यन्ति च ध्रुवम्।।
(*Udhyoga Parva*, 135: 33-35)

Sanjay was encouraged so vigorously by his mother that he became ready for the war. This teaching is the history of Vijay and gives encouragement, enthusiasm and has got importance for the war-politics–a principle of political science/law.

The King Dhritarashtra

Maharaja Dhritarahstra had a unique position and he has great importance in the history of India. Maharaja gave blessings to Yudhishtir on being the king after the Great War was over. The sermons given by the king signifies the gist of the political acumen he was carrying with him as being the experienced king of the great empire.

He has been given the most important place for the management of the kingdom on the basis of Dharma (*Mahabharat, Ashram*, 5:8-9).The king had given high position to the learned and people with skills and expertise. The king should have close contact with such persons to get advice from them in execution of the administration (*Ashram Parva*, 5:10). He has given further importance to the Indriya, with the control of the Indriyas one could control the kingdom effectively (*Ashram Parva*, 5:13). Emphasis is laid on effective, honest and loyal ministers, who have been engaged in the management of kingdom from the forefathers' regime (*Ashram Parva*,5: 14) and maintenance of secrecy in administration (*Ashram Parva*,5: 24). The law and order can be maintained by honest judicial officers. He has warned that people of doubtful character may not be engaged in the administration (*Ashram Parva*, 5: 29- 31). King Dhritirashtra gave almost the same direction to the king Yudhishtir for running the administration which Manu has given (Manu, 7:177,180).

Maharani Gandhari Niti

When the peace proposal given by Krishna failed and Duryodhan with his men left the hall, Dhritarashtra asked Vidur to bring Gandhari in the hall. When Gandhari came the king Dhritarashtra asked Gandhari to persuade Duryodhan and others to accept the peace proposal given by Krishna in the interest of the kingdom and the human kind as the war is dangerous and there would be loss to the kingdom as well as the loss of human life.

In the beginning Gandhari told the king that he was himself responsible for such behaviour of Duryodhan and others and for the war (*Udhyog Parva*, 129: 11 and 12). She told Dhritarashtra that it was not possible for Duryodhan to accept the peace proposed as he was drunk with greed, anger and all sorts of unbecoming behaviour. He was surrounded by all such wicked persons. She feels that the effect of the division among brothers and self would create bad impression and the king Dhritrashtra would never be happy. The crises which could be averted through solution could not be solved through confrontation (*Udhyog Parva*, 129: 14 and 15).

When Duryodhan came before the mother Gandhari, she gave him certain sermons –she told that in the interest of the relations –friends and society, in the interest of Guru Bhisma, father, mother, Acharya Drona– in the interest of the kingdom, peace proposal should be accepted and only through good wishes one can enjoy the fruits of the kingship. One should have control over the different indriyas and that would lead to prosperity. She further scolded and asked Duryodhan to leave the idea of war –confrontation and division and peace proposal should be accepted (*Udhyog Parva*, 129: 20-24). She friendly told Duryodhan that if he would like to be the king and carry out the administration of the kingdom peacefully, he should handover half of the kingdom to Yudhishtir (*Udhyog Parva*, 129: 46).

Lastly she persuaded him to accept the peace proposal as he would not be able to harm Srikrishna and Yudhishtir and he would not be happy with the kingdom if he tries to have it alone (*Udhyog Parva,* 129:54).

Maharsi Veda Vyasa

Veda Vyas was the great grand son of Vashist, grand son of Rikhi Shakti (son of Parashar). He was the father of Sukhadev. The Puranas say that Vyas was born in the Island of the Yamuna– so he was called Dwaipayan. He was shyam– so he was called Krishna Dwaipayan. He divided the Vedas: So he was called Vedavyasa. He was great author and authority on knowledge.

It is said that whatever is available, what everybody has learnt about Dharma is due to Vyas. Veda, Puran, Itihas – Mahabharata –Smritis are due to Veda Vyas. There are a few Smritis authored by Vyas.

Vyas Smriti

In Jivanand and in the Anand Sharma collection of Smriti, there is a Smriti ascribed to Vyas. The two texts are the same with a few variations. It is in four chapters and contains about 250 verses. Vyas is said to have declared the Smriti in Benaras (*Vyas Smriti*: 1.1). It demarcates the geographical boundary of the Dharma by stating that 'the Dharmas herein laid down prevail only in that region where the black deer roam'. In brief the contents are: the authoritativeness of Shruti, Smriti and puranas; mixed castes; sixteen sanskaras; duties of brahamachari; marriage; duties of a wife; the nitya, naimittika, and kamya acts of householder, eulogies of the householder and gifts. He is called Dana-Vyasa due to his contributions as gifts.

Vyas has mentioned 16 (sixteen) sanskaras: garbhadhana, prasavana, seemantonnayan, jaatkarma, naamkarna, nishakramana, annaprashana, chudakarana, mundana, karnaveda, upanayana, vedarambha, godana, samvartate, vivah agni-parigraha and tretagni-sangraha (*Vyas Smriti*: 1: 13-15).

Vishwarupa quotes a few verses of Vyasa. They are mostly taken from Mahabharata and are concerned with topics of marriage, daily duties, shraddha and prayaschita. Similarly Medhatithi quotes several verses from the Mahabharata as Vyasa's. Kalpatru quotes Vyasa 80 times on Vyavahara, 16 times in grihastha, 3 times in Rajadharma. Vishwarupa on Yagavalkya quotes three verses of Vyasa on theft the 2nd and 3rd of which say, 'on acquiring by theft one *suvarna,* one cow or even one fingerbreadth of land from the best of Brahamanas (the thief) certainly receives bodily punishment (or death sentences)'; and 'by gift or theft the reward (or result) is middling or lowest or highest, depending on the extent of the thing donated and the worth of the donee' (Kane, vol. I, part I: 530). Vyasa says, 'nobody is a friend or foe of anybody; friends and enemies arise on account of power' (Kane, 531).

Vyasa dealt with rules of procedure and the several titles of law (Vyavahar-Padas) and that his doctrines closely agreed in most respects with those of Narada, Katyayan and Brihaspati. He gives rules on the four kinds of Uttara (Mithya, Sampratipathi, Karana and Prana-Nyaya), divides documents into three varieties (Swahasta, Janapada, Rajashasana) divides Laukika documents into eight sub-varieties (just as Katyayana seems to have done) Yagavalkya provides that when a king makes a grant of land or of a permanent right to receive a certain sum of money or a certain parts of goods, he should inscribe on a piece of cloth the details of the grant with his seal. Brihaspati deals more elaborately with the same matter and Apararka quotes about eight verses of Vyasa one of which prescribes that the grant should record in it the merit for the one who grants and his successors who continue the grant as heaven for 60000 years and hell for the same length of time for him who resumes it (Kane, I.I: 532).

There are laghu Vyasa Smritis written on vyvahara. It is perhaps also written by the Vyasa. Vyasa flourished about the same time as Yagyavalkay and Brihaspati (5th Century

A.D.). There are 268 verses of Vyasa on judicial procedures and the substantive law. They relate to the king as judge, the qualification of a judge, the member of the court, the plaintiff, the reply, proof and burden of proof, document etc.

Bhagwan Vishnu Smriti or Vaishnava Dharmashastra or Vishnu Sutra

Bhagwan Vishnu Smriti is in the main collection of ancient aphorisms on the sacred laws of India and as such it ranks with other ancient works of this class which have come down to us.

It is very important and it can be easily said that where as the Dharmashastra of Manu, Yagyavalkya, Gautam, Vasistha, Parasara and others are through the Rishies, the present one is directly by the Vishnu, the creator of the Prajapati. This can be compared with that of the Srimad Bhagwat Geeta. Both the Geeta and the Vishnu Smriti are from the mouth of the Almighty.

It is also called Vaishnav Dharmashastra depicting the idea that it is the Vishnu who is the embodiment of Vaisanav cult– though we can keep him isolated. The Vaishnavas consider this book as the most precious one for them and worship this valuable Smriti. Great Vaishnavas–Ramanuj, Madhwa, Nimbark, Ballava, Vishnuswami and Ramanand etc. consider this book as their personal property and keep this with utmost importance.

These are 98 chapters. Though the number of chapters is so large, the sutra is not very extensive. There are several chapters such as 40, 42, 76 which contain only one Sutra and one verse. The first chapter and the last two are entirely in verse; the remaining chapters are in a mixed prose and verse, the versified portion being generally at the end of each chapter.

The size of the Vishnu sutra and the great variety of the subjects treated in it would suffice to entitle it to a conspicuous place among the five or six existing Dharma sutras; but it possesses a peculiar claim to interest, which is founded on its close connection with one of the oldest vedic schools, the Kathas on the one hand, and with the famous code of Manu and some other ancient law codes, on the other hand. There is 'Keshav-Vaijayanti', a commentary on this book by Acharya Nand Pandit. References for these books are available in the Manu Smriti, Srimad Bhagwat Geeta and Garuda-Puran in this Vishnu Smriti. Vishnu Smriti has been quoted in the Medhatithi Bhashya of Manu Mitakshara commentary on Yagyavalkya, Apararka and Smriti Chandika. This book is worth reading even for the points of clarity, brevity and fine language. It is also related to Varaha Puran. In this story, the earth goes to Maharshi Kashyap for its placing and he advises Prithvi to go to Lord Vishnu. Then she goes to Bhagwan Vishnu and prays for her safe position to stay. On her prayer, the God Vishnu remarked that the people who follow Dharma, who conduct their behaviour on the sadachar would bear the earth and she would continue to remain there only on this strength (*Vishnu Dharma*, 1/1/471).

The earth further requested the Lord for his blessing with certain sermons for the conduct of people *Dharmacharan.* Whatever the Vishnu explained formed the main contents of the Vishnu Dharma Sutra (*Vishnu*, 1: 76). There are following topics discussed in this book: Vishnu and the goddess of the earth, four castes, duties of a king, weights and measures criminal and civil law; law of debt, writing, witnesses, ordeals, inheritance, funeral ceremonies, funeral oblations, impurity, women, sacraments, studentship, crimes, hells, transmigration, penances, duties of a house holder, rules for a snataka, self-restraints, shradhas, pious gifts, the hermit, the ascetic and mediation on Vishnu. It emphasises that the king should have prime duty for the protection of the people and their welfare. We also come to konw that the state administration was divided into the following: Gramadhyaksha, Dashgramadhyaksha,

Shatadhyaksha, Deshadhyaksha. Able and efficient people who obey Dharma should be associated with the administration. Brahaman was exempted from tax payment. It is said that the king gets credit and gets punya if the king as well as the subjects follow the Dharma. And if subjects do not do good work the king gets cursed on behalf of his people for the unseeming acts done by the subjects. Naturally, it is the duty of the king to do works on Dharma and it is also the duty of the king to see that no unlawful works be taken up by the subjects and the king himself does not do improper works. There are six wings of the kingdom: Swami (King), Amatya (Ministers), Durga, Kosha, Danda and Mitra. The king should not hurt the following and they should be worshipped by the king: Sadhu, Sant, Mahatma. The king should take steps for maintenance of peace during the period of famine, epidemic, earthquake and such calamities. Ultimately the kingdom must have peace and calm for the welfare of the state and the people and through the welfare of the state the king gets punya. Besides the general Dharma, Rajaniti Dharma, the following are mentioned in the main book: matters related to *preta*, shradh, *kaala*, *sauch* by birth, *sauch* by death, *sauch* if death in the nation, *sauch* if death outside, importance of cow, black money, respect towards father-mother-wife, general welfare and place for the stands of the goddess Lakshmi.

It is said that there is concise Vishnu Smriti in five chapters with 115 slokas. It is related to Dharma, for Brahmacharya] Grihastha, Vanprasth and Sannyas. Four different kinds of Sanyasi are mentioned too: Kutichak, Bahudak, Hans and Param Hans (*Laghu Vishnu Smriti*, 4: 11).

Maharshi Apastamba

Maharshi Apastamba is one of the oldest Rishis, a great Yogi proficient in Veda-Vedanta and a great kind hearted sant. Maharshi Yagyavalkya has placed him in a very high and respectable place. He is placed as one of the important

Acharyas of Black Yajurveda and his name figures in Panini's Vidadi-Gan-Sutra. There are still many South Indians having Apastamba as their gotra. It is referred in the Matsya Purana that he was the chief acharya at the Yagya performed by the Kashyap's wife–Diti Devi on the occasion of Putreshti Yagya.

References are available in the Purana about his jalasmadhi during the period of king Navaga. The circumstance, as well as the fact that Apastamba's work is free from any suspicion of having been tampered with by sectarians or modern editors and that its intimate connection with the manual- teaching the performance of the great and small sacrifices, the Shrauta and Griha Sutras which are attributed to the same author, is perfectly clear and indisputable. This entitles it, inspite of its comparatively late origin, to the first place in a collection of Dharma sutra (Max Muller, II (I): XI).

The Apastamba Dharma sutra forms part of an enormous Kalpa Sutra a body of aphorisms, which digests the teaching of the Veda and of the ancient Rishi regarding the performance of Sacrifices and the duties of the twice-born men: Brahamanas. Kshatriyas and Vaisyas and which being chiefly based on the second of the four Vedas Yajurveda in the Taittiriya recension, is primarily intended for the benefit of the Adhvaryu priests in whose family the study of Spanguvedi is hereditary. The following are the works of Maharshi Apastamba: Apastamb Shrauta Sutra, Apastamb Dharma Sutra, Apastamb Grihya Sutra, Apastamb Sulba Sutra, Apastamb Yagya Parivasha Sutra and Apastamb Smriti.

Apastamb Dharma Sutra (C.600-200 B.C) is composed in sutras and is divided in two parts. This Dharmashastra has been familiar and popular among the authors of different Dharmashastras and references are there. Medhatithi or Manu Smriti Bhagya and Mitakshara have references of this book. There is a chapter by the name of Adhyatma Patal in which we have commentary of Acharya Shankar Bhagwatpad– Vivaran. Acharya Haradath has written bhashya on this by the name of Ujjwalavritti. Apastamb has drawn his base on the Veda as the base of Dharmashastra.

Apastamb discourages those who relish on achievement of being victorious and successful. This degenerates people from their normal dharma rituals and ultimately makes their lives hell. Therefore there is a main sutra in the work of Apastamb. Many commentators have given importance of this sutra of Apastamb and they have placed it on the commentaries on Srimad Bhagwat Geeta.

Apastamb Smriti

There is a small book by the name of Apastamb Smriti- with 10 chapters and 200 slokas.Apastamb says that those who conduct themselves on the Dharma are supreme and no harm can be made to them (Apastamb, 90/3). He further says that those who see the other's wife as mother, other's property as dust and treat all other persons as themselves are the true people (Apastamb, 90/90).

The gist of the Apastamb Dharmopadesh says that those who treat the Dharma as their base of livelihood/rituals/ daily conduct/their mannerly behaviour/ and those who are men of honest view and harmless creatures get the blessings of the Lord Almighty. And this life becomes immortal (Apastamb, 90:6).

Maharsi Vashishta Dharmasutra

Maharshi Vashishta is said to be the son of Mitravarun. Vedic Mantra Drista Rig Vedic Seventh Mandal is called the Vashishta Mandal. It is also said that he is the son of Prajapati, the creator Brahma. The clan gotra Vashishta is after this great Rishi. His name figures in Saptarsis. Arundhati is his wife and Vashishta–Arundhati are always together.

The Vashishta Dharmashastra is like that of Gautam, the last remnant of the Sutras of a vedic school, which, as far as our knowledge goes at present (Max Muller,14(II):XI) has perished, together with great part of its writing. We owe the preservation of its Dharmasutra probably to the special law school of India, which attracted, as it would seem by its title and the legend connecting it with Vashishta Maitra Varuni (one of the most famous rishis of the Rig Veda and a champion of Brahamnism), made it one of the standard authorities. The early existence of a legend according to which the Vashishta Dharmasutra was considered either to be a work composed by the Rishi Vashishta, or at least to contain the sum of his teachings on the duty of man, is indicted by several passages of the work itself.

Finally, the concluding sutra of the whole work gives expression to the devotion felt by the author for the rishi, adoration of Vashishta, Satayatu, the son of Mitra and Varuna and of Urvasi.

The epithets used in this last passage conclusively show that Vashishta after whom the Dharmasutra is named, is the individual, who according to the Brahamical tradition, is the rishi of the large portion of the seventh Mandala of the Rig Veda and the progenitor of the Vashishta clan (gotra) of the Brahmanas and who in some hymns of the Rig Veda appears as the Purohit or domestic Priest of king Sudas and the rival of Vishwamitra and in other suktas as a half mythical being.

Kumarila in his Tantravartik gives a very interesting observation on the point whether the Dharmasutra of Vashishta is an independent work or part of Grihya sutra. It tells us that Gautam Dharmasutra and Gobhil Grihya Sutra were studied by the chandogyas (samvedi), Vashishta Dharmasutra by the Rigvedins, the Dharmasutra of Sankh-Likhite by the followers of the Taittiriya Sakha. The Tantra Vartika establishes it as a siddhant of all the Dharmas and Griyha Sutras for all Aryan people. From this it appears that although originally all Sutra charanas might not have possessed Dharmasutras composed by the founder of the *charana*; yet gradually certain Dharmasutras were specifically taken over or appropriated by certain charanas. As the

Dharmasutras were mostly concerned with rules about the conduct of men as members of the Aryan community and did not deal with ritual of any kind at all, Dharmasutra gradually became autharitative (Kane, I.I: 20).

Thus Kumarila is of the opinion that the Dharma sutras of Vashishta was specially studied by the students of the Riga Veda, but that along with other Dharma sutras it is authoritative for all charanas. No Srauta and grihya sutra of Vashishta, if it were ever in existence, has come down to us. Therefore we have to fallback upon one of the two hypotheses, either the Dharma sutra of Vashishta is the solitary remnant of a school that might have once possessed a complete kalpa or that it was composed as an independent work on Dharma and was subsequently seized upon by the students of the Rig Veda, who had only Shrauta and Griyha sutras of Asvalayana. Kumarila suggests that it be the work of Dharmashastra alone.

There are 30 chapters in the Vashishta Dharmashastra: general rules for four castes, lawful occupation, duty of studying the Veda, definition, purifications, origin of castes, impurity, women, rule of conduct, studentship, house holder, hermit, ascetic, guests, shraddhas, sacrifices, initiation, snataka, study of the Veda, saluting, lawful and forbidden food, adoption, excommunication, legal procedure, inheritance, mixed caste, duties of a king, penance, secret penances, gifts.

In the Vashishta Dharmashastra/Vashishta Dharmasutra, the author has discussed the rules of conduct–where the Dharma has been explained श्रुति स्मष्टति विहितो धर्म:।। (Vashishta,1.3). Besides, the conduct of Mahapurush- great kings, rishis should be considered as the Dharma (Vashishta, 1.4). Explaining the meaning of shishta purusha, the rishi Vashishta explains that those who make sacrifies and are lustless are called shishta (Vashishta, 1.5). Those who are righteous are praise worthy and are worshipped at both places, loka and parloka alike (Vashishta, 1.2). Explaining the wickedness, he says that those who help the wicked, they are part and partial of wickedness. There are six types of bad people: संवत्सरेण पतित पतितेन सहाचरन्। (Vashishta , 1.22). They are fire sponsoring, poison giver, killer with arms, stealing wealth, usurper and abductor of wife/woman. अग्निदो गरछश्चैव शास्त्र पानिर्धनापहः। क्षेत्रदारहरश्चैव पठेते आततायिनः।। (Vasistha, 3:19). If they are killed, no prayaschita is imposed: आततायितं दश्त्वा नात्र प्राणच्छेनुः किंचित् किल्विषमाडः। (Vashishta,3.16).

Maharsi Vashishta discusses and praises righteous and criticises the non-righteousness. Righteousness brings happiness whereas nonrighteousness brings misery (Vashishta, 6.3). Vashishta has given certain characteristics of a Brahman: He gives Yoga, Tap, Dam (Indriya-nigraha), Dan, Satya, Sauch, Daya, Vedadhyayan, Vidya, Vigyan and Astikta (Vashishta, 6: 20). For Grihasthya Dharma - Maharsi Vashishta has given one sutra to all beings– the most important characteristics of the Grihastya Dharma यथाशक्ति चान्तेन सर्व भूतानि। (Vashishta, 8:13). For the king's role– one chapter has been devoted to Rajaniti: the king has been endowed with great power and he has to take responsibility of the welfare of the subjects of the whole kingdom. स्वधर्मो राज्ञः पालनं भूतानां तस्यानुष्ठानात् सिद्धिः (Vashishta, 19:1). The gist of the Vashishta Dharmashastra consists in the idea that one should always work on the path of Dharma which would lead to prosperity and would get the blessings of the Lord (Vashishta, 30.1).

Vashishta Smriti

Vashishta Smriti, with seven chapters and 1150 slokas, is mainly a smriti consisting of the Sanskar of the Vaishnavas from Aannprasan to marriage (Vaishnava Dharma, Vaishnava Sadachar and Vaishnava Sanskar) and the importance and duties of women. Lastly, he advises the people to follow the Dharma for prosperity of individual family and the state.

Parashara Dharmashastra

Maharshi Parashara was the grand son of Maharshi Vashishta; son of Mahatma Shakti; father of Krishna Dwaipayan Vedvyasa; grand father of Mahagyani Sukhadeo.

The name Parashara is an ancient one. The Parashara Dharmasastra must be very ancient–but we have doubts whether the old one is the present form. The extant work is probably a recast of it as is mentioned in the Yagyavalkya in the first chapter (Kane, 1, I: 460). The Garuda Puran in chapter 107 gives a summary (on 39 verses) of the Parashara Smriti. In doing so, it takes part of the latter and pieces them together. This establishes that the Garuda Purana regarded the Parashara Smriti authoritative and ancient. Kautilya mentions six times the views of Parashara on the various aspects of politics and state administration.

Therefore, it appears that there was a work of Parashara on politics in which it is possible that the Vyavahara also was dealt with.

The extant Parashara Smriti is divided into 12 chapters and contains only 592 verses. It deals only with achar and Prayaschitya. Madhav introduced his disquisition on Vyavahar, which forms about a fourth of his extensive gloss, in an indirect way by regarding Vyavahar as part of the duties of Kshatriyas on which the Parashara Smriti has something to say. There is a 'Vishnu Puran' by Parasara. This is very beautiful and useful Dharmashastra. There is a Parashara– Gita. It is a dialogue between Parashara and Janak and Parashara gives lectures on the rightful thinking to Maharshi Janak (*Shanti Parva,* 290:6). Parashara preaches Dharma which is beneficial to all beings and those who carry their works as per Dharma and get the blessings of the Parmeshwara (*Shanti Parva,* 293: 3.1).

The introductory verses of the Smriti say that sages went to Vyasa and requested him to instruct them in the Dharma and conduct beneficial to mankind in the Kali Age and that the great Vyasa took them to his father Parashara, son of Shakti, in the Badrikashram, who then propounded the Dharma of the four varanas. The first chapter recites the Smriti then known (19 in all) and lays down that in the four ages of Krita, Treta, Dwapara and Kali, the Dharmas proclaimed by Manu, Gautama, Sankh-Likhita and Parashara were respectively considered to be the guiding ones.

There are 12 chapters: introductory verses; duties of house holder; purification; concerning suicide etc.; expiation for minor things; expiation for killing various beasts and birds; purification of various articles; expiation for killing cows; proper thickness of stick for beating cows; other expiations; expiation for partaking food from chandalas; bath prescribed after evil doings. Prashara has cited Manu/ Baudhayan Sankh, Veda–Vedangas. Several vedic Mantras also are quoted by Parashara.

Parashara appears to have been a practical man. He exhorts his readers to save their bodies first from invasions, journeys, diseases, calamities and then care for Dharma. He recommends the non-observance of the rules of purity in times of difficulty and adherence to the strict rules of Dharma when one is at ease (Kane, I, I: 464).

Prashara emphasises on the importance of Achara-Vichar. He gives importance to all the varanas. Who are against achara they are against the Dharma (Parashara, 1:37). Besides, Parashara gives details on many aspects of human body.

Brihat Parashara Smriti

There are 12 chapters but there is very less commentary on this book. Mahatma Subrat is the chief spokesman. There are 3000 verses. The following are subjects matters: introduction; disquisition on the 6 daily kamas; duties and manners of house holder; forms of marriage; concerning shraddhas; impurity on birth and death; condrayana and other penances; gifts; rights for propitiating garsha-granths etc. Rajadharma: different varieties of Pranayamas and other angas of yoga.

Narada Smriti

Narada refers to four versions of the Code of Manu consisting of 100,000 slokas, 1080 chapters in 12000 slokas; 8000 slokas and 4000 slokas. The authorship of these four versions is assigned respectively to–Manu, Narada, Markandeya and Sumati, the son of Bhrigu, and the Narada Smriti is described as an abridgement made by Narada, of the 9th or Vyavahar chapter of the original code in 100000 slokas. The first part of Narada's abridgement of the 9th chapter of Manu's code is designed as a matrika or vyavhar-matrika (summary of proceedings on law or general rules of procedures).

Narada also figures in Manu when he says that ten rishis were made in the interests of the subjects along with the creation of the universe (*Manu Smriti*, 1:35-36).

If the date of Manu has been rightly placed between 2nd century B.C. and 2nd century A.D., the Narada Smriti can belong to 4th to 5th century A.D. The Narada Smriti agrees on many important points especially in the law of evidence, with the Dharmashastras or Smriti of Yagyavalkya, Vishnu, Brihaspati, Katyayana and Vyasa. It may be a little older than the three last named works which belong to the latest production of the Smriti epoch of Hindu Law, but its legal rules and judicial theories have a decidedly more advanced character than either Vishnu's or Yagyavalkya's. The Smriti of Vishnu cannot belong to an earlier period than the 3rd century A.D. and the Yagyavalkya Smriti is not likely to be anterior to it in date (Max Muller, 33(I): XVIII).

Narada follows the Manu Smriti to a considerable extent in the nomenclature and the arrangement of the 18 titles. Some of the titles are definitely named by Narada, e.g. he speaks of Upanidhi, while Manu employs the word nikshepa. The Smriti Chandrika expressly says that it follows the work of Narada in preference to that of Manu with regard to the nomenclature and the sequence of the titles of law (Kane, I,I: 469). Narada follows Manu in speaking of witnesses and in treating of theft after the eighteen titles have been dealt with.

The printed Narada Smriti contains 1028 verses. Narada is probably later than Yagyavalkya. Yagyavalkya mentions only five kinds of ordeals, while Narada knows seven and the former's treatment of them is not so exhausting as Narada's. The rules of judicial procedure in Narada are more systematic and exhaustive than those of Yagyavalkya. Narada is more conservative than Yagyavalkya. For example: Narada no where recognizes the right of the widow to succeed her deceased husband. Narada cites more definitions than Yagyavalkya. In some respects, Narada is more reticent than Yagyavalkya; Narada gives no rules about the succession of gotrajas and the bandhus as Yagyavalkya does. In few respects Narada agrees with the views of Manu instead of Yagyavalkya, such as allowing a brahaman to marry a shudra woman. Narada regards sexual intercourse with a pravrayita (female ascetic) as a mortal sin, while both Manu and Yagyavalkya treat it lightly. Taking all these things together into consideration it was said that Narada flourished nearly at the same time as or somewhat later than Yagyavalkya (Kane, I, I: 474).

Though these are indications in the Sanskrit literature about Narada's contribution to the Rajadharma, the extant Narada work can hardly be described as a treatise on Rajadharma. It deals only in an indirect way with one aspect of king's duties and is rather concerned with Vyavahara and the duties of the subjects towards each other from the strictly legal point of view. If we turn to Mahabharata and other works, we shall find that Rajadharma meant something different from what is treated in the Narada Smriti. Therefore Bana's reference to the Naradiya is of doubtful character (Kane, I, I: 475). The Rajaniti Ratnakar of

Chandeshwara frequently quotes Narada on politics (pp. 3, 13, 79). These quotations are not traced in the existing work of Narada. Therefore it is highly probable that Bana refers to a distinct work of Narada on politics which has not yet been recovered.

From the Rajaniti Ratnakar of Chandeshwara it appears that Chandeshwar knew a work of Narada on Rajadharma. On page 3 of that work Narada on Rajaniti is cited for dilating upon three grades of rulers viz. Samrat (an emperor to whom other kings pay tribute) also called Chakravarti and 'Sakara' and 'akara' rulers (*Rajaniti Ratnakar,* pp:3, 75 and 79).

Chandeshwar quotes the words of Harita and Narada to the effect that a king should transmit his kingdom to the eldest son after providing for the maintenance of other sons if he has several sons. The Vriddha Harit Smriti in the Anandashram collection of smritis says that Katyayana, Manu, Yagyavalkaya, and Narada described at length the Rajdharma which he himself dealt with (Kane, 1, I: 476).

The references to Narada on Rajaniti are available in the Mahabharata when Narada is called for in the meeting hall of the king Yudhishtir at Indraprastha where there were many other kings present. Narada was respected by the Pandavas and then Narada gave surmons to Yudhishtir on the Rajadharma (*Sabha Parva,* 5:17).

Narada dwells on the role of the king and the management of the kingdom. He mentions six virtues of a king and also provides seven remedies and fourteen places to examine self strength and to remain vigilant. Narada further asks Yudhishtir that wealth, treasury, agriculture, fort, construction of bridges, tax collection are the different wings or limbs of the kingdom (*Sabha Parva,* 5:23-23). There are eight important efforts for the increase of wealth for the kingdom as follows: increase in agriculture, protection of trade, construction of Durga and its protection, construction of bridge and its protection; to keep shepherds, to capture the mines of gold, diamond, tax collection and rehabilitation of people wherever there is complete destruction.

These are following important limbs of the kingdom: it is the duty of the king to keep a regular watch on: king, ministers, friends, treasury, nation, fort, army and purwari.

Narada further asks Yudhishtir to keep alert on the working of the kingdom of the enemy so that there might not be an attack from the enemy side (*Sabha Parva*, 5:38).

Explaining the eighteen Trithas it is said that the king should keep watch on the working of the following of the enemy side: ministers, purohit, yuvaraja (Crown), senapati, dwarpal, antahpur-adhyakshya, karagarchhata, sachiv, dandapala, koshadhyaksha, watchman, nagardhyakshya, karryaniman karta (patchalak), dharmadhyakshya, sabhadhyakshya, durgapala, rastra-simapala and vanarakshaka. These are eighteen Trithas. But of the 18, the last fifteen should also be watched from one's own kingdom. There are many such references which consider Narada the propounder of Rajaniti.

Mahamuni Atri or Aatreya Dharmashastra

Atri is one of the Mantra Drastas of the Rig Veda. He is ancient. Manu says that he is one of the ten rishis to whom Manu authorized the work of organization of the universe. He is also called Prajapati.

The fifth Mandala of the Rig Veda is authorized to this great Maharshi. That is why the 5th Mandala of the Rig Veda is named 'Aatreya Mandala'. It is said that Maharshi Atri was born from the eyes of the Prajapati Brahman.

He is one of the members of the Sapatarshis. There is a very famous Ashram of Atri in Chitrakoot. Aansuya, the daughter of Kandarav Prajapati is his wife. He got the husband of Saibya alive and got the mandakini in the Chitrakoot through his supermental power.

It is said that his language was very powerful and with full of love and affection and a source of respect towards seniors. When Ram, Lakshman and Sita visited the ashram of Maharshi at Chitrakoot, the prayer of the Rishi to them is masterpiece and forms an important part of the language:

नमामि भक्त वत्सलं। कृपालु शील कोमलं।।
भजामि ते पदांब्रजं। अकामिनां स्वधामदं।।

Maharsi Yagyavalkya has named Atri as an important propounder of Dharmashastra. The works of Atri are called as Aatrieya Dharmashastra. Atri Smriti or Atri Dharmasutra has nine chapters with about 90 slokas. The fourth and seventh chapters are in Sutra with 45 and 15 sutras respectively.

They treat gifts, prayers and tapas by which men can become free from all sins. Some of the chapters are in mixed prose and verse. The first three chapters are entirely in verse and some of the verses occur in the Manu Smriti एकाक्षरं परं ब्रह्म।।83।। (Manu, 2: 83). The fourth opens with a long sutra, which in style resembles later bhashyas and commentaries (Kane, I, I: 261). The fifth also is in verse and contains several verses found in Vashishta. The sixth part is of special holy hymns and verses of the Veda. Some of the verses here are the same as Vashishta. The seventh refers to secret prayaschita and the very first sutra after the opening words speak of some non-Aryan tribes such as the sakhas, Yamanas, Kambhages, Balkyas khasas, Varga, and Parasa. It is to be noted that the same sutra is quoted as Atri's by Apararka (on Yag. III. 266, p. 1123). The 7th and 8th chapters are in mixed prose and verse. The 9th is in verse and speaks of Yoga and its angas. It refers to the fact that Shishupal, son of Dansogha, because of his hatred of Govind went to heaven.

In this book, the Maharshi emphasises on Pranayam and the characteristics of the Pranayam and makes it clear that the bad elements in the mind and body are removed by the Pranayam (*Atri Smriti*, 3: 2-3). He has suggested that sins can be removed with the Japa of the Veda Sukta. He further gives suggestions for removing of the sins committed which would eventually lead one to happiness in the world and overall prosperity. This is a type of Prayaschita for the sins committed (*Atri Smriti,* 7: 4). If one regrets and does not commit sin again and pray the sun, then the prayaschita is complete and sin is removed (*Atri Smriti,* 7: 15). He has attached great importance to the Gayatri mantra and says that all sins will be removed if one makes 1000 of Gayatri japa (*Atri Smriti,* 8: 8). For the removal of the sin, he suggests that ultimate reality lies with the prayer of the God and pious works which will lead to happiness. Men should always remain engaged in the prayer of God– that is the ultimate reality (*Atri Smriti,* 9: 4).

Atri Samhita

This is in the form of slokas. There are about 400 slokas in it. It deals with Dharma for all the four varnas, Rajaniti or Rajadharma, sins and the efforts to remove sins, Dan,Ashauch, Prayaschita, rituals and sanskar.

He says that all the varnas should follow and work as per Dharma assigned to each one. Nobody should follow or work on the Dharma of the other varna. It leads to sins (*Atri Şamhita,* 18).

On the question of Rajadharma, he suggests that the king should perform Panchayagna for the welfare of the kingdom: these are: (1) Punish the weak, (2)Worship those working on Dharma, (3) Enhance the treasury as per Dharma or justice, (4) Administer justice impartially so that rights of the subjects are not violated, (5) Safeguard the interests of the kingdom, subjects and serve the subjects of the kingdom.

The king who does all the above works and performs Panchayagna gets Punya of performing 1000 Yagyas (*Atri Samhita,* 28.29).

The Maharshi suggests the following characteristics of a pious Grihastha:

1. Aansuya: Those who do not criticise or disobey those who are virtuous. Even those who possess a few virtuous characteristics should be respected. People should not laugh on the demerits of other either. This is called Aansuya.
2. Sauch: To leave out *abhakshya-bhakshan*. To remain aloof from those who are condemned. To consider what is acchaar vichaar is called Sauch.
3. Mangal: To obey the respected, senior, pious and virtuous people and those who follow Shastras. To discard critical or condemned behaviour. Maharshi calls this as Mangal.
4. Aanaayas: Not to indulge in any physical exertion which might harm the body notwithstanding whether it is good or bad. The work which can be done easily is called Aanaayaas.
5. Aspriha: To remain satisfied and happy with what one has, and not to be eager to get others'. This is Aspriha.
6. Dam: Those who do not try to harm physically or ethically or spiritually. Those who remain completely neutral will be people of Dam.
7. Daan: To give gifts with happiness daily and and enjoy the act of doing so.
8. Daya: To have sympathy in the cause of self, others and all beings. To remain sympathetic even at the times of distress. To treat all on par with oneself is called Daya.

Those who follow and remain dutiful to the above mentioned duties as per Dharma are never to be reborn. They get blessing of the Lord. Their lives are filled with happiness and they will be worshipped by people.

Those who have respect for others, who are always sincere about others' welfare and those who try to help others will help themselves. People should always be eager to extend help, cooperation and pray for others' help. By doing so their life would be always happy and God shall bless such people.

Sankha-Likhita

There is a story in the Shanti Parva (23. 18-23) about both the brothers –Sankha and Likhita. From the Tantra Vartika we learn that the Dharmasutra of Sankha Likhita was specially studied by the followers of the white Yajurveda (Vajaseya) (*Purva Mimansa Sutra*: 1: 3: 11)

In the Mahabharata it is said, "It is not possible to live if one adopts Sankha-Likhita mode of life, particularly, when one intends to secure the protection of the subjects. In another place, it is said in the Mahabharata that for some conduct or practice is the best characteristic of Dharma, others to whom Sankha-Likhita are dear do not like it. It is further said in the Mahabharata that Sankha-Likhita were present in the Indra Sabha along with other sages.

It is further said, न शंख लिखितां वृतिं शक्यमास्थाय जीवितुम। विशेषात: कुरुश्रेष्ठ प्रजापालन मीप्सया। The word Sankha, means also 'forehead' and 'Likhita' means 'written'. It was believed that Brahma writes on the forehead of a child (on the sixth day after birth) the child's future; compare the verse.

यद्धात्रा मिजमालपट्टलिखितं स्तोकं महद्धा धनं तत्प्राप्नोति मरुस्थलेऽपि नितरां मेरौ ततो नाधिकम्।'

Sankha-Likhita vritti would mean the conduct of the two brothers viz. extreme devotion to the rules of honesty and the like. The verse has also another meaning and asks the king not to rely on daiva if he desires to protect the subjects (Kane, I, I: 137).

Laghu Sankha Smriti

Written by Sankha, it has about 71 slokas. The smriti says that if one worships the God/Goddess, and do pious works, such as construction of Dharmashala, plantation of trees, construction of tanks etc–such people would get place in the heaven and people get Moksha for Purta works.

In the smriti, Agni Hotra, Tap, Satya, Vedadhyayas, Athithya are mentioned and Vaishwa Deva has been mentioned as Ishta Deva. Sankha has elaborately discussed the rites to be performed on the death of a man from Tilanjali–Jalanjali to the shraddha (final rites) (*Dharmasastra Ank*, *Kalyan*: 261).

Likhita Smriti

There is a great similarity in Likhita Smriti and Laghu Sankha Smriti slokas in that they are almost similar. There are 71 slokas in Laghu Sankha, whereas there are 96 slokas in the Likhita Smriti.

Like Laghu, in the beginning in this smriti also the Maharshi has mentioned about Ishta Purta and other rituals including that of the Shraddha. Vishvadeo description is also there. Prayaschita has also been mentioned.

Sankha Likhita Smriti

This is a joint venture of Sankha and Likhita and the Smriti has 32 slokas. In this Smriti, description has been made of the Ishta-Purta, Vishwa Deva and about food. Rajaniti has also been discussed. In the Smriti, it is said that people should perform valivaisava-deva karma and pay respect to the guests. Without worshipping the Vaishwa-Deva and the guests, people should not take meals.

In the matters of Rajaniti, the Smriti refers to the function of the king. There it is said that the king, for the interest of the king himself and for the interest of the whole kingdom and for the growth of the kingdom and the welfare of the subjects, must take efforts for the safety and protection of cow, territory, women and Brahaman.

Markandeya Smriti

Maha Muni Markandeya is a great saint and Bhakta of the great Lord Bhagawan Vishnu. He is alive at the feet of the great Lord. He is the son of Maharshi Mrikandu and belongs to Bhrigukula. Though his age is limitless, he is said to be of only 25 years of age as per the Mahabharata (*Vana Parva*, 183: 42-43).

Muni Markandeya is a perfect follower of the Dharmashastra, a devotee to the Lord and always meek with his respectful behaviour towards all beings. His respects to seniors and devotion to parents and guru have made him the embodiment of *avivadanshilata*. This virtue has great importance in the life of human being. Manu gives due importance to this aspect of human nature (Manu, 2: 121). The Mahabharata also recognises this aspect (*Anushasan Parva*, 104: 43-44).

Mrityunjay Stotra given by Muni Markandeya is very famous and useful for life of human being. God Shankar gave a boon to Muni and he is alive forever.

Muni Markandeya has great faith in the Dharma and devotion. The Durga Saptashati is a prayer to the Goddess Durga with the refrain *namastasyaiy, namastasyaiy, namastasyaiy*. The Muni has got this great arm with him and that is why through love, affection and prayer he wins the hearts of the seniors including the blessings of the God/ Goddess. Muni advises everyone to follow this sense of devotion and that would take one into the final achievement the moksha.

There is a Markandeya Smriti. There is a Markandeya Puran in which there is Durga Saptashati with 13 chapters. There is 'Markandeya Samasya Parva' in the Mahabharata. The sermons given to Yudhisthir by Markandeya form the contents of Markandeya Samasya Parva.

There is also a version that Markandeya was one of the senior Munis at the time of Manu and he helped Manu in the organisation of the universe.

The Narada Smriti says that Manu composed 100000 slokas 1080 chapters and 24 Prakaranas, Dharmashastra and imparted it to Narada, who abridged it into 12000 verses and taught it to Markandeya, who in his turn compressed it into 8000 slokas and passed it to Sumati Bhargava who again reduced it to 4000 slokas (Kane, I, II:309).

Markandeya devotes much of his works to love, affection, meekness, gentleness devotion to service, prayer to all seniors and the God/Goddess. He is of the view that one's prayer does not make one go astray. He also devotes space for the Sanskara for purification (such as upanayan samskara). The gist of his Dharmashastra lies in the fact:

सर्वहिंसामिवश्ता ये नराः सर्वसहाश्च ये।
सर्वस्याश्रय भूता ये ते नराः स्वर्गगामिनः
ये निर्जितेन्द्रिया धीरास्ते नराः स्वर्ग गाजिनः
...यान्त भरावतीभ्र। (*Manu Smriti*, 103-105.11)

A great length has been devoted for the young boy's upanayana balaka-samsakar, sauch and ashauch. M u n i Markandeya in his Markandeya Purana has discussed all sorts of welfare to the general people in his kind heartedness. His devotion towards general welfare is a great asset to the world literature (*Markandeya Puran*, 117: 12-19).

His devotion towards munis, saint-rishis–god/goddess are praise worthy and brings general welfare (*Markandeya Smriti*, pp. 78-79). Markandeya also gives his views and suggestions that one should not be attached to people, especially one's relations and friends. Even if some one is inclined to be attached, he should be close to saints, Yogis and good people who are attributed to the Dharma rituals (*Markandeya Puran*, Chapter 38). He emphasises on the importance of guests. This is Athithi Dharma (*Vana Parva*, 200: 23-24). He has also suggested remedies for prayaschita for sins (*Vana Parva*, 207: 51).

Raja Dharma

He has given sermons to Yudhishtir and has given general views of Rajaniti. He says that no one should consider himself as master, though he suggests this to Yudhishtir as a general advice for the king. The king should give due importance to the welfare of the people as a whole and should always keep his limbs under control (*Vana Parva*, 191: 23-25).

Lastly, he gives kindness the most important Dharma kshama (the most important power), satya the most important pious tap and the closeness with the Paramatama as the most important knowledge. He advocates that one must embibe these qualities (Vana Parva, 213: 30). Further for welfare of individual and for general welfare one must be a devotee of the supreme power that keeps oneself happy and free from fear (*Vana Parva*, 216: 28).

Maharshi Gautama Dharmashastra

Maharshi Gautam is one of the saptarshis. कश्यपोऽत्रिर्वसिष्ठश्च वि श्वामित्रोऽथ गौतमः जमदग्निर्भारद्वाज इति सप्तर्वयः स्मृताः।। (*Srimada Bhagawat*: 8.13.5; *Vishnu Puran*: 3.1.32). Devi Ahalya is his wife. The character of Gautam is superb. The Gautam Dharmasutra and The Gautam Smriti are the two great works of the Rishi Gautam.

The Gautam Dharmasutra

This appears to have been held in high esteem by Kumarila. He starts with Gautam as the first in enumerating the Dharmasutra and remarks that Gautamiya and Gobbiliya are accepted and adopted by Chandogas or Samavedins. Not only Kumarila but an earlier famous writer on logic and philosophy viz. Dharmakirti in his Nyayabindu appears to suggest that Gautam was chief among the exponents of Dharmasutra (Kane, I,I: 26). Dharmakirti says: there is a close relation between the Sama Veda and Gautam."

Gautam Dharmasutra is composed in Sutra and some parts of if are also in prose, but there is no sloka. There are commentaries on Gautam's works by Acharya Haradatta, Acharya Maskarsi and Sri Aasahaya. There are about 29 chapters in the Gautam Dharmashastra. Important among these are: Initiation, purification, Studentship, The Ascetic, The Hermit, the House holder, Times of distress, A king and Brahaman versed in the Vedas, the duties of a Snataka, Lawful occupation and livelihood, the Duties of a king, civil and criminal law, witness Impurity, Funeral oblation, The Study of the Veda, Eating, Forbidden food, Women, Penance and Inheritance.

Maharshi Gautam has dealt in his Dharmasutra almost all the matters related to a human being during his life time. In the beginning he has given the most importance to the Vedas, *vedo Dharma mulam.* He has also devoted a lengthy section to the Grihastha Jiwan.

Gautam suggests to take shelter with parents, gods and rikhis besides fore-fathers. Gautam suggests that men should follow Satya Dharma and follow the seniors who are versed in Dharma. Non-violence is also one of the key aspects of Dharma. To give alms, to give gifts– to keep control on one's limbs and to be respectful and submissive are the core principles of his Dharma sutra.

Bridha Gautam Smriti

There are 22 chapters consisting of Dharma, Dan, characteristics of a Brahama, Pious and non-pious works, Tapyogya, Rites, Tirth, Godan and Srikrishna–Yudhishtir dialogue.

Dharma Mahima

Srikrishna tells Yudhishtir about the Dharma. He says that father, mother, seniors, guru, saints and gods are the Dharmas and one should obey them. Those who obey get the heaven and blessings of the Lord. One must follow them (*Dharmashastranka, Kalyana: 306*). Lord Krishna tells Yudhishtir that he was successful with the cooperation of Brahman. He therefore always suggests that Brahman must be respected (*Bridha Gautama, 4:57; Dharmasastranka, Kalyana*).

He also praises devotion for cow. Lastly he cites the dialogue between Krishna andYudhisthir saying that the king must have only one thing in mind: to serve the subjects for their benefit. God will bless such kings: चिन्तयस्व सदा विणुम प्रमत: कुरुद्रह लोका गच्छन्ति नान्येन तद्विष्णो: परमं पदम्।। (*Bridha Gautama, 22: 47; Dharmasastranka, Kalyana*).

The Yagnavalkya Smriti

The name of Yagyavalkya is one of the most illustrious among Vedic Sages. He is credited with having promulgated the white Yajur Veda. He has been named as the avatar of Brahma as per the Puranas. He is the son of Devaraat as per Srimad Bhagawat Purana (12.6.64). He is the disciple of Maharshi Vaisampayana. He learnt Vedas from his Guru Vaisampayana.

In the Mahabharata Shanti Parva (312), we are told that there was a rupture between Vaisampayan and his pupil Yajnavalkya and that by worshipping the sun the latter received the revelation of the white Yajur Veda the Satpath etc. अहमयातया मयजु: काम उपसरामीति। (*Srimad Bhagawat*, 12.6.72). The sun pleased with Yagyavalkya of his Tapas stood before him and gave him the summons which none had received so far.

Because it was given by sun in his Ashvarupa, this branch of Sukla Yajurveda came to be known as Vajasnay and Yagyavalkya is the founder of this branch of teaching. Yagyavalkya is the main Acharya of the Veda. He is also the drashta of Satpatha Brahman, the Brihadaupanishad.

There is a dialogue between the king Janak and Yagyavalkya. He was the teacher of the king Janak. Maharsi Yagyavalkya belonged to Mithila. Yagyavalkya Smriti contains 1010 verses. His place is not lower than that of Manu. Almost all slokas of Manu Smriti have been commented upon in the original as well as commented books of Yagyavalkya. There are other books besides Yagyavalkya Smriti. These are 1. Brahmokta Yogi Jagayalkya Smriti, 2. Brihadyagiya Yagyavalkya Smriti, 3. Yagyavalkya Geeta, 4. Yagyavalkyapanishad, 5. Yagyavalkya Shiksha.

Gayatri Bhashya was fully commented upon in which there are many slokas in each letter of the Gayatri. Rishis asked Yagyavalkya on the issues of Dharma and what Yagyavalkya replied has come to be called Ygyavalkya Smriti. It is said, मिथिलास्थः स योगीन्द्रः क्षणं ध्यात्वाब्रवीन्मुनीन्। (*Yagyavalkya Smriti,* 1:2). It deals with Achchar, Vichar and Prayaschita.

The whole of Yagyavalkya Smriti is written in the classical Anustubh metre. The style is flowing and direct. Yagyavalkya's works are more systematic than that of Manu. He divides the work into three sections and relegates all topics to their proper positions and avoids repetition. He treats almost all subjects that we find in Manu, but his treatment is always concise and he makes very great and successful efforts at brevity. The result is that for 2700 verses of Manu, he requires only a little over 1000. He often compresses two verses of Manu to one. For example: Manu II 243, 247, 248 are equal to Yagyavalkya Smriti (1.79). The first part of the Yagyavalkya Smriti contains *acharadhyaya* which consists of fourteen Vidyas, twenty expounders of Dharma, sources of Dharma; the Sanskara from Garbhabhan to the end of man (Shraddha). These are Upodhaghat, Brahmachari, Marriage, Varna Jati Viveka, Grihastha Dharma, Snataka Dharma, Bhakhya Bhakhya, Dwavya Sudhi, Dan (gift), Shradha, Ganpati Kalpa, Grahshanti and Rajadharma.

The second part, *Vyavaharadhyaya* consists of sadharan vyavahara matrika, asadharana vyavhara matrika, Krinadaana and Upanidhi. It also lists following departments and concerned people: Sakshi, Lekhya, Divya, Daana Vibhaga, Seema-Vivaada, Swamipala vivada, Swami Vikraya, Dutta Pradanika, Kritanushaeya, Abhyupetyaassshrusha, Samvida Vyatikrama, Vetanadaana, Dhutas Madhya, Vaak Parushya, Danda, Parushya, Sahas, Vikraya sampradaana, Sambhuyasamuthan, Santeya, Stree Sangrahana and Prakirnaka.

The Third part, *Prayaschita Adhyaya* details Asaidakshauch, Aapdharma, Vanprastha Dharma, Yatidharma, Prayaschita and Prakrinaka Prayaschita.

Thus whole Dharmashastra is mentioned in the Yagyavalkya Smriti. Agnipurana/ Garuda Purana are full of slokas from Yagyavalkya Smriti. There are commentaries on the Vishwaroop: Balkrira of the Yagyavalkya Smriti; Mitakshara of Vigyaneshwar; Apararka Vyakhya of Aparaditya and Dip Kalika of Acharya Sulpani. There are commentaries called Balabodhini, Subodhini and Balambhatti. These are addressed to different Smritis of Yagyavalkya. Yagyavalkya gives due respects and importance to atmadarshana, atmabudhhi and bhagwadbuddhi for the realisation of Yoga gyan. अयं तु परमो धर्मो यद्योगेनात्मदर्ष्ठनम्। (*Yag. Achardhyaya*: 8).

On Rajadharma, he emphasizes on the kings' duties and Dharma, protection of the Brahmanas of the kingdom and not to procure extra money to help the subjects.

नातः परतरी धर्मो नृपाणां यद्रणार्जितम् विप्रभ्यां दीयते द्रव्यं प्रजाभ्यश्चाभ्यं सदा। ब्राह्मणेषु क्षमी स्निग्धेष्वजिधाः क्रोधनोऽ रिषु स्याद्राजा मृत्युवर्गेषु प्रजासु च यथा पिता।। (*Yag. Smriti Acharadhyaya*, 323-324)

Besides the four Vedas, Yagyavalkya refers to the Vedangas as six and enumerates forteen Vidyas. He refers to the Aranyaka and Yogashastra composed by himself. He enumerates at the commencement 19 authors on Dharma, besides himself. Upanishads are mentioned. Itihas, Purnana Vakavakya and Narasansi gathas are also mentioned.

It is remarkable that in the body of the work not one individual author of a Dharmashastra is mentioned by name. He speaks of metaphysics and Dandaniti. He lays down the dictum that where Dharmashastra and arthashastra conflict, the former shall prevail (II, 21).

Brahmokta Yagi Yagyavalkya Smriti

A composition of twelve chapters and about 500 verses, this corpus contains Veda Shakhas, Daily rituals of Grihastha, Shradha Kalpa, Brahmachari Dharma, Tithi Nirnas and Prayaschita.

Brihadhogya Yagyavalkya

There are 12 chapters of greater sizes detailing Yoga description. Yagyavalkya gives the highest priority to Atmagyan-Parmatma Gyan. सर्वेषामपि चौतेशामात्मज्ञानं परं स्मृतम्। (*Brihadhogya*, 11: 38).

Prajapati Daksha- Daksha smriti

Daksha is one of the writers on Dharma enumerated by Yagyavalkya. Daksha is the Manas-Putra of Brahman himself. Among the Ten-Manas Putras of Brahma, Daksh is one. He came out from the right thumb of Brahma. दक्षोऽङ्गुष्ठात् स्वयम्भुवः (*Srimad Bhagwat* 3.12.23).

He was the leader of the nine Prajapatis, those who were Manas Putras of Brahma for the organisation of the creation of the universe. Daksha was very efficient, so he was called the Prajapati of all Prajapatis under the leadership of Daksha Prajapati the rest nine Prajapatis engaged themselves in the creation of the great universe.

Bhagwat Sati was the daughter of Daksha and wife of Shankar. Aditi was the daughter of Daksha and was the mother of the Devas. Aditi, Diti and from them Kashyapa Dharma and Chandrama came out. All of them helped in the organisation of the universe and the credit was given to Prajapati Daksha. Hence it is said that the off springs of Daksha filled the whole universe and they spread over all the directions. यासां प्रसूतिप्रसवैर्लोकाआपूरितास्त्रयः। (*Srimad Bhagwat* 6:6:3).

Upon the organisation of the universe, there arose a need for a constitution by which they can be guided to follow the rituals, the aachaar etc. Daksh aprepared these laws and these laws took the form of Smriti.Hence the laws prepared by Daksha were called the Daksha Smriti.

Apararka cites numerous verses of Daksha on achara, asauch, Shradh and similar topics. In Jibanand's collection there is Daksha Smriti in seven chapters and 220 verses.

Daksha Smriti contains the names of Daksha himself and shows that he was a thorough going Advaitin. यस्त्वात्म व्यतिरेकेण द्वितीयं नैव पश्यति। ब्रह्मभूतः स विज्ञियो दक्षपक्ष उदाहृतः।। (*Daksha Smriti,* VII. II).

Daksha himself gives importance to this Smriti and says that if someone reads the Smriti and follows the laws enumerated therein, such a person will be free for generations from the sins. Even on the occasion of Shradh if the Smriti is followed the Shradh becomes important for the Pitr.

Major portion of the Smriti devotes on the different aspects of Grihasthashram.He has given emphasis on the daily morning rituals– bath, sandhya vandana etc. for keeping the body clean. Nav-Navak of Daksha Smriti is very important. It is related to nine important different rituals– what to follow and what not to follow.

ईषद्यानानि चान्यानि भूमिरापस्तृणानि च
पादशौचं तथाभ्यङ्गमाश्रयः शयनं तथा
किंचिच्चाश्रं यथाष्ठाक्तिनाश्यानश्यन्न गृहे वसेत्।।
मृज्ञतं चार्थिने देयमेतान्यपि सदागृहे। (*Daksha Smriti,* 3. 6. 7)

Maharshi Vishwamitra -Vishwamitra Smriti

Viswamitra is one of the writers on Dharma enumerated by Vriddha–Yagyavalkya as quoted by Vishwarupa. Apararka, the Smriti Chandrika, the Kala Viveka of Jimutavahana and other works quote verses of Vishwamitra on almost all topics of Dharma except Vyavahara, such as on the five deadly sins, Shradhas, prayaschita. Vishwamitra defines Dharma as that which is esteemed by Aryas (respectable people) who know the Vedas.

यमार्याः क्रियमाणं तु शसन्त्यागम वेदिनः।
स धर्मो यं विगर्हन्ति तमधर्म प्रचक्षते।। (*Smriti Chandrika*)

Apararka quotes 18 verses from Vishwamitra on Prayaschita and the Smriti Chandrika also quotes several verses of his Kalpataru (on Brahamchari). Similarly Kalpataru states that Yagyavalkya also occurs in Vishwamitra Smriti. His verses on Mahapatakas are frequently quoted.

ब्राह्मणे न च हन्तव्यः सुरापेया न च द्विजैः। ब्राह्मण स्वर्णहरणं न कर्तव्यं कहाचन।।
गुरुपत्नीं न गच्छेच्च संसर्गं तैश्च नाचरेत्। महापातकि संज्ञा तु निर्दिष्टैषा मनीषिभिः।।

(Aprarka, 1044).

Hardly one can get a rishi like Vishwamitra who became Brahmarshi from Rajarshi by virtue of his courage, efforts, determination and Purushartha. He was a Kshatriya but got Brahmanatwa by dint of his tapasya and his fighting power. He was ranked the highest among the Saptarshis and became the Drasta of Gayatri Mantra just by his unique determination.

Vishwamitra was a Kausik as he was in the lineage of Kush. He was a Gadhija-Gadhinandan and Gadhitanayana as he was the son of king Gadhi. People are aware of the dialogue and war between Vashishta and Vishwamitra and ultimately Vishwamitra was defeated by Kamadhenu of Vashishta. After renouncing his kingdom he engaged himself in a great tapa and after many odds he was successful in his mission and got Brahmarshi by Brahma. Vishwamitra is the mantra drastra rishi of third mandal of the Rig Veda, that mandal is called Vishwamitra Mandal. His important contributions are Viswamitra Kalpa, Vishwamitra Singhita and Vishwamitra Smriti.

Gayatri Upasana

Vishwamitra did a great tapasya in Pushkar (in Aravali mountains). On the completion of tapasya, all of a sudden the following mantra came out of the mouth of the rishi Vishwamitra ऊँ भूर्भवः स्वः ऊँ तत्सवितुर्वरेण्यम् भर्गो देवस्य धीमहि धियो या न प्रचोदयात् ऊँ।

Vishwarath became brahmarshi, became Vishwamitra from Vishwarath and became friends with all human beings (*Aitarek Aranyaka* 1.2.2; *Panini Sutra* 6.3.130).

Maharshi Deval– Deval Smriti

Maharshi Deval figures in the Rig Veda as mantra- drashta. It shows that he is one of the ancient Rishis and he is referred to as a great tapaswi and Yogacharya. He is the disciple of Maharshi Veda Vyasa: नाम्ना वै देवलः पुत्रो योगाचार्यो महातपा (Kurma Purana, 19: 5).

It is mentioned in the Brahamand Purana that Aak Parna was the daughter of Heemvan. Aak Parna was married to Maharshi Asit, son of Kasyap. Maharshi Deval was the son of Maharshi Asit. He has been described as the greatest among the Sandilyas (Brahman Purana, 3.10. 18-19 and 3.8.32).

There are references to Deval in the Mahabharata and he has been shown as associated with Asit. References have been seen in the Srimad Bhagawat Geeta also (Sabha Parva, 59: 9). It is said in the above slokas that Maharshi Asita and Deval who roam over the universe and visit people are of the opinion that victory should be assured through war fought on Dharma and not through cunning victories as after playing dies (*Sabha Parva*: 59.10).

Arjun asks Vasudeva Krishna offers respects to him and therein he says that great rishis, mahapurush, deva-devadi including the rishis Narada, Vyas, Asit and Deval praise the God Vasudeva Krishna. The Geeta refers to this as follows:

परं ब्रह्म परं धाम पवित्रं परमं भवान्
पुरुषं शाश्वतं दिव्यमादिदेवमजं विभुम्।।2।।
आहुस्त्वामृषयः सर्वे देवर्षिर्नारदस्तथा
असितो देवलो व्यासः स्वयं चौव ब्रवीषि मे।।3।।
(*Srimad Bhagwad*, 10: 12-13)

Thus, we find that high priority has been given to Maharshi Asit and Deval in the Geeta. Shankaracharya in his bhashya on Vedanta Sutra states that the Sankhya System is nearer to Vedanta than other systems like the atomic theory since it espouses the doctrines of the non-difference between cause and effect and adds that some writers of Dharmasutras such as Deval do rely on it in their works. So Deval Dharmasutra not only precedes Sankaracharya but was also regarded as early as the Sutras based purely on logic or atomic theory.

There is a Deval Smriti which has about 90 slokas. But we get references profusely from Deval Smriti in the commentary of Yagyavalkya Smriti in Mitakshara, Apararka, Smriti Chandrika but these are not available in the present Deval Smriti. References are available on the topics related to Aachar, Vyavahar, Shradh, Prayaschita, division of property, Deeds Stridhan.

Mitakshara as Yagyavalkya

तानि च देवलोक्तानि। शूद्रधर्मो द्विजाति शूषूशा पापवर्जनं कलत्रादि पोषणं कर्षण पशुपालन मारोद्वहन पण्यव्यवहारचित्र कर्म नित्य गीत वेणु वीणामुर जमृदङ्गवादना दीनि। (Mitakshara as Yagyavalkya, 1:120).

There is a Sutra on the Dharmas of the Shudra, and on the advocations open to him above aid there is a sutra dividing house holders into Yayavara and Salina and describing each of them as follows:

यथाहि देवल:। क्विविधो गृहस्थो यायावर: शालीनश्चच। तयोर्यायावर: प्रवर: याजनाध्यापन प्रतिग्रहरिकथ संचय वर्जनात्। षट्कर्माधिष्ठित: प्रेश्य चतुश्पगृहग्रामध नधान्य युक्तो लोकानुवती शालीन इति। (Mitakshara. as Yagyavalkya: 1.128)

In Aparарka and the Smriti Chandrika there are several prose quotations from Deval on Yagyavalkya III. 58. Aparарka quotes a long prose passage on the rules of conduct for a Yati on Yagyavalkya III. 109. Aparарka cites a very long passage in which Sankhya and Yoga are defined. Reference is made to extensive Tantras as the two systems and a brief resume is given to the Sankhya system, which greatly resembles the Sankhya-Karika and the Tattavasamsa. On Yag. II. 227. Aparарka has a prose quotation from Deval about Patita:

देवलः। देवमानुषयोद्विविविधः पुरुषार्थः अभ्युदयो निःश्रेयसमिति। तयोरभ्युदयः पूर्वोक्तः। द्विविधं निःश्रेयसम्--सांख्य योगा विति। पंच विंशतित्वज्ञानं सांख्यम्। विषयेभ्यो निवत्र्याभि प्रेतेऽर्थे मनसोऽवस्थापनं योगः। उभयत्रापवर्गः फलम्। जन्म मरण दुःख योरत्यन्ता मासोऽपवर्गः। एतो सांख्य योगौ चाधिकृत्य यैर्मृक्रितः समयतश्च पूर्वप्रणीतानि विशालानि गम्भीराणि तन्त्राणीर संक्षिप्योद्येशतो। वक्ष्यते। (Apraraka on Yagyavalkya III, 109: 996-97).

In the Smriti Chandrika there is lengthy passage from Deval on the daily duties of the brahmachari. A Sutra is quoted about brahmacharya for 48 years and in another place there is prose passage about the duties of a wife: पतिशुश्रुषा सहधर्मचर्या तत्पूज्यमान पूजनम्। (*Smriti Chandrika,* 1, p. 63).

It is presumed that there was a very famous and long (volumnous) book by the name of Devala Smriti. But at present that book is not available whereas the references on the commentaries referred above are from the original Devala Smriti not the one which is available at present.

In the present Devala Smriti there are contents related to purification: jati-shuddhi, purification of body: deh-shuddhi and references to different Prayaschitas, special importance has been given to the Panchagavya in which it has been remarked that the following Gods reside in the Panchagavya so it is very important: Varun in Gomutra: Copper colour cow; Agni in gomaya: white colour cow; Soma in dugdha: gold colour cow; Vayu in dadhi: blue cow; Surya in ghrita: dark cow.

वरूणो देवता मूत्रे गोमये हव्यवाहनः
सोमः क्षीरे दधि वायुर्धृते रविरूदाहतः
गोमूत्रं ताम्रवर्णायाःश्वेतायाश्चैव गोमयम्
पयः कांचन वर्णायाः नीलायाश्चापि गोर्दधि॥
धृतं वै कृश्ण वर्णायाः। (Deval, 62-64)

Deval in his Smriti mentions that those who take Panchgavya as per prescribed rules above are free from sins and they become pure:

उदरं प्रविशेधस्य पंचगव्यं विधानतः। भक्तिं चिदृस्कृतं तस्य सर्वं नृयति देहिनः।। (*Deval Smriti*,79-80)

Yama -Yama Smriti

Yama is one of the sages enumerated in the list by Yagyavalkya. Dharmaraj Yama is the son of Bhagwan Sun. Sangya is the mother of Yama. Yami (Yamuna) is the sister. He is also called the Vaiwaswata Yama.

He is called Dharmaraja as he regulates the animal kingdom and works on the Dharma. He is held in a very high esteem as people are afraid of Yama. He examines the right or wrong doers and people get rewards or punishments as per their work on the bases of the Dharma or adharma. The Vishnu Puran elaborates the views of Yama himself that he is the administrator duly appointed by the creator to reward and punish people as per their deeds. Those who work as per Dharma are rewarded and those who follow adharma are punished and they are placed in bad position. It is said:

अहममरवरार्चितेन छात्रायमइति लोकहिताहिते नियुक्तः।
हरि गुरुवशगोऽस्मिं न स्वतन्तः प्रभवति संयमने ममापि विष्णुः।। (*Vishnu Puran*, 3:7.15)

Dharmaraja Yama is a disciple of Vishnu. He resides in Yamaloka and it is also called Sanjivini Puri. Though people have an awful and fearful idea of his character and nature, his image is very attractive and people are impressed by his image as a great God, Dharmaraja. Dharmaraja is one of the twelve Bhagwats as mentioned in the Srimada Bhagawat:

स्वयम्भूर्नारदः शम्भुः कुमारः कपिलो मनुः।
पद्मादो जनको भीष्मो वलिर्वैयास किर्वयम्।।
द्वादशैते विजानीयो धर्मं भागवतं महाः। (*Srimada Bhagawat*, 6:3:20-21)

Dharmaraja says that only twelve persons know the terse Bhagwat Dharma. They are Brahma, Narada, Shankar, Sanat

Kumar, Kapildeva, Manu, Prahalad, Janak, Bhisma Pitamah, Bali, Sukhdevajee–Dharmaraj. Vashishta Dharmasutra (18. 13-15 and 19. 48) cites four slokas of Yama and quotes (11.20) one verse in which Yama is spoken of as an authority. All the slokas except one are found in Manu as quoted by Kane in his History of Dharmashastra, (Kane, I.I: 523).

Vashishta quotes a sloka of Prajapati, wherein Yama's view is set forth. Govindaraj and Apararka quote a verse of Sankha wherein Yama's view that the flesh of certain birds could be eaten is referred. Apararka also cites a verse of Sankha in which the view of Bhagwan Yama that one should save one's life in all ways (even by incurring sin) is mentioned and relied upon त्तित्तिरिं च मयूरं च लावकं च कपिंजलम् वाघ्रीणसं वर्तकं च भक्ष्यानाह यमः सताम्। (*Sadachara Yama*, V. I. Apararka:1167).

Maharaja Yama is the Lord of the South. He is one among the Dashadikpala. Yama is specially worshipped when there is Shani. People get his blessings by worshipping him on certain occasions especially on Yam Devitiya.

The dialogue between Yama-Yami and the Yama Sukta are famous and prominent in the Vedas. Dharmaopadesha given by Yama as mentioned in the Vishnu Purana, Nrisingh Purana and Agni Purana are called by the name of Yama-Geeta. Dharmashastra as given by Yama is called Yama-Smriti.

Yama-Stuti or Yama was praised by Savitri when her husband was made alive by dint of her tapa and works devoted towards her husband. And when worshipping Yama that stuti is always read. It is a solace to everyman.

Yama has been called the Lord of Pitar and tarpan is given to him, besides god, rishi, high people and high pitar. Yam is given *jalanjali* by the various names: i.e. yama, Dharmaraja, mrityu, anta-kaya, kala, audambraya etc.

It is said that those who comm sins should be the only people afraid of the Lord Yama but those who are pious get his blessings. Lord Yamaraj tells his men to let the disciples or those who obey or worship the Brahma free as Lord Yama is in the authority of those who commit sins and not the followers of the Lord Vishnu:

स्वपुरुषमभिवीक्ष्य पाशहस्तं वदति यमः किल तस्य कर्णमूले।
परिहर मधुसुदन प्रपन्नात् प्रभुरहमन्यनृणां न वैष्णवानाम्।।

(*Nrisingh Puran*, 9:1).

Lord Yama formulated certain rituals called Yama Smriti or Yamya Samhita. There are three Smritis given by Yama: Yama Smriti, Laghu Yama Smriti and Brihad Yama Smriti.

Yama Smriti

There are 78 slokas in the Smriti. The Smriti contains many aspects of Prayaschita. He has quoted the ideas of the great Dharmashastrakaras, Maharshi Atri, Maharsi Satatapa and Maharshi Uddhalakjee. It is said in the beginning of the Yamasmriti that prayaschita Dharma has been elaborately explained in the Smriti:

No sin can be committed from the boys between the age of 5 to 10 years. But Prayaschita should be done for the sins committed by such boy through close relatives of the persons concerned– that amounts to the Prayaschita for the sins by the boy. Yama Smriti remarks: ऊनैका दश वर्षस्य पंचवर्षात् परस्य च प्रायश्चिचतं चरेद् र्भ्रीता प्रिता वान्योऽपि वान्धवः।। (*Yama*, 5.15).

No sin can be committed below the age of five years,even if committed no Prayaschita is considered for such sins. Yama Smriti says: अतो वाल तरस्यापि नापराधो न पातकम् राजदण्डो न तस्याति प्रायश्चिचतं न विद्यते।। (*Yama*, 5. 16).

Persons above the age of 80, below the age of 16 and those who are diseased, if they make Prayaschita even half for the sins committed, they are free from the paapa.Yama Smriti says: आशीतिर्यस्य वर्षाणि वालो वाप्यून शोड़शः। प्रायश्चिचत्तार्धमर्हन्ति स्त्रियो रोगिण एव च।। (*Yama Smriti*, 17). Besides, there are guidelines for the prayaschita which are prescribed.

Laghu Yama Smriti

There are 99 slokas. Mostly prayaschitas and the other aspects of Vyavahar have been cited in the book. It covers morals related to touching a menstruating woman, abhkshya bhakshan prayaschita, agamyagamana prayaschita, gohasta prayaschita, ishtapurta mahima, panchgavya nirman, asaucha janya ashuddi, shradha and tarpana, pinda daan, asthi sanchaya and brishotsarga mahima.

Laghu Yama Smriti mentions Ishta Purta. People get heaven by Ishta where they get Moksh by the Purta works. इष्टेन लभते स्वर्गपूर्ते मोक्षं समश्नुते।। (*Laghu Yama Smriti*, 68; here *ishta* is *Yagya-Yagadi karma* and *Purta* is digging the tank, contruction of temple, garden, hospital etc.)

Girls before marriage are guided by the gotra and works of the father– but as soon as they are married and they complete saptapadi karma (seven parikrama of Agni) girls are separated from the gotra of the father. After chaturthi Karma girls become equal to pinda, gotra and sutak.

स्वगोत्राद भ्रश्यते नारी विवाहात् सप्तमे पदे
स्वामिगोत्रेण कर्तव्यास्तस्या: पिण्डोदक क्रिया:
विवाहे चौव संवृते चतुर्थेऽकृति रात्रि धु
एकत्वं सा व्रजेद् भर्तु: पिण्डे गोत्रे च सूतके।। (*Laghu Smriti*, 78: 86)

Asthi Sanchay and Ganga Prabah

So long the ashes/bones remain in the river the pitra is supposed to live in the heaven and then they get Moksh. Laghu Yama Smriti says:

गंगातोयेषु यस्यास्थि प्लवते शुभकर्मण:
न तस्य पुनरावृति व्र्ह्मलोकात् कथंचन।।
यावदस्थि मनुष्याणां गङ्गातोयेशषु तिष्ठति
तावद्वर्ष सहस्त्राणि स्वर्ग लोके महीयते।। (*Laghu Yama Smriti*, 90.91)

Brihad Yama Smriti

There are 182 slokas. It deals with Prayaschitas for various lapses, purifications from various kinds of contacts (Shuddhi) Shradh, partition and a few matters of medical procedure. Satatapa is frequently quoted by Yama in their smriti.

Suicide is considered the most heinous human crime. Such people get hell. However, if one stays alive by chance or by accident, one is called Pratyawasit. Such people are bycotted by all. Such people are purified by Chandrayan Vrata or by two Tapta Krichcha Vrata as mentioned in the Yama Smriti–2.3. (*Laghu Yama Smriti*: 22-23)

Sandhya Vandhana

Sandhya Vandhana is the purification for all the three sins committed by people.sins are of three types: Kayik (Bodily), Wachik, Vani (utturances) and mental.Yama says that all these are removed by the Sandhya Vandhana on three fixed times and by Utterances of Gayatri. It says:

मानसं वाचिकं चौव कायिकं पातकं स्मृतम्।
तस्मात् पापाद्विशुधर्थं प्रायश्चिचतं दिने दिने
त्रिविधं पापशुधर्थं सन्धयोपासन मेव च।। (*Brihad Yama Smriti*, 4:49-51)

Besides, there are many such references by which people are liberated from sins if they follow Prayaschit as according to Lord Yama. People must therefore pray to Lord Yama for his guidance in the Dharma–Karma–so that they might get place in the heaven and acquire moksh.

Maharshi Satatapa- Satatapa Smriti

Yagyavalkya and Parashara have named Maharshi Satatap as great law propounder. Vishwarupa, Haradatta and Aparарka quote several prose passages of Satatap on Prayaschita. Vishwarupa in his commentary on Yagyavalkya tells us that Satatap spoke of Eight Upapatakas, and that without dealing with Shradha as a principal topic he spoke of some of the subsidiary details of Shradhas: यथा शातातपः

श्राद्धमनुकल्वैव तदुतान्गुणा नाह विना यज्ञोपवीतेन गन्धैर्यस्तु सभालभेत् इति (Vishwarupa on Yagvalkya, 1: 1-5).

Haradatta on Gautam Dharmashastra quotes a prose passage of Satatapa about a penance for killing a cow. The Smriti of Satatapa says that Satatapa is the teacher of Maharshi Sarabhanga. इति शातापत प्रोक्तो विपाकः कर्मणामयम् शिष्याय शरभंगाय विनयात् परिपृच्छयते।। (*Satatapa Smriti*, 6:47). On the requests of Maharshi Saravrja and other Rishis, Satatapa gave discourses to them on different aspects of Dharma– those discourses are called by the name of Satatapatiya Dharma Samhita, Satatapatiya Smriti and Satatapatiya Dharmasastra or Satatapatiya Karmabipak.

Karmabipaka has been considered an important work of Satatapa. There are following three Smritis of Satatapa: Laghu Satatapa Smriti, Bridha Satatapa Smriti and Satatapa Smriti or Satatapatiya Karmabipak

Laghu Satatapa Smriti

There are 173 slokas–both prose as well as poetry mainly dealing with Prayaschita, purification, Abhakcha Bhakchan, Shradh and Dan- gift. Mahapatak, Upapatak, Gobadh and Prayaschita for general sins. There is marriage and its characteristics, especially of girls' marriage etc. Then we have dealings with the gods– worshipping of gods and atithi. The Laghu Satatapa Smriti contains several verses of Manu. The verses 103, 105, 106 are respectively the same as that of Manu (III : 237, III: 235; III: 174).

Satatapa says that there are three important pious articles and three important praise worthy matters in Shradh. These are– son of daughter *Kutap Bela* (12.30-1.00 P.M) and *Tila.* These are very pious and praise worthy: *satya,* angerlessness and simplicity. These are for the satisfaction of the *Pitaras.* Smriti says:

त्रीणि श्राद्धे पवित्राणि दौहित्रः कुतपस्तिलाः
त्रीणि चात्र प्रशंसन्ति सत्यम् क्रोधमार्जकम्। (107.11)

Satatapa says that people should not wear shoes or Paduka in the following places: where there is fire (agnishala), where there is god (deva mandir), at the time of taking food and at the time of mediation.The Smriti refers to this as follows:

अग्न्यगारे गवां गोष्ठे देवतानां च संनिधौ
आहारे जपकाले च पादुकां च विवर्जयेत

Maharshi Satatapa describes that people should observe the following: not to take meal putting on a cloth, not to take bath naked, not to spit on road, on ashes and on dung. One should speak good even in inauspicious occasions and ashubha should be avoided.The smriti says:

नाश्रीयादेक वस्त्रेण न नग्नः स्नानमाचरेत्
न विण्मूत्र पथि कुर्यान्न मस्मानि न गोमये
भद्रं भर्द्रमिति व्रूयाद्भद्रमित्येव वा पुनः
शिष्क वैरं विवादं च न कुर्यात् केनचित् सह।। (139-140)

Satatapa further says on guests that those who come without any prior information without any work, any time, from any place are called Atithis. If we have full information of someone's arrival, then such a person is not considered a guest.

अनिमित्त मनाहूतं देशकालमुपस्थितम्
अतिथि तं विजानीयान्नातिथिः पूर्व संगतः।। (*Laghu Smriti*, 55)

Brihad Satatapa Smriti

Bridh Satatapa is quoted several times in Kalpataru. Apararka in several places quotes the views of Satatapa immediately followed by quotation from Brihad Satatapa and vice-versa. There is a Brihad Satatapa Smriti with 64 verses on Prayaschita for various things, on Shradh and on washing the teeth. It is further said that Brihad Satatapa Smriti has

97 verses on defilement and purification. It is further remarked that it has 68 slokas as prayaschita, purification for various defilements and other miscelleneous matters. Hemadri mentions brihad Satatapa along with several other Smritikaras. In the Vyavahar Matrika of Jimutavahan Satatapa is cited on the six kinds of Uttara (defendant's reply). This shows that Brihad Satatapa had matters written on Vyavahar also. On Uttara (defendant's reply), the sloka is as follows:
वृद्धष्ठाातातपवचनं तु बहुज्ञजीर्णकृत निबन्धे स्माभिर्दृश्टं न पुनर्मोजदेवे।

Mitakshara on Yagyavalkya cites Brihad Satatap where as Hemadri speaks a bhasyakar on Brihad Satatap.

Maharshi Satatapa has given messages for the welfare of people. Poeple should keep themselves Sankalpa Sunya. Sankalpa produces Kama which harms people. People should discard all sorts of kama which is produced by sankalpa. Maharshi says,

काम जानामि ते मूलं संकल्पात् किल जायसे।
संकल्पं न करिष्यामि मूलच्छिन्नो भविष्यसि।। (64)

Maharshi gives very important teaching when he says that one should always feel that time is very short and that anything can happen any moment. So one should not waste even a Single moment, one should always have in mind the god, bhakti and worship the Almighty (65-66).

Satatapa Smriti

There is a Satatapa Smriti in twelve chapters dealing with Prayaschitas for Mahapatakas, Prayaschitas for injuries to various beings, marriages, Vaisavadeva, Shradh, Pitra tarpan, rules about taking one's dinner, prayaschita for dog bites and similar matters; impurity on birth and death, rules of conduct (achara). In Jivanand's collection there is a Smriti ascribed to Satatapa called Karm-bipaka in six chapters and about 231 verses. Its contents are: certain diseases are concomitants of certain sins; gift of lands, cows etc., eulogy of Brahamanas; penances for killing a Brahaman, a cow etc., penances for drinking wine, incest and forbidden sexual intercourses of various sorts; theft; rites for those who meet with violent and accidental death. The last verse declares that the Smriti was promulgated by Satatapa to his pupil Sarabharga. It is a late production. It prescribes the reading of Harivans as a penance for infanticide. The Smriti has 6 chapters and 240 slokas. Maharshi Satatapa gives summons to the people that there are many sins and those who commit sins must take steps for their prayaschitas otherwise they have to suffer from different diseases tantamount to their sins as mentioned in the Smriti. People should be cautious not to commit sins, and even if they are committed there should be prayaschita for the sins so that they may be given places in the heaven. –If they remember Brahma, they would get Moksha. Smriti says:

प्रायश्चिचत विहीनानां महापातकिनां नष्टणाम्
नरकान्ते भवेज्जन्म चिह्नाकिंत ष्टारीरिणाम्
प्रति जन्म भवेत् तेषां चिह्नं तलापसूचितम्
प्रायश्चिचते कृते याति पश्चचातापवतां पुनः
महापातकजं चिह्नं सप्त जन्मनि जायते
उपपापोद्भवं पंच त्रीणि पापसमुद्भवम्
दुष्कर्मजा नृणां रोगा यान्ति चोपक्रमेः शमम्
जणैः सुरार्चनैहौं मैदानं स्तेषां शमो भवेत्।। (*Satatapa Smriti*,1:1-4)

Importance has been given to Brahman. He says that if one takes care of a Brahman one is freed from sins, because to please a brahman is to please the god. Brahman is Sarvadevomaya.

ब्राह्मण यानि भाषान्ते मन्यन्ते तानि देवताः
सर्वदेवमया विप्रा न तद्वचन मन्यथा
तेषां वाक्योदकेनैव शुधयन्ति मलिना जनाः। (*Satatapa Smriti*, 1:27-30).

Mahatma Budha: Budha Smriti

Budha is the son of Chandrama. Chandrama (Moon) is called Adi Raj. So Budha, being his son, is also called Rajputra.

Pururba is the son of Budha and later as this lineage expanded, it became Chandra vansha.

Brahma Vaivarta Puran mentions that Dhanwantari, Devodas, Aswanikumar, Nakul, Sahdev, Yam, Chyavan, Augustya were among the sixteen Ayurvedacharyas. Budha is one among them. It is mentioned that mahatma Budha has one very important work on the medicine called Sarvasartantra.

Mahatma Budha is rarely cited. The work is very brief and speaks of Upanayana, marriage, the Sanskaras from garbhadhan to upanayana, the five great daily yagnas, shradh, substance for Brahma, the duties of vaishyas and shudras, the order of the foremost hermits and sanyasis, removal of thorns by the king, administration of justice, kings' duties. There is a very famous and important Vedic mantra for the Buddha Mahadasa.

उद्बुध्यस्वाग्ने प्रतिजागृति त्वमिष्टापूर्ते स सृजेथाम यं च
अस्मिन्त्सधस्ते अध्युत्तरस्मिन् विश्वेदेवा यजमानश्च सीदत।।
(*Yajurveda*, 15: 54)

Budha is called awahana: प्रियंगुकलिका मासं रूपेणाप्रतिमं बुधम् सौम्यं सौम्यगुजोपेतं बुधमावाह याम्यहम्। The tantrik mantra is as follows: वु वुधाय नमः Budha is in Navagrah. He is one of the nakshatra mandala.

Budha has been mentioned as welfare doer. He is kind to all who are working in the path of Dharma. Explaining Dharma it is said: श्रेयोऽभ्युदय साधनो धर्मः For the worship of God it is said तस्मिन् गृह्यामि देवपितृमनुष्यव्रतयज्ञ कर्माणि कुर्यात्।

Grihasta should respect atithi, अतिथीन् पूजयेत। Friends and relatives should also be taken care of भृत्यान् बन्धून पोष्यवर्गाश्च। King has been given authority so that he oversees whether people follow Dharma or not and he should also control people: विहितमकुर्वतो राज्ञा कारयितव्याः वलतश्चौतात् स्वधर्म स्थापयेत्।।

It is further said that even if the king has to use Danda to control the Dharma he should follow it to maintain Dharma which would bring good to the king and to the people also. The Dharmashastra says, ए तथा कुर्वतः कारयितुश्चेभयोधर्मसिद्धिः।

Baudhayana–Dharmasutra

Baudhayana originally was the follower of the Taittiiriya Veda of the Yajurveda alone,but later on it became one of the important sources of the sacred law for all Brahmanas.

According to Dr. A Burnell who is the authority on the literature of the school of Taittiriya Veda, the sutras of Baudhayayan consists of six sections: Shrauta Sutra (19 chapters); The Karmanta Sutra (20); Dwaidha Sutra (4); The Grihya Sutra (4); Dharma Sutra (4); The Sulva Sutra (3). It is very popular in south India specially Karnataka, and Tamil Nadu.

In Baudhayana, Dharma refers to the Grihya and pre supposes it in several places. In the Baudhayayan Grihya we have a reference to *Padakara* Atreya, Vittikara, Kaundinya, Prarachanakara Kanva Bodhayayan and Sutkara Apastamba. The extant Baudhayan Dharmasutra is certainly later than Gautam as it mentions Gautam twice by name and at least one quotation of Gautam is found in the extant text. Besides Baudhayan, quotes by several teachers on Dharma are found, while Gautam quotes only one that is, Manu. Baudhayayan is renowned from the time of the Upanishad. In the tarpana, Baudhayan has several appellations of Gautam, Vishnu, Vinayaka, Sthula, Varada, Lamboder, but this affords no certain due as to date.

Harita —Dharmasutra

The Harita Dharmashastra is ancient. Harita as an ancient Sutrakara on Dharma is quite patent from the fact that the Dharma sutra of Baudhayayan, Apastamba and Vashishta quote him as an authority. Harita's views are quoted by Baudhayan Dharma Sutra. Apastamba refers to Harita,

Vashishta quotes Harita. The Tantra Vartika mentions Harita along with Gautam and other Sutrakaras on Dharma. From Vishwarupa down to the latest writers on Dharmashastra Harita is most profusely quoted. From the quotation it appears that his Dharmasutra was perhaps the most extensive of all the Dharmasutras.

From the numerous quotations from Harita in the Nibandhas it appears that the Dharmasutras dealt exhaustively with the same topics as are dealt with in other Dharmasutras viz.: sources of Dharma, brahmacharya of two kinds, snatakas, the house holder, the forest hermit, prohibition about food, impurity on birth and death, shradh, general rules of conduct, the five yagyas, vedic study, holidays, duties of kings, rules of state craft, court procedure, the various titles of law, duties of husband and wife, various kinds of sins, prayaschitas, expiatory prayers etc.

According to Kulluka, the Harita Dharmasutra opened with the words 'now then we shall explain Dharma,. Dharma is based upon revealed texts (Shruti); revealed texts are of two kinds, the Vedic and the Tantrik.

अथातो धर्म व्याख्यास्याय:। श्रुति प्रमाणको धर्म:। श्रुतिश्च द्विविधा वैदिकी तान्त्रिकी च। (Kane, I, I:729)

Some of the doctrines of Harita are worth noting. He speaks of eight forms of marriage but two of them are styled ksatra and Manusa, while Arsa and Prajapatya are omitted. Vashishta has the same nomenclature. Harita speaks of two sorts of women–brahmavadins and sadyovadharma and states that the former were entitled to have the upanayan performed, to keep the sacred fire and to study the Vedas.

द्विविधा: स्त्रिय:।ब्रह्मवादिन्य: सधोवध्वश्च तत्र ब्रह्मवादिनीभ्रणनयन मग्नीन्धनं वदान्ययतं स्वगृहे च भिक्षाचर्या। (*Smriti Chandrika* I, p. 24).

He speaks of the twelve kinds of sons. Both Mitakshara and Aparарka quote Harita's verses eulogising the sati. The Smriti Chandrika quotes his verses that refer to signs of the zodiac. The Dharma sutras of Harita appear to have been very extensive and were in mixed prose and poetry.

Vaikhanasa Dharma Prashna

Mahadeva in his commonly called Vaijayanti on the Satyasadha Shrauta Sutra speaks of six Shrauta Sutras of Black Yajurveda: Baudhayan, Bharadwaja, Apastamb, Hiranyakasin, Vadula and Vaikhanas.

He was a very ancient writer as we find his references in the ancient Dharma works. In Gautam, Vaikhanasa occurs as the name in the order of the forest hermits and he lays down that the fire was to be consecrated according to the Sramanaka श्रावणकेन अग्निमाधाय, which later is explained by Haradatta as Vaikhanasa shastra. Baudhayan has the same sutra and defines Vaikhanasa as one who follows the rules of conduct laid down in Vaikhanasa sutra. Govind Swami, the commentator of Baudhayan says,

वैस्वानसोपि वानप्रस्थ एव। संज्ञान्तरकरणं तु संव्यवहारार्थम। विखनसा ऋषिणा प्रोक्तं वैखानस शास्त्रम्। तत्र हि वहवो वानप्रस्थास्योकवा ग्रीष्मे पंचतया इत्यादहः समुदाचाराः।

The Vashishta Dharmashastra also has the same sutra as that of Gautam. The Manu Smriti speaks of Vanaprastha as one who abides by the views of Vaikhanasa. Manu says that in Vanprastha one should take the fruits (which automatically fall from the tree once they are ripened). पुष्पमूल फलैर्वापि केवलैर्वर्तयेत्सदा काल पक्वै स्वयंशीर्षे वैखानसमते स्थितः।। (Manu 6: 21).

It is also clear that Manu knew the Shastra called Vaikhanas. Kalpataru quotes a long passage from Harit which says that four ashramas are a ladder by which Gods and the pitras reached immortality.

Vaikhanasa Dharma Prasan is divided into three prasanas, each pranasana being subdivided into Khandas. There are all in all 41 khandas. The work is a small one. The contents of the works are: four Varnas and their privileges, and the four ashramas, brahmachari, duties of the house holder etc.; vanprasthas with patni (sapatnika or apatnika); kinds of Yogini and subdivision; details of forest hermit; achaman and sandhya; abhivadan of relatives– salutation to relatives; roads; burial of sanyasin; tarpan.

Nigamas or Vedas are the basis for Agamas, particularly Vaikhanasa Agamas. The statements in Rigveda (II-2-26) like *idam Vishnuh..ajayamano bahudha...rupe rupe pratirupam bahuva, prava panta mandhano dhiyayate maheshurya 'Vishnave Charchata'* etc. instruct various forms of Vishnu as objects of meditation by mind and are considered as foundation on which the auspicious forms of Lord Vishnu and His worship are propounded by the Agamas leading to the welfare and bliss of the people in this and other worlds respectively. This worship in iconic form is considered as superior to even performance of sacrifice etc. Like puranas, the Agamas amplify the meaning and significance of Veda *'Ithihasa–Puranabhyam Vedam samupabrahmayeta'*. The all-pervading Almighty takes the form of a particular deity as desired by devotee, as the Lord is compassionate to confer grace on the devotees. Vaikhanasa Agamas are ritual handbooks first written by Vikhanasa sage and the same matter was further developed by four of his famous disciples viz.. Bhrigu, Atri, Kashyapa and Marichi. Only those texts, dealing with religious devotion and spiritual practices which contain a lakh of granthas (a grantha being 32 letters in anustubh verse) are extant, and not more than a crore and half are entitled to be called as Agamas (as stated in Pauskar Samhita, 39.11). According to Vimanarchana kalpa, the teachings of the sage Vikhanasa were a crore and half in extent (*sardha koti pramanam grantham dattavam*). The last Patala (101st chapter) gives the extent as four lakhs of granthas "*Catur laksham Proktam*", through the treatises composed by Vikhanasa's four disciples Bhrigu and others. The great lore of Vaikhanasa literature is based on the Vedas and as such is the very essence of the import of all the Vedas and is authoritative and flawless and is followed by adherents of Vedic tradition as the doctrine of worship of Vishnu. It was taught by Lord Vishnu to sage Vikhanasa for the good of all beings and by Vikhanasa to Bhrigu and by Bhrgu to Kashyapa and Marichi through the texts called Tantra-Adhikara Kanda–Samhitas–all totalling four lakhs. The patal further gives the details of the texts by each of the four sages. Atri composed four tantras– purva, atreya, vishnu, uttartantra. These cover 88 thousand granthas. Bhrigu composed 13 tantras called khila, puratantra Vasadhikara, Chitradhikar, Manadharaka, kriya, archa, yagna, varuna– prakima– pratigrihya– niruktha– khila– adhikaras the works cover 64000 granthas. Kashyapa composed three kandas viz., Satya– Tarka–Jnana and these also covered 64000 granthas. Marichi wrote 8 samhitas– viz., Jaya– Anand–Samjuna– Vira– Vijaya– Vijit– Vimala– Jnana. These covered 1 lakh 84 thousand granthas.Thus altogether we have 28 works and four lakh granthas.

These are the texts of canonical status. Of these 28 texts only 8 are printed. These are: Samurtarcanadhikara of Atri, Jnanakand of Kashyapa, Kriya-khila-prakirna-yagna Adhikaras of Bhrigu, Vimanarchana kalpa and Anandasamhita of Marichi. Archana– Nirukta –Vasadhikaras are in manuscript form. Thus together these total ten texts of which Jnanakanda of Kashyapa and Vimanarchana kalpa of Marichi are in prose and the remaining 8 are in verses. Chapters in Vimanarcana Kalpa are labelled as 'patala' whereas in all other texts, they are labelled as Adhyayas. The texts of Vaikhanasa Agamas are mentioned by four sages in their works and also those of other sages like Vimanarcana Kalpa, Samurtadhikarana, Vasadhikara, Ananda samhita and yagnakadhikara etc. However, there is no unanimity with regard to either number (some say they are 58), and name. Kasyapa's Jnanakanda is translated into English by T. Gaudrian of Netherlands and many of the important Vaikhanasa works namely V.K. of Marichi, Samurtarcanadhikarana of Atri, Jnana Kanda of Kashyapa and Kriyadhikara and Khiladhikara of Bhrigu have been published and critically edited by Agamacharya, and Asthanvidwan late Pandit R. Parthasarathy Bhattacharya has edited with excellent introduction in Sanskrit including the original Vaikhanasa kalpa sutra by Vikhanasa which forms the basis for all these texts.

'Vimanarchana kalpa sutra' is one of the full-fledged kalpa sutras and is an important auxiliary among the six Vedangas. These Kalpasutras which pertain to the systemic exposition of performance of various rites enjoined in Vedas and Smritis have three distinct parts: Shrauta, Smartha and Dharma sutra. The Smartha sutras treat the rites beginning with impregnation (Nisheka) and ending with funeral rites (Anteysti). Shrauta sutras deal with various sacrifices such as agnistoma, Chaturmasya etc. The Dharmasutras prescribe a set of rules which regulate the duties of a house holder with reference to society and himself and also pertaining to law both civil and criminal. The difference between shrauta and smartha rites is that the latter is to be performed by the house-holder (yajamana) himself, with or without single consecrated fire whereas the former is to be performed by Ritviks (priests) in 3 or 5 consecrated fires. A part of Shrautasutra is called Sulbhasutra wherein the details of construction and measurements of altars and firepits are given. Similarly Adhyatmasutra is a part of Smarthasutra which is devoted to the science of self. Among the 18 kalpa sutras mentioned by 'Agnivaisya Kalpasutra', the prominent ones are Apasthamba, Asvalayana, Agniveshya, Katyayana, Gautama, Kaushika, Jaimini, Parashara, Vashishtha, Bharadwaja, Bodhayana and Hiranyakesi and Vaikhanasa. Many of these kalpasutras are incomplete but 'Vaikhanasa Kalpasutra' is counted by all as 'Complete kalpasutra' as explained above and even Manusmriti is based on it. In this Vaikhanasa sutra, mantras from Khila, Sukta, Exagnikanda, Rig Veda, Yajur Veda, Sama Veda and Athar Veda are there. Brahmana, Aranyakas are collected for various samskaras or rites. Mantras from Rig Veda are less in number than those from Yajur Veda and their application is mentioned in 32 prasnamantras as follows. For 1-4 prasnamantras -apply to human beings, for 5-8 apply to Divinity of the 32 Chapters, 21 prasnas pertain to Shrautasutra, 7 to Smartha sutra and 3 pertain to Dharmasutra, and to pravara. The Vaikhanasa mantra samhita or pravara prescribes mantras for various Smartha rites and Vaikhanasa Daivika mantra prasna (in 4 chapters) lays down specific mantras that are applicable to the worship of Vishnu in idols in temples and houses. The later works by 4 sages elaborately deal with temple worship in all its aspects. The important sutra is– *Agnau nitya homante vishnor nityarcha grhe devayatane va bhaktya bhagavantam narayanan Carcayeta (V.S.)*. This Vaikhanasa sutra is termed as scripture i.e., Bhagavatshastra as it mainly deals with installation and consecration and other procedures of worship of icons of Vishnu both in the house and temple.

The main contents of all these texts are as follows: Lord Vishnu is the supreme principle and obtaining him is moksha; and means to this end is two-fold– worship of Vishnu with form and second one without form. The former type is further classified into two– worship in the house and worship in the temple and the latter of course is considered superior as it is a direct means to moksha. All the manuals on Vaikhanasa as referred to earlier eulogise Vishnu. He is to be worshipped with Vedic mantras. Each of these manuals has four parts - Jnana, Yoga, Carya (arca) and Kriya. In Jnanapada, nature of the supreme self, the nature of universe and individual soul and their mutual relations are expounded. In yogapada, the method and means of attaining moksha or God is described through practice of eightfold components of yoga. 'Vimanarchana kalpa' describes this in detail in 97th patal. In kriyapad there is an elaborate discussion on the construction of temple, types of temple, architecture, fashioning of the icons and their installations and consecration, various images of Vishnu and other accessory divinities. Iconometry is also dealt with. Vaikhanasa-agama combines both carya and kriya elements in contrast to Pancharatra and Saivagamas. In carya, procedures for daily worship, materials required for it, Vedic hymns that should accompany the various sequences of worship, occasional rites, expiation rites for the lapses of various kinds, various periodical ceremonies like Brahmotsava, ritual prescriptions for temple priest are mentioned. Only some information about Jnana and yoga is scattered here and there in these Vaikhanasa texts (For the extant of Vaikhansa literature see the tables below). The tradition that began with Vikhanasa, regarding the temple worship (with Vaikhanasa sutra as its authority) is continued in temples in South India particularly in famous Lord Venkateswara temple at Tirupati.

Apart from main texts there are separate texts, Adhikar texts which deal with specific topics like Bhagavadachaprakarana of Nrsimhavajapeyi, Brahmostavanukramanika, Samprokshana (periodical purification), expiations (prayaschita), installation and consecration (pratishtta). Nrisimhavajapreya, Srinivasa Dixit or makhin and Kesavacarya, Vrittikara on Vedanta sutras are prominent prolific writers and commentators on Vaikhanasa standard texts.

These Vaikhanasagama texts lay down that God i.e., Vishnu is to be worshipped according to the procedures 6 times, or 3 times or 2 times or at least once during the day and night. This will lead to prosperity in the world.

The value of iconic worship was justified in great detail and with zeal. Kashyapa's 'Jnanakanda' (28th Ch.) and Bhrigu's 'Prakirnadhikara' (37, 126-144) offer elaborate explanation as to why iconic worship is to be performed. The Vaikhanasa scripture prescribed the qualifications for the priests who specialise in both kinds of worship, at home and in the temple and prescribe in minutest detail the sequence of worship, procedure without lapses or interruption in consonance with the scriptural norms and urge the priest to discharge his duties diligently and resolutely.

A priest who was in later period known as Bhagavat and who was properly initiated and consecrated, and who was a man of learning with sterling character and conduct, was invested with the power of transforming the stone image into a deity–*Archakasya Prabhavena shila bhavati sankarah.*

These Agamas equally underline the responsibility of the public or the management committee to arrange regular worship of the deity and also for proper maintenance of the livelihood of these priests who are unflinching and ardent devotees of the Vedic tradition.

This Vaikhanasa mode of worship is described as pacific (saumya) and beneficent to all people (srikar) and as such it contributes to the national and spiritual welfare of the entire population. The same mode of worship is conducted at the famous temple of Venkateswara at Tirupati with unbroken tradition and till today it stands as representative of the Vaikhanasa Agama in action (Aralikatti).

1. Adhikar Granthas Source text; 2.Samhita Granthas; 3. After commentary Samhita Granthas; 4. Verses in Adhikar Granthas; 5. Verses in Grantha samhita.

Kanva and Kaanva

P.V. Kane says that from the Apastamba Dharmashastra it appears that Kanva and Kaanva are two distinct writers on Dharma. On the issue of food, Apastamba was of the opinion that food is to be taken at anybody's house provided the latter offered it with a request, and that the opinions of Eka, Kunika, Kanva, Kutsa and Puskarasadhi were that only food that was offered by a pure and religious man should be taken. Kanva is quoted a few times in the Smriti Chandrika on daily duties and shradh and one of these quotations is in prose. Haradatta in his commentary on Gautam cites verses of Kanva in several places. Though Mitakshara, Maskarin have frequently quoted Kanva and Kaanva, it is not very clear whether both are different people or same.

Table I: Extent of Vaikhanasa Literature

1	2	3	4	5
Chapters of various texts Granthas	Bhrigu Granthas	Marichi Granthas	AtriGranthas	Kashyap
Puratantram	6000	Jaya-sam.	Puratantra	Satya Kanda
Vasadhikara	4000	Ananda-Sam.	Atreyatantram	Tarka Kanda
Manadhikara	6000	Samjnana-Sam.	Vishnuatantram	Jnana Kanda
Kriyadhikara	9000	Veer-Sam.	Uttaratantram	Karma Kanda
Archadikara	6000	Vijaya-Sam.	Padmatantram	Kasyapa Kanda
Yanjadhikara Kanda	3000	Vijita-Sam.	Mahatantra	Samjnana
Varnadhikar	2000	Vimal-Sam.	—	Santana Kanda
Prakirnadhikara	2000	Jnana-Sam.	—	—
Niruktadhikara	2000	Anantakhya-Sam.	—	—
Khila tantra	6000	Satya Sam.	—	—
Uttar tantra	4000	Para Sam.	—	—
	50000 Kalpa Sam			
Khiladhikara				
Chitradhikara	14000			
Pratigrhyadhikar	64000	84000	63000	51500
Adhikargranthas	1000000	25000	12500	
Total	**64,000**	**1,84,000**	**88,000**	**64,000**

The grand total of these becomes 4,00,000 (four lakhs).

Table II: Another classification of Vaikhansa Literature

Author	1	2	3	4	5	Total
Bhrigu	14	~	~	64000	~	64000
Marichi	11	12	8	100000	84000	184000
Atri	6	6	4	25000	63000	88000
Kashyapa	5	8	5	12500	51500	64000
Total	**36**	**26**	**17**	**201500**	**198500**	**400000**

Kaashyapa or Kashyapa

Dharmasutra of Kashyapa comprised all the usual topics such as daily duties, shradh, asauch, prayaschita. Vishwarupa and all downward writers have quoted the Kashyapa Dharma sutra. Boudhayan cites a verse which contains the view of Kashyapa that a woman who is bought cannot be a wife and that she is not authorised to take part in religious deva rites or rites for the man.

क्रीता द्रव्येण या नारी सा न पत्नी विधीयते
सा न दैवे न सा पित्र्ये दासीं तां कश्यपो व्रबीत्।।

Vishwarupa quotes Kashyapa on the prayaschita for contact with Chandalas and for killing a cow when the sinner is a brahman or a member of another caste. Secondly, Maskarin on Gautam 23.19, quotes a verse of Kashyapa providing prayaschita for homosexuality and masturbation.

Pumsi Maithuna Masevya Yatnotsarge Krte Tatha,
Brahmacari tatha bhyasat Snatvatha havisa Yajet.

The Vanaparva sets out five gathas which Kashyapa declared about Kshama (forbearance or mildness). Two of the five verses on kshama are quoted: क्षमा धर्मः क्षमा यज्ञः क्षमा वेदाः क्षमा श्रुतम् ...क्षमा तेजस्विनां तेजः क्षमा ब्रह्म तपस्विनाम्।। (*Vana Parva*, 29.36.40). *Udyoga Parva* (33.48) points out the defect about forbearance or mildness: एकः क्षमावतां दोज़ो द्वितीयो नोपध्यते। यदेनं क्षमयायुक्त मष्ठात्तं मन्यते जनः।।

Gargya

Vishwarupa quotes a verse of Braddha Yagyavalkya in which Gargya is enumerated among the expounders of Dharma (Dharmavaktah). He quotes two sutras, one from Gargya and the other from *Briddh Gargiya* :

Gargya: पतिताः स्त्रियस्त्याज्या भर्तृवध प्रतिज्ञायां च।
Briddha Gargya: अनेकोद्धार्ये काष्टशिले भूमिसमे।

Thus it is clear that there is a Gargya Sutra on Dharma. The Mitakshara, Apararka and Smriti Chandrika quoted several verses of Gargya on atnika, shradh and prayaschita. Parashara mentions Gargya as one among the writers on Dharma. Apararka is also one of the writers who quotes Gargya as a writer on Dharma (topics of Dharma). He is also enumerated as writer on astronomical matters, nomenclature of the months (such as Chaitra) in connection with the signs of the zodiac

Anushasan Parva states that Garga acquired on the banks of the Saraswati astronomy with its 64 angas. In the same Parva it is said that Vidha Gargya inquired about Vrsotsarga. Salya Parva narrates that old Garga by his tapas acquired on the banks of sacred saraswati the knowledge of Kala, movements of the plannets, of evil and good utpatas, and the place is called Gargastrotas. Vishwarupa mentions a verse of Gargya on the proper times for morning sandhya and evening sandhya and a prose passage of Vridhya Gargya.

चतुः षष्टन्यङ्गम् ददत् कलाज्ञानं ममाद्भूतम्
सरस्वत्यास्तरे तुष्टो मनोयज्ञेन पाण्डव।। (*Anushasana Parva*, 18: 38)

पितृणां भावितं श्रुत्वा दष्टरोमातचोधनः
वृद्ध यार्ग्यो महातेजः स्तानेवं वाक्यम् ब्रवीत
के गुणा नीलषण्डस्य प्रमुक्तस्य तपोधनाः। *(Anusasan Parva, 125: 77)*

गर्ग स्त्रोतो महातीर्थ माज गामैक कुण्डली
तत्र गर्गेण वृद्धेन तपसा भावितात्मना
काल ज्ञान गतिंचौव ज्योतिषां च व्यतिक्रमः
उत्पाता दक्तणाश्चैव शुभाच्च जनमेजयः।। (*Sulya Parva*, 37: 14-15)

Chyavan

Chyavan is a famous name in the Rig Veda. The Aswaras are often praised as having endowed the old and the aging Chyavan with youth.

युवं च्यवानमश्विवना जरन्तं पुनय्रुवानं चक्रशुः शाचीषिः
युवो रथं दुहिता सूर्यस्य सह श्रिया ना सत्या वृणीत्।। (Rigveda, 1: 117.13)

The Mahabharata tells certain stories on Chyavan. He married Sukanya, daughter of king Sanyati and the asvins made him young and handsome. He then helped the Asvins to get a share after paralysing the arms of Indra who at first opposed them (*Adi Parva*, 6: 2 and *Vana Parva*: 122-124).

Mitakshara, Aparарka and Kalpataru cite a sutra of Chyavan on the Prayaschita for coming in contact with a dog, a suapaka, smoke from a funeral pyre, wine, wine-vessel etc. Apararka cites prose passing of Chavan on the Prayaschita for killing a cow for touching, carrying or burning the corpse of one who commits suicide, on the method of purification of houses, vessels, articles of food when touched by Chandalas.

Apararka with reference to the great rewards of the gift of a cow when she is about to deliver, sets out from Chyavana a long prose passage with ten mantras and provides details of expiation for causing the death of a cow, for touching or carrying a corpse to to the cemetery or for cremating the body died from a suicide, and for close contacts of chandalas with houses, earthen pots. He also states that for children, the aged and the woman the expiation is only half of what is prescribed for a grown up man.

Jatu Karnya

Vishwarupa quotes a verse of Briddha Yagyavalkya in which Jatukarna is mentioned as the expounder of Dharma:

भूयां सो धर्मवक्तार उत्पन्ना माविजस्तथा।
निधानं सर्व धर्मा वेद एव हि शाश्ववतः।
नारदः प्रलहो गार्ग्यः पुलस्त्य, शौनकः ऋतुः।
वौधायनो जातुकर्णो विश्वामित्रः पितामहः।।

Smriti Chandrika quotes a passage from Angiras in which Jatukarnya is enumerated among writers on Upasmriti.

Vishwarupa quotes prose passage from Jatukarna on many occasions. He gives a sutra about 'Pratilomas'. There is a Sutra saying that a pupil should not all of a sudden put a question to his teacher in an assembly of people; about a Kshatriya and Vaisya wearing an upamit of hemp and wool when initiated for sacrifice; as to the age when a Brahma became a Vratya, about prohibition of marrying another woman of a different caste when one has already married a savarna wife; about the time of shradh. These are the proofs which shows that Jatukarnya composed a sutra work on achaar and shradh which was comparatively ancient.

The name Jatu Karnya is an ancient one. The Katyayana Shrautsutra mentions the view of Jatu Karnya on Pind Pitryagyna when all the three paternal ancestors of the performer are not dead and the Kalpataru on Shradh remarks जीवत पितृकस्य ऋय: पकाश

Katyayana

Narada, Brihaspati and Katyayana form a triumvirate in the realm of the ancient Hindu Law and procedure. Katyayana is enumerated as one of the expounders of Dharma by Sankha Likhita, Yagyavalkya and Parashara. Katyayana is quoted as an authority in the Baudhayan Dharma Sutra. A Shraut Sutra and Shradh Kalpa of the whiteYajurveda are ascribed to Katyayan.

Katyayana has considered Narada and Brihaspati as his models in the order and treatment of the subjects to be dealt with Vyavahara. Narada lays down that Vyavahara has four padas–Dharma, Vyavahara, Charitra, Rajashasana and then Narada very briefly in one verse explains the four terms; Katyayana on the other hand, devotes at least nine verses to the elucidation of the rules as to each succeeding one prevailing over its predecessors. Katyanyana's treatment of Stridhan has attained classical rank. It appears that he was probably the first to carefully define several kinds of Stridhan such as adhyagni, adhya Vahanika, Pritidatta, Sulka,

Anvadeya, Saudayika, to lay down women's power of disposal over the several variations of stridhan and to prescribe lines of devolution as to stridhan

Smriti Chandrika alone quotes about 600 slokas from Katyayana as Vyavahar. Katyayana several times refers to the views of Manu; Katyayana says that the views of Manu were valid 'In those disputes or crimes for which ordeals are forbidden (to be administered to perpetrators) and that the king should make efforts to have them performed by good men on their behalf; he should not abondon the person charged (without testing his guilt by proxy)'.

He is lived in about 3rd or 4th century AD. Medhatithi ascribes to Katyayana the rule that in case of conflict between Dharma shastra and arthashastra the king should prefer the Dharmashastra.

Angiras

Angiras is one of the ten primordial sages mentioned in the Manu Smriti: Marichi, Atri, Angira, Pulasatya, Pulah, Kratu, Pracheta, Vashishta, Bhrigu and Narada. It is a very ancient name even in the Rig Veda. Vishwarupa quotes a verse of Angiras saying that what is done according to one's own will without following the dictates of shastra is fruitless. स्वामि प्राय कृतं कर्म यत्तृ धर्मविवर्जितम् क्रीड़ाकमैव बालानां तत्सर्व निष्प्रयोजनम्।। It is doubtful but yet it is mentioned that Angiras Smriti is in 72 verses altogether.

Pulastya—Pulastya Smriti (4th & 7th century A.D)

Pulastya's name also figures among ten primordial sages mentioned by Manu.

Mitakshara cites a verse from Pulastya that a Brahaman should in principle use ascetic food (Vegatable food) in Shradh. Danaratanakara of Chandeshwar cites a prose text from Pulastya on the gift of deer-skin.

Marichi

He is the first among the ten primordial sages. Marichi's views are similar to modern transfer of property acts. The sage is relied upon as an authority by Mitakshara, Apararka, Smriti Chandrika on asaucha, shradh, prayaschita and vyavahar.

Kautiliya Arthasastra

Arthsastra in its technical sense is some what wider in meaning than Dandaniti and includes politics, economics, law and justice, but was narrower in scope than Dharmashastra. It was said to be an upaveda of the Artharva Veda according to Vishnu Puran. आयुर्नेदो धनुर्वेदो गान्धर्वश्चेति ते त्रयः अर्थशास्त्रं चतुर्थ च विधा अष्टादशेवताः।

No commentary on Arthashastra of Kautiliya has yet been completed. The Kautiliya is the oldest extant work on Arthshastra. It is really a branch of Dharmashastra as the former deals with the responsibilities of the kings for whom rules are laid down in many treatises on Dharma.

Kautiliya contains two sections (called Dharmasthiya and Kantakaso Dharma) on the administration of justice. The purpose of this shastra as stated by Kautilya himself is to prescribe means for bearing and preserving power over the earth.

तस्याः पृथिव्या लाभपालनोपायः शास्त्रमर्थ शास्त्रमिति। (Kautilya, 15-12)

पृथिवव्या लाभे पालने च यावन्त्यर्थ शास्त्राणि पूर्वाचायैः प्रस्थापितानि प्रायशस्तानि संहत्यैक मिदमर्थ शास्त्रं कृतम्। (Kautilya,1-1)

Vishnu Gupta/ Chanakya/ Kautilya

Kamandakiya–Nitisara pays a rich tribute to Vishnugupta who single handedly brought the downfull of the Nandas and bestowed the earth to Chandragupta by force of his political strategy. Kamandak looks upon him as the guru. That there was in India a great deal of thinking on politics, economics, law, and administration several centuries before Christ is clear from the Mahabharata and early Dharmasutras of those of Gautam, Baudhayan and Apastamba.

Dandin in Dashakumaracharita refers to Vishnugupta– 700 A.D. In Mudrarakshasa byVisakhadatta there is an earlier reference to Kautiliya. Vishnugupta was the original name, but Vishnugupta, Chanakya and Kautilya are the same.

Chandragupta acqired the thrown in 317 B.C./680 B.C. There are 15 chapters in the Arthashastra.

The Ramayana and the Dandaniti

Lord Ram during Vanvaas at Chitrakoot gave certain ideas of the kingdom and its administration when Sri Bharat met him. He says that well versed in Rajaniti–Acharya Sudhanwa must be respected.

इश्व स्त्रवर सम्पन्नमर्थ शास्त्र विशारदम् सुधन्वानमुपाध्यायं कंचित् त्वं तात मन्य से।। (Valmiki, 100.14).

About the characteristics of Mantri, Ram suggests that well versed men who are aware of the working of the kingdom should be appointed as advisors–Amatya and Mantri. He suggests that good counsel is the main reason for the king to be victorious. Thus the advisors must be well acquainted with the system of administration and the Niti as well as that should be strictly secret (Valmiki, 16-18). Lord Ram is critical of bribe and says that no such person should be associated with the administration (Valmiki, 26).

There are 18 posts which are being called Tirth in ancient Dandaniti. They are : Mantri, Purohit, Yuvaraj, Senapati, Dwarik (chief gate keeper), Antah Puradhyaksh; Karagaradhyaksh; Koshadhyaksh; Karya Niyojak; Pradh Vivak (chief); he who gives salary to the army; Nagaradhyaksh; Karmantik; to safeguard the boundary of the kingdom, Durg Rakshak; Rashtrapal; Dandapal; Dharmadhyaksh. These are called Ashtadasha Tirth.

कच्चिदष्टादशान्येषु स्वयज्ञे दश पच्च च
त्रिभि स्त्रिभिर विज्ञातैर्वेत्सि तीर्थानि चारकैः।।

Lord Ram gives 14 demerits of a king. He suggests Bharat that he should not imbibe such characteristics: these are called Rajadosha. These are Nastikta; Asatya-Bhashan, Krodh; Pramad; Dirgh Sutrata; Yagi Puruko ka sang na karna; alasya and subordination to Indriyas, to think on the general administration alone, to accept advice from uneducated etc. and further he suggests that the king should leave the following ten habits:

नास्तिक्यम नृतं क्रोधं प्रमादं दीर्घसूत्रताम्।
अदर्श नं ज्ञानवतामालस्य पंचवृतिताम्।
एकचिन्तन मर्थानामनर्थ ज्ञैश्च मन्त्रणम्।
निश्चितानाम नारभ्यं मन्त्रस्या परिरक्षणम्।
मंगलाध प्रयोगों च प्रत्युत्थानं च सर्वतः।
कच्चित् त्वं वर्जयस्येतान् राजदोषांश्चचतुर्दषः।।65-67।।

Ten evil habits come out of kama. These are to be neglected by people who follow Dharma specially the king. They are called dashavarga. Lord Ram asked Bharat not to associate with the dashavarga. Manu has given the following names of the dashavarga.

भृगयाऽक्षो दिवास्वप्नः परिवारः स्त्रियो मदः
तैर्यत्रिकं वृथाच्चा च कामजो दशको गणः।।

These are *akhet*; gambling; sleeping in day; to elaborate others' evil; to associate with women in plenty numbers; to take wine; to dance, to sing; roaming-aimlessesly. These are available in the Manu smriti. Thus the importance of these can be understood.

The whole chapter 100 of Ayodhyakand is full of poliical statecraftship, which Sri Ramchandra advised to Sri Bharat. One should follow the sayings of the Purushottam Sri Ram.

Mahabharata

The Mahabharata, the Ramayana and the Manu Smriti give us the details of the Dharma, Rajaniti and all sorts of the rituals that can be sorted out through these authorities of the Epic and the Manava Dharmashastra.

Once Maharaja Yudhishtir was holding a darbar in his Darbar hall in the Indraprasth along with his relations, well-wishers, advisors and others. Maharshi Narada went to see how the king Yudhishtir is managing administration of his newly kingdom. Narada who was himself a great scholar of the Veda and who was aware even of the ticklish problems of the administration and Rajaniti gave advice to Sri Yudhishtir on almost all aspects of politics– Dandaniti, Dharmashastra and all the general vyavahar of the society.

After well recieved by the king, Yudhishtir along with his people, the great Maharshi Narada asked certain questions relating to Dharma–aachar and other rituals both in respect to the working of the kingdom as well as of the society (*Sabha Parva,* 5: 21-23).

The whole Mahabharat, if one goes through it in minute details is a great work of the Dharma. The advices given by the different Maharshi are worth considering to know more about Dharma.

People should read these authorities. The Arthshastra of Kautilya also gives references to these great authorities of the Dharma.

Bhatti Kavya

It is said that there was a time when people in general and intellectuals in particular used to discuss and participate in the deliberation of the Dandaniti–Rajaniti and Dharmashastra. Poets and play writers also played important and dominant roles in shaping politics through deliberations. Bhatti Kavya is also one of such important deliberations.

Bhatti has commented through his poems focusing on

the 14 slokas of the 12 chapters of the Yuddhakand of the Ramayan. The whole chapter 12 is full of the Dharma/ Rajaniti.

Ravan explained before the Darbar hall about the merits of Seeta whom he had abducted and kept in the Ashok Batika. Ravan also explained the duty of Seeta before the sabhasad. Bhatti Kavya has taken clue from this sloka and has thrown light on the politics through his Kavya.

वधस्तु रामस्य भया त्वया च
प्रहस्त सर्वैरपि राक्षासैर्वा
कथं भवेदर्थ विशारदस्य
महार्णवं तर्तुमिवा प्लवस्य
धर्म प्रधानास्य महारथस्य
इक्ष्वाकुवंश प्रभवस्य राज्ञः। (*Ramayana*, 14: 11-12)

In the Ramanyana, the relatives of Ravan explained the characteristics and power of Ram and said that he was the authority on economics/Dandaniti. Ravan was advised not to have enmity with Sri Ram.

What has been explained in the Ramayana by Ravan in chapter 12 of Yuddhakand is full of Dandaniti and Dharmaniti and it is about the functioning of the kingdom. The same theory is mentioned in the Manu Smriti in 7th chapter and 154 slokas, which is almost the same in Kautiliya chapter 7: 11.

Ramayan: Yuddhakand- 12th chapter

Manu Smriti: 7th chapter- 154 slokas

Kautilya: 7th chapter - 11 slokas

Kamandak Nitisar: 11th chapter- 56 slokas

Katyayana: 2nd chapter- 12 slokas

Mahabharat: Shanti Parva- 56th chapter

What Bhatti Kavya suggests on the Rajaniti, it endorsed in the above mentioned authorities. But Bhatti Kavya has impressed upon the poeple to follow the righteneousness so that the life of the people of the kingdom remains happy. One should follow what the authority of Dharmashastra has been mentioning on the Dharmashastra.

Kiratarjuniya Kavya: Dandaniti

In this book the author has based the story of the Mahabharata's Vana Parva- Virat Parva when the Pandavas had to spend 12 years in the vanavaas. One must take stock of the enemy's movement because the victor and the vanquished, both have to fulfil their missions.

In this authority steps have been taken to show how to follow the political intricacies i.e., one needs to keep alert on the enemy because when one is in the secret place, the opposite party would always be alert to find out the working and management of the victor-vanquished relations.

What has been given in the Manu Smriti should have had impact on the people and that is why the Manu Smriti/ Ramayan/Mahabharat/Kautiliya are almost intentical. One must take care of the movements of enemy so that one can remain careful every moment (Manu, 7:177-178). Further it is said that one must be aware that the remaining work has to be done in cooperation (Manu, 7: 180).

The poet Bharavi has drawn from the Mahabharat on the basis of the role of Duryodhan in matters of the state craft. Kavi Bhamal says that even the poets should have discussions on the points of Rajaniti– that is healthy politics (Kautiliya: 6: 97).

Sisupalvadha: Kavya

There are references of this text in Shanti Parva (75.10), Vishnu Samhita (3.46), Udhyog Parva (84) and in Chhandogya Upanishad.

अव्रताद्यनधीयानाः यत्र भैक्ष्यचराद्विजाः। तं ग्रामं दण्डयेद् राजा चौर भक्त प्रदोहिसः।।
(Atri Samhita: 22; Parashara Samhita: 3.46)

Again Manu says that if the villagers do not take steps to control groups who are engaged in creating chaos in villages or those who do not help in cases of emergency in villages, such villagers are not entitled to remain in the village as a part of the kingdom:

यश्चापि धर्म समयात्प्रच्युतो धर्म जीवनः
दण्डेनैव तमप्योषेत्स्वकाद्धर्माद्धि विच्युतम्
ग्रामधाने हिता भंगे पथि भोषामि दर्शने
शक्तितो नाभिधावतो निर्वास्याः सपरिच्छदीः।। (Manu : 9: 273-274)

Kasiraj Dibodas: Dibodasiya

Among the Nibandhakaras, people have considered 'Dibodasiya' authored by Kasiraj Dibodas who has been noted as the incarnation of Bhagwan Dhanwantari as important. Previous to that the commentaries written by Medhatithi, Devaswami and Asahay were already available. General author Kamalakar Bhatta has given references of the book 'Dibodasiya' in his own book Nirnay Sindhu. But this is not available in its original form. Kritya Kalptaru written by Acharya Lakshmidhar who was the Chief Minsiter of Kanyakubja Naresh Govind Chandra becomes the first Nibandhakara and his book is available. Lakshmidhar belongs to the first half of the 12th century. Prithwi Chandrodaya of about the same period has been prominent; references of these books are available in the book Nirnay Sindhu of Kamalakar Bhatta.

Royal Patronage of Scholarship

It is said and we have also noted earlier that श्वेदोऽखिलो धर्ममूलम्श्‌ The Veda is the authority for Dharma, for the welfare of the humanity but as Veda is the direct offspring of the Brahma sometimes even the general rishis and mahatmas have difficulties in grasping the substance of the Vedas and they are put in great dilemmas. To make it easier for the knowledge of the mass, efforts were made by the scholars, rishis, munis to interpret the Vedas. That brought Itihas, Puran and later on the Shruti, Smriti to collectively form the basis of the Dharma and all the relevant matters related to Dharmashastra were incorporated in these books. Many of these texts were also composed under the patronage of royal houses. These writings have greater impact on the general Dharmashastra- Vyavahar. Among those, important ones are: *Chaturvargachintamani* (Hemadri), *Birmitrodaya* (Bir Mishra), *Bhagwant Bhaskar* (Neelakanth Bhatt), *Smriti Tatwa* (Raghunandan Bhatt), *Dana Sagar* (Ballala Sen), *Pratistha Sagar* (Ballala Sen), *Madan Parijata, Bidhan Parijata* and *Nrisingh Prasad* (Dalapati Raj), *Smriti Chandrika* (Devanna Bhatta). Some of these scholars were also directly involved in running the administration. Sayanacharya who was quite an influential person in the administration of Vijayanagar Kingdom during the regime of Maharaja Harihar Bukka.

The following books were authored by the intellectual remaining in the courtyard of Maharaja Harihar Bukka among which *Tirtha Sudhanidhi, Shraddha Sudhanidhi, Vrata Sudhanidhi, Subhashit Sudhanidhi* and *Ayurveda Sudhanidhi* are important.

Similarly from Bengal we have important contributions including *Shradh Kaumudi, Dana Kaumudi* and *Sudhi Kaumudi* written by Govindacharya or Kavi Kankanacharya; Smriti Viveka by Sulpani; Haralata and Pitridayita by Annirudha; and Daya Bhag and Kal Viveka by Jimut Vaahana.

Mithila's contribution in this field will include prominent scholars like Sridatta Upadhyaya, Chandeshwar Thakur, Vachaspati Mishra, Kamalakar Bhatt (*Tirth Kamalakar, Brat Kamalakar, Shradh Kamalakar, Daan Kamalakar*) and Nagesh Bhatt (*Tirthendu Sekhar, Shradhendu Sekhar and Bratendu Sekhar*).

Mithila Varanasi have been major centres of learning and scholarship. Here we have scholars like Narayan Bhatta who wrote *Triyasthali Setu.* But Kamalakar Bhatta was not quite in agreement with Narayan Bhatts on certain points and he himself wrote *Nirnay Sindhu* which was appreciated and liked by people. Yet, the Scholars of Kasi doubted and did not agree on certain specificities raised in the *Nirnay Sindhu.* This is to suggest the significance of the popular appericiation of intellectual works in Varanasi. It may be interesting to note in this context that Kashinath Upadhyaya wrote *Dharma Sindhu* and sent it to Kashi from Poona and suggested that if this be useful then it should be retained otherwise it should be thrown into the Ganga. But people in Kashi were very pleased with the text and for four days it was taken in procession in the town on a palanquin. This book became quite decisive and was followed by few more books on the subjects which were not touched in *Niranay Sindhu and Dharma Sindhu* that supplemented these two seminal texts. Among them particular mention should be made of *Niranayamrit, Purusharth Chintamani, Ranbir Singh Brat Ratnakar, Brataraj, Bratark, Utasabh Sindhu, Vratotsabh Kaumudi, Jaisingh Brat Kalpadruma.*

Krityakalpataru: Lakshmidhara

This book exercised great influence over the Dharmashastra writers of Mithila, Bengal and North India in general. The period of Lakshmidhara falls in the first half of the 12th century. He was the Mahamantri of the Kanya Kubja Naresh Govindchandra. There were other great scholars in the courtyard of the Naresh Govindchandra and all those scholars in company wrote many important works on Dharmashastra. Of all the works, the works of Lakshmidhar got precedence and the contemporary as well as later writers have given references to the works of Pt. Lakshmidhar such as Annirudh, Ballal Sen, Sulpani, Raghunandan, Chandeshwar, Harinath, Sridatta. Hemadri, the author of Chaturbarg Chintamani has addressed Lakshmidhar for his work Kalpataru as Bhagwan.

The work is very extensive and is divided into 14 kandas: Brahmachari Kand; Grihastha Kand; Niyatkal Kand. In these kands all matters relating to Dharmashastra and daily routine have been incorporated– brushing teeth, bath, japa, tarpan, daily yagya rules related to monthly illness of women. Pawar tithi; care of cows, and rules listing to puranas; shradh kand; daan kand; Vrata kand: This kand is principally based on Puranas and is eleven in number, among which Bhabisya, Matsya and Varah are the most prominent. P.V. Kane states that it is written in the kand in the Krita, Treta, Dwapara and Kaliyuga respectively. Sujaya, Rama, Dhananjaya, Vikram attained position of Supreme rulers by performing vratas and that Vasundhara, the virtuous daughter of Vikrama dwelling in the Dasarna country (Malva) secured moksha by performing vrata. Further it quotes 16 verses from Sumantra, the last of which a verse that the Haiyas, Talanganas, Turuskas (Turks), Yavanas, and Sakas observing, facts in Bratas reached the status of brahmanas in this very world; Pratistha kand is not very clear about its contents as the manuscript begins with an incomplete verse and ends also abruptly: ...सर्वस्य तथैवेन्द्रिय संगमम्। ज्ञापयेत स्वयं... समाहितः ...शामीगर्भारिणिः कार्या दैध्रयाद्धस्त प्रमाणतः। वितस्तिः परिणाहार्ध मध्यं वै षोड्शाङ्गुलम्।। वृतं कर द्वयोपेतं दशाङ्गल सुविस्तृतम्।।...Tirth Vivechana Kand: Visiting holy places– Kashi, Prayaga, The Ganges, Gaya, Kurukshetra, Pauskara, Mathura. This kand speaks of starting on the Mahapatha (the great Journey). The same with Yudhishtir and his four brothers and the Dog:

युधिष्ठिर मतं ज्ञात्वा वृष्णिक्षय मवेक्ष्य च।
भ्रातरः पंच कृष्ण षष्ठीश्वा चौव सप्तमः।। (*Mahaprasthak Parva*,1.24)

Smriti Chandrika: Devan Bhatt

Son of Keshwaditya: Devenna Bhatta is a great author of Dharma belonging to south India in 12th century. He is also called Somaiyajee. This book is considered as an authority especially in south India where it is taken as a sacred book on the laws covering the Vyavahar, daily rituals–Sanskaras as well as sauch and asauch and Shradh, and Prayaschita. All matters related to the Dharmashastra mentioned in the Smriti–Shruti Itihas–Puran have been included in the Smriti Chandrika. Many commentators of the Dharmashastras and authors of the repute whose works are authority on Dharmashastra have been given as references in the Smriti Chandrika especially we find Apraraka , Deva Swami, Dhurta Swami, Dharmadeep, Medhatithi, Vigyaneshwar, Vishwarupa Chaturbarg Chintamani, Saraswati Vilas, Bir Mitrodaya. Naturally there is a great importance attached to this book.

There are about 750 pages in the book Smriti Chandrika, covering about 90 pages on Sanskaras, 144 pages on Ahnika, 350 pages on Vyavahar, 175 pages on shradh. In the end the author clearly remarks that the book is based on authorities and nothing is based on his own imagined idea and that all are based on the different writers or authorities on Dharmashastra.

स्वामि प्रायेण हि मया न किंचिदिह लिख्यते।
किं तु वाचनिकं सर्वमतो ग्राधैव निर्भयैः। (*Smriti Chandrika*)

Prof. P.V. Kane remarks that the book is very extensive and almost all important writers have been quoted in the Smriti Chandrika including Manu, Katyayana, Narada, Brahaspati and even the commentries given by Apararka, Medhatithi.

Dharmaratna—Jimutvahan

Jimutavahan is the first of the triumvirate of Bengal writers on Dharmashastra, the other two being Sulpani, and Raghunandan. He wrote Kala Viveka, Vyavahar Matrika and Dayabhag. All these three books combined together take shape of a big book called Dharma Ratna. Vachaspati Mishra has given references of Jimutvahan in his different works. He belonged to a respected saint in the distinct Radha. He has given references of Raja Bhojadeva and Govind Raj.

Haralata: Pitri Dayita or Karmopadesani Paddhati of Aniruddh

Aniruddh of Bengal–12th century–a resident of Biharbatak on bank of the river Ganges belonging to

Champahattiya Brahmin caste was the teacher of the king of Bengal at that time.

The Haralata deals with impurity on birth and death, with the acts allowed to be done or forbidden during impurity, with periods of impurity on death in a distant land, or on the deaths of infant and women, with rules when two periods of impurity overlap each other, with impurity on the death of Sapindas, the meaning of Sapindas, persons who need not observe periods of impurity, cremation and burial, offering of water to the deseased, observances during mourning, persons entitled to perform rites after death, observances after the period of mourning, persons to whom no water should be offered.

The Pitridayita is a work for the use of the followers of the Sama Veda. Its contents are– the duties on rising from bed, brushing the teeth, bath, sandhya, tapa, Vaiswadeva Parwar Shradh, eulogy of gifts, Sapandikara, and other shradhas, antyeshta and rites during the day of mourning after death, the letting loose of a bull.

The Haralata is named as an authority in the Suddhi Viveka of Rudradhar. The shradh Kriya Kaumudi of Govindanand (1510-1545 A.D.) frequently quotes Aniruddh and includes him among ancient authors. Raghunandan in his Ekadasi Tattava makes a casual but striking remark on Aniruddh. Thus, we find that Anirudh is an important authority.

BallalSen and Lakshman Sen

Ballala Sen and Lakshman Sen, the two famous kings of Bengal composed five works on Dharmashastra in the later half of the 12th century. These are: Aachar Sagar, Pratistha Sagar, Vrata Sagar, Daan Sagar and Abdhut Sagar.

Out of five, Abdhut Sagar was started by Ballal Sen but was completed by Lakshman Sen. Daan Sagar is a huge book. The text covers about 750 pages. There are 75 chapters and about 1400 daans have been dealt with in it. The work is mentioned in the Chandeshwar by Daan Ratnakar.

Lakshman Samvat was started by Lakshman Sen when he lost Bengal and came to north Bihar and ruled North Bihar for some time. In the Daan Sagar itself it is distinctly stated that Ballal Sen composed it under the distinction of his guru (Aniruddh).

The Smrityarthasara of Sridhara

Sridhar Acharya was the son of Vishnu Bhatta Upadhyaya of Viswamitra gotra. Sridhar was himself a performer of vedic sacrifices.

The contents of the book cover –sanskaras rituals including shradh,rituals of death, purification of bodies, Sanyas, Prayaschita, various grades of sins and lapses. It was probably written between 1150-1200 A.D. It has given references of Mitakshara, Kamdhenu, Kalpataru and Govind Raja. The Smriti Chandrika and Hemadri both quote it as an authority. It is mentioned that Tulsi should be avoided in Shradh.

Chaturvarga Chintamani of Hemadri

It is a very vast authority especially popular in the south. It is an encyclopaedia of ancient religious rites and observances. It is of the 13th century. From ancient time in India the goals of human life are said to be four: Dharma, Artha, Kaam and Moksha– Chaturvarg.

Kamdeb was his father– Batsa. He was the Mantri of Yadava Raja of Deogiri and later on he became Amatya of Ramchandra.

Sankalpas framed by Hemadri are very famous works called Hemadri Mahasankalpa, Prayaschita Sankalpa and Tirth Sthana Sankalpa. The book is in four volumes containing six parts with about 6000 pages. He was a great authority on Purva Mimansa:

Brat Kand: 32 chapters

Daan Kand: 13 chapters

Parisekh Kand : (a) Kaal Nirnay: 17 chapters

(b) Shradh Kalpa: 25 chapters.

Prayaschita Kand: 10 chapters.

Acharya Sayan—Madhavacharya

Both Sayan and Madhava were brothers. Madhava was the founder of Vijaynagar kingdom and the kingdom of Srinagar. Madhava got Maharaja Bukka enthroned as the Vijaynagar king. He was the Minister of Maharaja Bukka and Maharaja Harihar. His father was Mayan and mother Srimati. His third brother was Bhogavath. They belonged to Yajurvedi Brahman family. Sayan Bhashya is very famous. The joint efforts of the brothers Saayan-Madhava made them immortal in the field of Dharmashastra works popular all over the country. Their significant contributions are: *Purusharth Sudha Nidhi, Dattaka Mimansa, Smriti Sangrah, Kurukshetra Mahatya, Parashara Madhaviya, Kaal Nirnay, Sri Vidyaranya, Madhaviya Dhatubriti, Jaiminiya Nyaya Mala Vivaran, Vivaran Prameya Sangrah, Pancha Dasi* and *Jivan Mukti Viveka.*

Sridatta Upadhyaya

Mithila has made extremely valuable and substantial contributions to Dharmashastra literature. From the days of the Yagyavalkya Smriti down to modern times the land of Mithila has produced writers whose names are illustrious. Sridatta Upadhyaya is one of the earliest among the medieval Maithili Nibandhakaras. He belongs to the first half of 14th century. His works are *Aacharadars, Alias Kritchar, Chandogyahik, Samaya Pradeep, Pitri Bhakti, Shradh Kalpa, Suddhi Nirnaya* and *Vrata Saar* or *Vrata Paddati.*

Acharadarsha

It is a manual of the daily religious duties of the followers of white Yajurveda (Vajasnaya) such as Achaman, Bath, Sandhya, Tarpan, Jap, Brahma Yagya.

अहो रात्राश्रितो धर्म इह वाजसनेयिनाम्। निबध्यते निबद्धी यो धर्मशास्त्र निबन्धभि:।।
समूल वचना भोगो मीमांसा न्याय निर्मल:।श्री दलेन सता मेष आचारे दर्पण: कृत:।।

There is a commentary on this book by Gauripati son of Damodar (Mishra) titled Acharadarsha Bodhini. Sri Datta has given references of the predecessors specially the works namely *Acara Chintamani, Kalpataru, Kamdhenu, Kalika Puran, Harihar* and *Halayudh-Nibandhas.*

Samaya Pradeep

It treats of the proper time for various vratas श्री दत्तेन व्रतादीनां सारमाकृष्य लिख्यते।। It is divided into three chapters: (i) Samaya Parichccheda (details of fasts etc.); (ii) Samvatsar- Krita Praichheda which treats of vratas from the Pratipada to Amavasya in several months; (iii) The Prakiranya dealing with fasts and sankranti.

Pitri Bhakta

It is a manual of shradh rites for students of Yajur Veda. Details of rites have been mentioned.

Shraddha Kalpa

It deals with the shradh rites for students of Samavedin. The author was liberal enough to assert that a Shudra can perform Vaiswadeva and the offering of *bali* but he can not adopt the procedure of Sakala as it includes Vedamantras; he can however, perform those rites with *namah* as the mantra. The author relies on Yagyavalkya and Vishnu Puran to support his claims.

Chandeshwar

Chandeshwar is the most prominent figure among Maithil Nibandhakaras on Dharmashastra. He compiled an extensive digest called Smriti Ratnakar (Kane, I (II): 763-775). This digest was divided into seven sections: Krtya; Daan; Vyavahar; Sudhi; Puja; Vivada; Gryhastha.

Out of these, the Vivad Ratnakar dealing with Daya bhag and other titles of law (Vyavahar padas) has been printed and has been translated into English by Mr. G.S. Sarkar and by Justice Digamber Chattarjee. The Vivad Ratnakar of Chandeshwar and Vivada Chintamani of Vachaspati are of paramount importance in the matters of Hindu Law in Mithila so far as British Indian courts are concerned.

Krityaratnakar

The Krita-Ratnakar deals in 22 tarangas the discussion on Dharma–its real nature, its rewards, means of knowing it and the occasion for it; the various vratas and observances for several desires from Chaitra, the observance in the intercalary month, various sratus on senhal days of the week, the sun's passage into a new sign, eclipse on the new moon day etc. This work is referred to in his Daan Ratnakar, which in turn is quoted in the Grihastha Ratnakar. अत्रोक्तमापि यद्यानं कृत्य रत्नाकरे पुनः। मासादि कृत्य सामसस्त्यं गौरवात दुहीरितम्। (*Daan Ratnakar*); असत्प्रति ग्रहाक्ष्चन्यमिर्दानरत्माकरे देयादेव तरंग प्रदर्शिताः (*Grihastha Ratnakar*, Folio 76).

The work was printed in the *Bibliotheca Indica* series in 1926. This was probably the first of the seven Ratnakars, since it is mentioned first in the verse quoted and since it has a large number of introductory verses. The verses in the *Kritya Ratnakar* 24.25 are

विभ्राणः कल्पवृक्षं क्वचन परिसरे कामधेनुं दधानः क्राप्यन्तः पारिजातं क्वचिदपि च दधद्योशया दो विमुक्तः। श्री मच्चण्डेश्ववरेण श्रुति निगम विदा तन्यते तेन तद्दद् विष्णु व्यासादि वारूचस्फुटदमृतमयः कृत्यरत्नाकरोऽयम्।। यस्मिन् किंचिदपि शंसति कामधेनुयत्रैष्ट मल्पपि कल्पतरूणं दत्ते। धत्ते न गन्धामपि कंचन पारिजात स्तत्सर्वेमेव विविनामि नयप्रवीणः।।

The words कल्पतरू कामधेनु and पारिजात are paronomastic i.e. they are names of specific literary works and also have other meanings.

Grihastha Ratnakar

The *Grihastha Ratnakar* is a very extensive work in 68 tarangas on the duties of householders. The work was printed in the *Bibliotheca Indica* series in 1928. It is a large work of 591 pages. It has only two introductory verses. This *Ratnakar* is full of Mimansa verses (3.20) which enumerate briefly the topics of 68 *tarangas* (waves, chapters) of this *Ratnakar* (which also means Sea). They are:

what girls may be chosen or not chosen for marriage; examining the gunas of the proposed bridegroom; proper order of choosing a girl from the several varnas; the proper ages of girls and bridegrooms; order of persons entitled to give away a girl in marriage; when a girl can choose her own husband; form of marriage and merits and demerits; passing over a wife marrying another girl; condemnation of a younger brother marrying before elder one; setting up grihya fire and performing the worship of fire; worship of Gods and officiating as a priest; ahnice (daily observances from morning onward i.e. aachaman, brushing the teeth, morning bath, sandhya observance, the five daily Yagyas honoring guests, rules about food to be taken or not to be taken, observance for women proper, observance and actions for Brahmans and for war of the three other varnas; maintaining oneself in calamities; the observance of Shataka, about Yama and Niyama; impurity on birth and death, to the ruin of families; proper abode and a house for married man; what a householder should speak or not utter or what he should not look at, abstaining from adultery; avoiding mixture of caste; paying off debts; listening to Mahabharat and etc.; actions proper for Kshtriyas, Vaisyas and Sudras.

Daana Ratnakar

The *Daana Ratnakar* contains 29 tarangas and deals with the following: meaning of daan, what may or what may not be gifted, fit objects of charity, the mahadanas; gifts of a thousand cows and heaps of corn; various gifts, such as those of food, books, gifts appropriate to certain months, Nakshatras; and tithis; miscellenous gifts; dedication of wells and tanks for public use and planting of trees etc.

Vvivad Ratnakar

The *Vivad Ratnakar* is an extensive work (671 pages) in 100 tarangas on civil and criminal law and deals with 18 titles of law and *Dayabhag*, recovery of debts and others. It formed the basis of *Vivad Chandra*, the *Vivad Chintamani* of Vachaspati and the *Danda Viveka* of Vardhamana. It is mentioned in his own *Grihastha Ratnakar*: इत्यादिनि चान्यानि पुत्रदेशे विवाद रत्नाकर एवास्माभिर्वर्णितानीति। (*Grihastha Ratnakar*, Folio 133 b).

Vyavahar Ratnakar

The *Vyavahar Ratnakar* deals with judicial procedures such as the plaint, the reply, the burden of proof, means of proof, judgement etc.

Suddhi Ratnakar

The *Suddhi Ratnakar* is in 34 tarangas and deals with impurity on birth and death, persons who have to observe asauch, meaning of sapinda, rites on death upto the end of period of mourning, purification of food and various substances.

Kritya Chintamani

It is one of such works. The date of its compostion is not known. In his Grihastha Ratnakar he says that certain architechnical and decorative construction called Sribriksha, Vardhaman, and Nandhabarta have been spoken by him in the Kritya Chintamani. The Krityachintamani says that he has already composed the seven Ratnakaras: आम्नाय स्मृतिनिर्णयाय कृत वां स्तान्सप्त रत्नाकरात्।

The Kritya Chintamani is divided into sections called prakas. It deals with astrononical matters related to the performance of several religious ceremonies, and sanskaras such as Tara suddhi, the intercalary month, garbhadhan, Srimantonnayana, birth of a child on the mula Nakshatra, the rites on the 6th day after birth, Namakaran, the movement of saturn, sun's passage from one sign into another, the results of eclipse etc. The Kritya Chintamani expressly states that it was composed after all the seven Ratnakaras. The Kritya Chintamani is frequently quoted by Rajdharma. Besides, Chandeshwar compiled several other works and the Pooja Ratnakar is one among them.

Rajaniti Ratnakar

The *Rajaniti Ratnakar* was published at Patna by the K.P. Jayasawal with a learned introduction dealing with the personal history of Chandeshwar, his reletions with the Mithila king and the medieval Indian literature on politics. It appears that Chandeshwar did not contemplate the writing of a work on politics, when he compiled this great object. He wrote the work at the command of the king Bhavesh or Bhaviswara of Mithila.

राज्ञा भवेशेनाज्ञाप्तो राजनीति निबन्धकार तनोति मन्त्रिणामार्या: श्री मान् चण्डेश्वर: कृती।

The work contains 16 tarangas on the following subjects: definition of a king; duties of king; the characteristics and duties of amatyas; the characteristics of a purohita; the characteristics of the hall of justice (sabhya)- the number and qualification; concerning forts; the time, place and access of royal policy; the state treasury; the army; the commandar-in-chief and the discipline of the army; the ambassadors, allies, spies, the general obligation of king, conflict of Dharmashastra and Arthasastra, the six gunas–Samadhi etc., the Mandala of kings; the king's power of punishment, abdication of king, the heir apparent, impartiaility of kingdom, the eldest son's right to succeed, the seven constituent elements of the state; obligation towards the poor, the helpless etc., the coronation of the heir-apparent or his investiture.

There are two more works composed by Chandeshwar: *Daan Vakyavali* and the Siva Vakyavali. Chandeshwar quotes in *Kritya Ratnakar* and the *Vivada Ratnakar* a host of writers and works he has taken note of Kamdhenu, the Kalpataru, the Parijata, the Prakasha, (Smriti Maharnava) and Halla Yudha. At the end of the *Vivada Ratnakar* he boasts that whatever is of essence in the above five works and even more is comprehended in his single work *Ratnakar.*

कल्पद्रुमे वाप्यथ पारिजाते हलायुधे वाप्यथवा प्रकाष्ठो। यत्सार मस्मादधिकं च यत्तद्यधाति रत्नाकर एक एव। यं कामधेनु रनुयाति सकल्पवृक्षो यं सेवते निजफलाय स पारिजातः तं वैरिगोत्र मिद्मुच्चसहस्त्रदष्टिं चण्डेश्वर तुलायितुं कतमे भवन्तु।

Dr. K.P. Jayaswal rightly points out in Introduction to *Rajaniti Ratnakar*, from Lakshmidhar's Kalpataru as Vyavahar that Chandeshwar borrows into his *Vivada Ratnakar* practically the whole book. The boastful reference to himself and highly slighting remarks about Kamadhenu, Kalpataru and other works which occur in his works are felt by modern readers as very objectionable and offensive, since he appropriates without express acknowledgement the valuable parts of such works as Kamadhenu, Kalpataru etc.

Besides, these in his *Rajaniti Ratnakar*, he names Kamandaka, Kulluka Bhatta, Pollava and Pollavakara, Srikar. What is printed as *Nata Sutra* in the *Vivad Ratnakar* is really Latyayan Shrauta Sutra. Chandeshwar mentions many vernacular works in *Krityain Ratnakar.*

Chandeshwar was a mantri, and was intrusted with the office of the minister of peace and war. He was from Nepal and weighed himself against gold on the banks of Bagmati in 1314 A.D. The grand father of Chandeshwar was Devaditya who was a minister of Hara Singh Deva who belongs to Karnata family (1097 A.D.— 1324 A.D.). Devadatta–grand father of Chandeshwar, was the Chief Minister of the king. After Devadatta his son Vireshwar became Chief Minister and Chandeshwar, the eldest son of Vireshwar held several offices such as Chief Justice, also minister for peace and war and chief Minister. He was a favorite Minister of the king and that is why he weighed himself with gold. Hara Singh Deva began to rule in 1304 A.D. He after being defeated went to Nepal and Delhi emperor replaced him with Kameshwar Rajapandit.

Chandeshwar was the son of Vireshwar. The *Kritya Ratnakar* says that he touched the very idol of Pashupati in Nepal and worshipped it after commencing the commentary. From the *Vyavahar Ratnakar* it appears that Chandeshwar was the Chief Judge as well as Minister of Peace and War. The several Ratnakaras were composed between 1314 and 1324. The literary activities of Chandeshwar existed for about fifty years.

Chandeshwar exercised great influence over Mithila and Bengal writers. Misaru Mishra, Vardhaman, Vachaspati Mishra and Raghunandan very frequently quote him. The Virmitraday called the Ratnakars 'Paurastya Nibadh' (Easter Digest).

Sulpani — Smriti Viveka

Jimutavahan, Sulpani and Raghunandan are the three leading and very eminent writers on Dharmashastra from Bengal.

The earliest work of Sulpani appears to have been his *Dipakalika,* a commentary on the Smriti of Yagyavalkya. Besides, there are many other Dharmashastras and they have been called 'Viveka':

Ekadasi Viveka, Tirtha Viveka, Dattak Viveka, Durgotasava Viveka, Dolayatra Viveka, Prayaschita Viveka, Kal Viveka, Sudhi Viveka, Samkruti Viveka, Pratistha Viveka and *Sambandh Viveka* are the examples. All these *Vivekas* are called *Smriti Vivekas.* He must be dated after Chandeshwar (1375-1460).

Visheshwar Bhatta —Madan Parijat

Madan Parijat, compiled under the patronage of king Madan Pal by Visheshwar Bhatta, is a famous work like Raja

Bhoja's. Madan Pal seems to have been a great patron of learning and several works are attributed to him (c. 14th century A.D). Four works on Dharmashastra are attributed to him. These are: *Madan Parijat, Smriti Maharnnava or Madan Maharnava, Tirtha Nirnayasar* and *Smriti Kaumudi.* Besides the above four books on Dharmashastra, there are following books: *Madan Vinod Ani Ghantu, Surya Sidhant Viveka, Sidhanta Garb* and *Yantra Prakas.*

Madan Parijat is an extensive work in 995 pages. It was composed by Visheshwar Bhatta, the author of Subodhini. There are 9 Stabakas: *Brahmacharya Stabak, Grihastha Stabak, Aahnik Stabak, Garvadhan Sanskar Stabak, Asauch Stabak, Dravya Sudhi Stabak, Shradh Stabak, Bibhag Stabak* and *Prayaschita Stabak.*

Nri Singh Prasad

Nri Singh Prasad is considered as the encyclopaedia of Dharmashastra. The author was Dalapati or Daladhish, son of Valabh–Bharadwaja Gotra of Yagyavalkya Sakha. 15th century is the age of this work.

Nri Singh Prasad is divided into 12: Sarasa Samskar Sar, Ahnik Sar, Shradh Sar, Kala Sar, Vyavahar Sar, Prayaschita Sar, Karmbipak Sar, Brat Sar, Daan Sar, Santi Sar, Tirth Sar, Pratistha Sar. People give this book a great respect and Bhagwan Nri Singh has been attributed with respects in the end of the each chapter.

Madan Ratna

It appears that the work was composed under the patronage of king Madan Singh Deva, son of Shakti Singh. It is further said that Madan Singh called together four learned man i.e., Ratnakar, Gopinath, Viswanath, Gangadhar Bhatta and entrusted the composition of this digest to them.

तेनाहूय मनीषि मण्डनमणि सान्मिश्र रत्नाकरं
गोपीनीय मनुत्तमं च सुधि चं श्री विश्वनाथं तथा।

मुग्धं पण्डितं मुन्नतम्द्र्यति मतिं भट्टं च गंगाधरं
राजा शक्तिन सू नुना सकृतिना ग्रंथोय मारभ्यते।।

There are seven udyoth: Samyodhyoth, Acharodhyoth, Vyavaharodhyoth, Prayaschita Udhyoth, Danodhyoth, Shuddhi Udhyoth and Shanti Udhyoth. Period of the work is the middle of 14-15 century. It refers to Achar, Vyavahar, Kala, Prayaschita, Dan, Shuddhi, Shanti.

Raghu nandan Bhattacharya: Smriti Tattva

Raghunandan is the last great writer of Bengal on Dharmashastra. He compiled an encyclopaedic work on different branches of Dharmashastra styled as Smriti Tattva which is divided into 28 sections called Tattvas (Smriti Tattva). There are :*Malamas Tattva, Daya Tattva] Samskar Tattva, Shuddhi Tattva, Prayaschita Tattva, Vivah Tattva, Vidhi Tattva, Janmasthami Tattva, Durgotsava Tattava, Vyavahar Tattva, Ekadasi Tattva, Jalasayotsarga Tattva, Rigvedi Krikhotsarga Tattva, Yajurvedi Vikhotsarga Tattva, Samanga Vrikh, Vrat Tattva, Deva Pratistha, Divya Tattva, Jyotish Bastuyag Tattva, Diksha, Ahik Tattva, Kriya Tattva, Math Pratistha, Purushottam Kshetra, Chandogya Shradh Tattva, Yajurvedi Shradh Tattva* and *Shuddhi Kritya Vichar Tattva.* Besides these, he wrote *Gayashradh Paddhati* and *Rasayatra Paddhati.* Raghunandan, son of Harihar Bhattacharya (Bihra 1490-1570) was a contemporary of Chintamani Maharatha.

Harinath: Smritisar

Harinath is the author of a digest called Smritisar on several topics of Dharmashastra. The manuscript contains the portion of the Smritisar on Sanskaras, rites on death, shradh and prayaschita. No portion is published. Vachaspati Mishra has given references of Harinath in his works. His period is between 1300-1400 A.D. He was a Maithil.

Rudradhar

This is a well-known Maithila writer on Dharmashastra, who composed several works. He was the son of

Lakshmidhara (Mahamahopadhyay) and the youngest brother of Haladhara. His works are quoted by Vachaspati in Dwaita Nirnay, by Govindanand in the shradh Kriya Kaumudi; by Raghunandan in several of his Tattva by Kamalakar and Nilakantha. His period is between 1425-1460 A.D. His works are *Shuddhi Viveka, Shradh Viveka* and *Varsh Kritya.*

Varsh Kritya is very popular and famous in Mithila. Rudradhar has mentioned Ratnakar, Smritisar and Sulpani. Therefore he must be junior to them.

Mishru Mishra: Vivad Chandra (c. early 15th century)

Mishru Mishra is famous for his work called Vivad Chandra and Padarth Chandrika (on Nyay Vaisekhik System). The Vivad Chandra is a work of authority on Hindu Law in Mithila and has been recognised from very early days in the British courts. It is said that the book was compiled under order of the wife of Bhaikur's Chand ... younger brother of Bhairabh Singh.

Vachaspati Mishra

Vachaspati Mishra is the foremost nibandh writer of Smriti in Mithila. His Vivada Chintamani was recognised by the judiciary in India and by the judicial committee of the Privy Council as a work of paramount authority on matters of Hindu Law in Mithili. His literary activities were closely connected with the reigns of two kings of Mithila: Bhairvendra or Bhairab Singh also styled Hari Narayan and his son Rambhadra called Rup Narayan, both of the Kansherer Dynasty. He was an extremely voluminous writer and appears to have composed a dozen of works. These are: *Aachar Chintamani, Ahnik Chintamani, Sudha Chintamani, Krit Chintamani, Tirth Chintamani, Vyavahar Chintamani* and *Vivad Chintamani.* Besides these, he has written a few of the works *Tirth Nirnay, Dwait Nirnay* and *Sudhi Nirnay.*

The Vivad Chintamani was published from Calcutta in 1837 and was translated into English by Prassan Kumar

Tagore in 1863. A translation into English of Vivad Chintamani is by Dr. Ganganath Jha with an introduction by Dr. Umesh Mishra. The Vivad Chintamani was elaborately examined by the Patna High Court. It explicitly states that the author carefully studied the Kritya Kalp drum, Parijata and Ratnakar. The work deals exhaustively with the eighteen titles of law. He has given references to Rudradhar whereas, Raghunandan has cited Vachaspati Mishra. He is belongs to the middle of the 15th century.

Govindanand (Kavikaukanacharya)

Govindanand wrote several works out of which four have been printed. A great Nibandhkara of Bengal, his father was Ganpati Bhatta. His period was 16th century. He was of Vaishnav cult of Bagri Village. His works are *Dan Kaumudi, Kriya Kaumudi, Shradh Kaumudi, Barsh Kriti Kaumudi, Shuddhi Kaumudi* and *Govindanandiya Dharmashastra.* He also wrote comments on the Prayaschita Viveka of Sulpani and Tattva Kamaudi. He has quoted Madan Parijat, Rudradhar and Vachaspati.

Todaranand (c. 16th century)

Raja Todarmala, the celeberated finance minister of Akbar, compiled an extensive encyclopaedia of civil and religious law, astronomy and medicine. He was a Kshatriya of Oudh. His books are: *Achar Saukhya, Vyavahar Saukhya, Dan Saukhya, Shradh Saukhya, Viveka Saukhya, Vivah Saukhya, Prayaschita Saukhya, Vastu Saukhya* and *Samaya Saukhya.*

Nand Pandit

Nanda Pandit resided in Kashi in the 16th century. He was the son of Dharmadhikari Rama Pandit. Prodsh called him by Vinayak Pandit. His compositions are *Dattaka Mimansa,* his commentary on *Vishnu Smriti* (famous by the name of *Kesav Vaiyajanti* or *Vaijayanti*), commentary on *Parahsara Smriti (Vidwan Manohar), Shradh Kalpalata, Shradh Mimansa, Navaratra Pradeep, Shuddhi Chandrika, Madhvanand*

Kavya, Smriti Sindhu, Harita Vilas. Narada Pandit has commented on *Mitakshara* of Vijayneswara which is famous by the name of *Pramitakshara.*

Narayan Bhatt

Narayan Bhatt was the most famous of the celebrated family of Bhattas of Benaras. His famous works are *Tristhali Setu, Prayoga Ratna, Antyesthi Paddhati* and *Rudra Paddhati.*

Bhagwant Bhaskar: Smriti Bhaskar (early 17th century)

Neelakanth Bhatta was the son of Shaunak Bhatta and grand son of Narayan Bhatta. Neelakanth Bhatta wrote Bhagwant Bhaskar or Smriti Bhaskar. The book is divided into 12 chapters: (i) Sanskar Mayukh (ii) Achar Mayukh, (iii) Samaya Mayukh, (iv) Shradh Mayukh (v) Niti Mayukh (vi) Vyavahar Mayukh, (vii) Dan Mayukh, (viii) Utsarg Mayukh, (ix) Pratishtha Mayukh, (x) Prayaschita Mayukh, (xi) Shuddhi Mayukh, (xii) Shanti Mayukh.

Vir Mitroday: Pt. Mitra Mishra (early 17th century)

Gwaliar resident and son of Pt. Hans Mishra, Mitra Mishra was scholar in the Raj of Sri Vir Singh Deo. He wrote a Dharmashastra which is known as Bir Mitroday. In this text, there are twenty sections– all independent. The Bir Mitrodaya takes all these together: Paribhasa Prakas, Sarkar Prakas, Ahik Prakas, Pooja Prakas, Pratishta Prakas, Rajaniti Prakas, Vyavahar Prakas, Sudhi Prakas, Shradh Prakas, Tirth Prakas, Dan Prakas, Brat Prakas, Samay Prakas, Jyotish Prakas, Santi Prakas, Kam Bipak Prakas, Chikitsa Prakas, Prayaschita Prakas, Prakeern Prakas, Lakshman Prakas, Bhakti Prakas, Moksh Prakas.

Pt. Mitra Mishra wrote a commentry on the Yagyavalkya Smriti which is famous as Vir Mitrodaya. There is Anandkand Champu by the same author.

Smriti Kaustabha: Anantdeva

Anant Deva was a Mahaastrian Brahmin, though he

resided for a long period in Kurmachal (Kumayu) in the kingdom of Naresh Bag Bahadur Chand. He, at the direction of the king, wrote Smriti Kaustubh. He also belonged to the early 17th century. There are 15 works of Pt. Anant Deo out of which *Smriti Kaustubh, Prayaschita Dipika* and *Kalavindu Nirnay* are very prominent.

Smriti Kaustubh is a very extensive work divided into following sections: *Sanskar Kaustubh; Aachar Kaustubh; Raj Dharma Kaustubh; Daan Kaustubh; Uttasarga Kaustubh; Pratishtha Kaustubh* and *Tithi Sambatsar Kaustubh.*

Dharmashastra Sudha Nidhi: Pt. Diwakar Bhatt

Pt. Diwakar Bhatt belongs to South. But his famous works on Dharmashastra made him popular not only in South but through out the country. He was son of Pt. Mahadeo Bhatt. His mother was Ganga. Ganga was the daughter of Neelkanth Bhatta, son of Shankar Bhatt. Pt. Diwakar Bhatt in 1683 wrote a book which is very extensive.

Nagesh Bhatt

Nagesh Bhatt was the son of Pt. Shiva Bhatta. Pt. Hari Dikshita was his guru. He belonged to South but his study centres was Benaras, where he got impetus of great scholars living there at that time (period 18th century). He wrote more than 30 works on Dharmashastra.

Prominent among those are: Acharendu Sekhar; Tithindu Sekhar; Tirthendu Sekhar; Prayaschitendu Sekhar or Prayaschita Sar Sangrah; Shradhendu Sekhar; Lakshman Ratna Malika; Sapindya Deepak; Sapindi Manjari. There extensive references to the predecessors in these writings. These books are very useful and are popular.

Kashinath Upadhyaya (late 18th century)

Kashinath Upadhyay composed an extensive work called Dharma Sindhusar or Dharma Sindhu. It is now the leading work in matters of religious observances in the Deccan and has been referred to even in judicial decisions.

He has consulted many authors previously referred. He composed the work which sets forth only the established conclusion after eliminating the original Smriti texts. He was the great disciple of Bhagwan Bithal Deva.

The Dharma Sindhu is divided into three sections and contains 433 printed pages.

Part - I: *Kal Nirnay, Sankranti Nirnay, Malamas Nirnay, Singhasth Guru Mimansa, Vratopbas Nirnay, Pratipada Tithi Nirnay* and *Sthalipak Vichar Grahan Mimansa.*

Part - II: Details of V*ratopabhasha* for each month.

Part - III: Section I: Rites of all *Sanskar, Aahik rites, Deva Pratistha* and *Daily rites.* Section II: *Shradh.*

Pt. Ratnakar Bhatt

Pt. Ratnakar Bhatt was the son of Pt. Deva Bhatta. He was the scholar in Maharaja Jai Singh's darbar. Maharaja Jai Singh was a great Maharaja of Surya Dynasty. He extended his patronage to great intellectuals and scholars.

Pt. Ratnakar Bhatt at the initiation of the Maharaja compiled an extensive work on the Dharmashastra. Details of Vrat and the Tithi calculations were included in the work– Vrat Kalp Drum or Jai Singh Vrat Kalpa Drum. The book is divided into 19 chapters: Monthly Tithi, a Vrat, monthly Vrat, special festivals, Sankranti Vrat, Kayik, Bachika, Mansik Vrat, Nakshtra Vrat, Prakeern Vrat.

Pt. Vishwasharma: Vrataraj

Pt. Viswa Sharma who resided in Benaras was a great scholar of Dharmashastra. He compiled a book called Vrata Raj depicting the details of the Vratas. Pt. Gopal Sharma was the father of Pt. Viswa Sharma.

The book is divided into chapters: Definition of Vrat, then *Panch Pallava: Panch Gabya; Panchamrit; Madhur Traya*; different procedures for *pooja, homa* etc. The book is just like an encyclopaedia for *vrata* and is very useful.

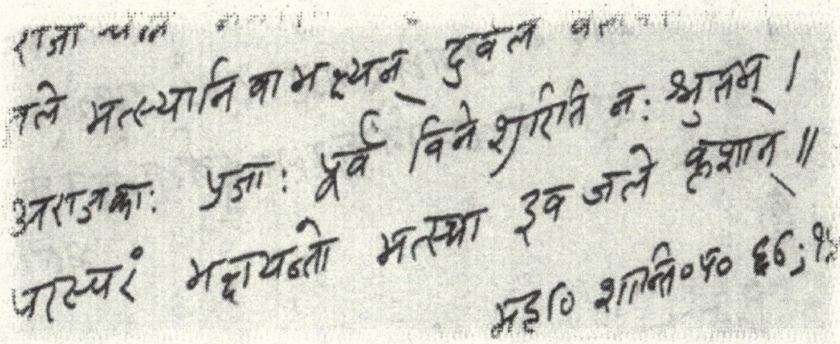

राजा [illegible]
जले मत्स्यानिवाभक्ष्यन् दुर्बलं
अराजकाः प्रजाः पूर्वं विनेशुरिति नः श्रुतम् ।
परस्परं भक्षयन्तो मत्स्या इव जले कृशान् ॥
महा० शान्ति०प० ६६;१६

APPENDICES

A.
Chronology of Sanskrit Literature

The chronology of classical Sanskrit literature starts with the Mahabharat war and Kaliyug.

1. Kaliyug commenced on 18 February 3102 BC.
2. The day Krishna departed to his divine abode: 18 February 3102 BC.
3. The Kuru-Pandava war was fought 37 years before Kali age: 3139 BC.

From the commencement of Kaliyuga, Puranas contain accounts of various kingdoms that flourished from time to time and successive dynasties that ruled and fell during the course of 35 centuries.

To an impartial observer, the tenor of these accounts warrants their accuracy. Ancient sages/seers/rishis perceived divine hymns of the Vedas and passed them on for the edification of posterity. Since the advent of Kali, a prospective crop of vice and folly was predicted and to wean the erring world from such sin and misery, Vyasa formulated the Puranas, with the object of Vedopabrahmana, which supplemented the exposition of Vedic teachings, and that too in the garb of a language and narrative that would be easily assimilated by the masses. To such philosophical minds, the rise and fall of kings and kingdoms was not worth remembering, save as another realistic means of illustrating the tenets of philosophy, e.g., the truth of the divine essence, Brahman, the unreality of sensual pleasures, the liberation of individual soul and the attainment of eternity in beatitude or oneness with the spirit Divine and above all the inevitable occurrence of God's mandate, shortly termed Destiny or otherwise called Kala or Niyati.

The Puranas uniformly give two methods, which are corroborative of each other, in calculating the dates of Hindu dynasties. One starts with the close of the Mahabharata War and almost co-eval with the commencement of the Kaliyug, from which time the number of years that each king reigned is given. The other starts from the Sapatarshi Era or the Laukikabda, whose cycle consisting of 2700 years is accepted by all authorities to have commenced about 4992 years ago corresponding to 3676 BC. Now the Puranas state that the first cycle of the Sapatarshi era commenced at the time of Parikshit, that the Saptarshis were in Magha at this time, that they move in a retrograde motion and take 100 years to pass one Nakshatra to another, that they were in *Purvashadha* (or the 16th Nakshatra from Magha) at the time of the commencement of the Nanda dynasty, and that they were in Chitra Nakshatra or the 24th Nakshatra from Magha at the commencement of Andhra dynasty and that at the beginning of the reign of the 27th king of the Andhra dynasty, the cycle repeated itself, the Saptarshis having come back to Magha. So there must have elapsed at least 1500 years between Parikshit and Mahapadma Nanda, 2300 years between Parikshit and Andhra Simuka (Sri Satakarni), the founder of the Andhra dynasty and 270 years between Parikshit and Siva Sri Shatakarni, the 27th king of Andhra dynasty, and that this king Sivasri must have commenced his reign in the year 377 BC.

The Mahabharat War is the reference point for the Puranic chronology, that is, at 3139 BC. The periods assigned to the Eight dynasties that ruled over Magadh, Barhadratha to Andhra is made up of 2811 years. Thus, 2811 years after the Mahabharat war or about 328 BC. The Sovereignty of Magadh passed with the hands of a time called Purvatiya and Andhrabhatiya, the first king of which was Chandragupta.

The Saptarshi Era is fully described in all Puranas almost similar to one another and the following passage from the Kaliyuga-Raja-Vrittanta may suffice as example:

In the circle of the Lunar Asterisms (Nakshatra) where in the great constellation of the Sapt Rishis constituting the great Bear or the Ursa Major revolve, and which contains 27 asteris (like Aswani, Bharnim Kritika etc.) in its circumference (ecliptic contain of 360Ī of each Nakshatra or Lunar asterism being equal to 13Ī.20Ī of the ecliptic), the seven sages remain for 100 years in each asterism in turn (The Rishis taking 2700 years to make on circuit of the heavens).

This is the cycle of the seven seers (consisting of 2700 human years) and is reckoned in the term of Divine years (360 human years being equal to 1 Divine year). And the total period is equal to 7 Divine years and 6 Divine months (i.e., 7´times 360 or 2700 human years).

The constellation of the seven saints (or the seven stars of the wain consisting of Marichi, Vashishta accompanied by Sukshmatara Arundhati, Angiras Atri, Pulastya, Pulaha and Kratu) takes a period of 100 years to go over each of the 27 asterisms (and it goes through these 27 asterisms in a retrograde order and, as the twelve signs of the Zodiac which comprise these 27 asterisms are arranged in a retrograde order around the ecliptic). Thus the Sapatarshikala consisting of a cycle of 2700 years has come to be constituted.

The two front stars (Pulah & Kratri) of the great constellation of the seven sages which are seen (in the northern region) when risen at night, the lunar asterism or Nakshatra which is seen situated equally between them in the sky is said to govern the same– the constellation of the Sapta rishis being known as conjoined with that asterism for 100 years. This is the exposition of the conjunction of the Lunar asterisms and the constellation of the Sapta Rishis.

When the constellation of the seven sages remained conjoined with the asterism of Maghas, then the Kaliyuga comprising 1200 Divine Years (or 432000 common human years) began.

According to the southern school of (astronomers), when Lord Krishna returned to heaven, (i.e. left this mundane world) then in that very same year on the first day of Chaitra of the year the present Kali Yuga (of the 28th Mahayug comprising 12000 Divine years) commenced.

As long as the great incarnation of the Divine Vishnu continued to touch the earth, (with His Holy Feat) so long the Kali Age was unable to approach the Earth.

When the seven rishis shall pass from the Maghas and reach the asterism of Purvashard, then will indeed the Kali Yug begin to grow.

When Prince Yudhishtira was for the first time crowned as king, at Indraprastha then the seven rishis of the constellation of the Ursa major entered the Lunar asterism of Maghas which were sacred and propitious of the pitris.

The seven rishis of the great Bear entered the asterism of the Maghas, just 75 years before the beginning of the Kali Yug (in the year 3137 BC) at the commencement of the reign of the great king Yudhishtir who ruled the earth during the said period.

These seven sages will enter the asterism of Aslesha on the expiry of 25 years from the commencement of the Kali Age (in the year 3077 BC) and they will continue to remain in that asterism for a period of 100 human years from 3077 BC to 2977 BC.

In that very same year (3077 BC) with Dharmaputra Yudhishtir ascending to heaven after wandering on the earth for a long time (having abdicated the throne in favour of Parikshit (The grand son of his brother Arjun and started as his mahaprasthan with his brothers and on hearing the sad and sudden news of the departure of Sri Krishna from the world), then will the Laukika era consisting of a cycle of 2700 years be started in the world in commemoration of the Ascension of Dharmaputra into heaven.

These divine sages will reach Ashlesha a second time at the time of commencement on the reign of the 27th king of the Andhra dynasty who began to rule Magadha in the year 2762 corresponding of 377 BC–one complete cycle of 2700 years having elapsed since the expiry of the 25th year of Kaliyuga, when they first reached Ashlesha after the Mahabharata War.

These seven sages were conjoined with the asterism Magha for a period of 100 years during the time to Yudhishtir and at the time of the commencement of the reign of king Nanda, Mahapadma, they will be conjoined with the asterism Shravan the 15th Nakshatra from Magha (calculated of course in a reverse order).

From the commencement of the Andhra dynasty at Magha, the seven rishis will be found conjoined with chitra the 24th lunar asterism.The interval of time between the birth of Pariskshit (son of Abhimanyu by Uttara and the grand son of Arjun who was in the womb of his mother at the time of Mahabharata war) and the inauguration of the Mahapadma Nanda is to be known as 1500 years. According to competent authorities, the interval of the time between the coronation of Mahapadma Nanda who came to the throne of Magadh in 1504 A.Y. and the commencement of the Andhra Dynasty which began to rule Magadh in 1305 A.Y. is stated as full 800 years.

When the great constellation of the seven sages of the Ursa Major shall again reach of asterism Punarvasu in its second revolution after the Mahabharat War, the Empire of the great Gupta kings shall begin to decline; and when they shall actually enter the asterism of Purva bhadra therefore, the kingdom of Magadh will pass from the Guptas to the Pal kings.

The 422 BC is the starting point backwards and forwards in the Puranic calculation. 1763 BC is the year after the great war. Pargiter arrives at the year 1810 BC as the date of the great war of Mahabharat.

B.
Samskara

Samskara means making something good, refining or purification. The Dhramashastras deal with such samskaras so as to make a man fit to be united with the Paramatma. From the Dharmashastras we know in detail the forty samskaras that are based on the Kalpa-Sutras and that are to be performed by a man during his life's journey.

The forty samskaras which are meant to purify the individual self are: 1.Garbhadhan; 2. Pumsavana; 3. Simanta; 4. Jatakarma; 5. Namakaran; 6. Annaprasana; 7. Kaula; 8. Upanayan; 9-12: Four rites like Prajapatya (Veda Vratas) performed during Guru Kulavas (The years the celibate student spends in his guru's house); 13. The ritual bath on completion of Gurukulavasa; 14. Marriage; 15-19: The five Mahagyayam, performed everyday by the house holder. We have listed nineteen so far. Then there are seven Pakayagya, seven Haviryagas and seven Sonayagas to be conducted by the house holder. Thus 19 + 21 = 40.

7 *Pak Yagnas:* Astaka (anvastaka), Sthalipak, Parvan, Sravani, Agrahayani, Caitri, Asvayaji.

7 *Havir Yagnas:* Agniyadhana, Agnihatra, Darsa-purnawasa, Agrayana, Chatumasya, Nirudh pasubandha, Sautramani.

7 *Soma Yagnas:* Agnistoma, Atyagnistoma, Ukathya, Shodasi, Vajapeya, Atiratra, Aptoryarma.

Out of the forty samskaras some are to be performed everyday, some at certain times and some at least once in a life-time. In the first category are the five Mahayagnas (Panch Mahayagna). Panch Mahayajnas are:

Brahmayagna: Chanting of Vedas is Brahmayagna.

*Devayagna:*Sacrifices and pooja is Devayagna.

Pitrayagna: Tarpan is Pitrayagna.

Manushyagna: Feeding guest is Manusyajna.

Bhutayagna: Offering bali to various creatures is Bhutayana (Saraswati, 521 and *Kalyan*, January 1949).

Garbhadhan, Simantonayan, Vishnu-Bali, Jaat-karma, Naam-karan, Upanishkraman, Annaprashana, Churakarma, Karnaveda, Aksharrambha, Upanayana, Vratarambha, Samavartana, Vivah, Upakarma and Utsarjana(17); Sapta Pak Yagna: Huta, Prahuta, Aahuta, Shulagav, Baliharan, Pratyavarohan, Ashtaka and homa(7); Sapta Havi yagna: Agniyadhana, Agnihotra, Darsha, Purnamaas, Chaturmaasya, Agryanesthi, Nirudh Agnia Pashubandha and Sautramani (7); sapta Soma Yagna: Agnisthoma, Atyagnisthoma, Ukathya, Shodshi, Vajpeyi, Atiratra and Aptoyarma (7). Along with these above Vanaprastha and Sanyas make for the forty samskaras. Further, by adding Saucha, Santosha, Tapa and Swadhyaya the list goes upto forty-four.

C.
Available Upnishadas

1. अक्षमालोपनिषद्
2. अक्षि उपनिषद्
3. अथर्व शिखोपनिषद्
4. अर्थवशिर उपनिषद्
5. अदूयतारकोपनिषद्
6. अद्वैतोपनिषद्
7. अद्वैत भावनोपनिषद्
8. अध्यात्मोपनिषद्
9. अनुभवसारोपनिषद्
10. अन्नपूर्णोपनिषद्
11. अमनस्कोपनिषद्
12. अमृतनादोपनिषद्
13. अमृतविन्दुपनिषद् (ब्रह्मविन्दूपनिषद्)
14. अरूणोपनिषद्
15. अल्लोपनिषद्
16. अवधूतोपनिषद् (वाक्यात्मक एवं पद्यात्मक)
17. अवधूतोपनिषद् (पद्यात्मक)
18. अवयतोपनिषद्
19. आचमनीयोपनिषद्
20. आत्मपूजोपनिषद्
21. आत्माप्रबोधोपनिषद्
22. आत्मोपनिषद् (वाक्यात्मक)
23. आत्मोपनिषद् (पद्यात्मक)
24. अर्थवर्ण द्वितोपनिषद्
25. आयुर्वेदोपनिषद्
26. अरूणिकायनिषद्
27. आर्शेयोपनिषद्
28. आश्रमोपनिषद्
29. इतिहासोपनिषद्
30. ईषावासोपनिषद्
31. ऊर्ध्वपुण्ड्रोपनिषद्
32. एकाक्षरोपनिषद्
33. ऐतरेयोपनिषद् (अध्यात्मक)
34. ऐतरेयोपनिषद् (खण्डात्मक)
35. ऐतरेयोपनिषद् (अध्यात्मक)
36. कठरूडोपनिषद् (कण्ठोपनिषद्)
37. कठोपनिषद्
38. कठश्रुत्युपनिषद्
39. कलि संतरणोपनिषद् (हरिनामोपनिषद्)
40. कात्यायनोपनिषद्
41. कामराजकीलितोद्धारोपनिषद्
42. कालाग्निरूद्रोपनिषद्
43. कलिकोपनिषद्
44. कालीमेधादीक्षितोपनिषद्

45. कुण्डिकोपनिषद्
46. कृशोपनिषद्
47. केनोपनिषद्
48. कैवल्योपनिषद्
49. कौलोपनिषद्
50. कौशीतकिब्रह्मणोपनिषद्
51. क्षुरिकोपनिषद्
52. गणपत्यर्थव शीर्षोपनिषद्
53. गणेशपूर्वतापिन्युपनिषद् (वरदपूर्वतापिन्युपनिषद्)
54. गणेशोत्तरतापिन्युपनिषद् (वरदांत्तरतापिन्युपनिषद्)
55. गर्भोपनिषद्
56. गान्धर्वोपनिषद्
57. गाय॥युपनिषद्
58. गायत्री रहस्योपनिषद्
59. गरूड़ोपनिषद् (वाक्यात्मक एवं मन्त्रात्मक)
60. गुह्यकाल्युपनिषद्
61. गुह्यषोढ़ात्यासोपनिषाद्
62. गोपालपूर्वतापिन्यूपनिषद्
63. गोपालोत्तरतापिन्यूपनिषद्
64. गोपीचन्दनोपनिषद्
65. चनुर्वेदोपनिषद्
66. चाक्षुणोपनिषद्
67. चित्युपनिषद्
68. छलालेयोपनिषद्
69. छान्दोग्योपनिषद्
70. जावालदर्शनोपनिषद्
71. जावालोपनिषद्
72. जावाल्युपनिषद्
73. सारतरोपनिषद्
74. तारोपनिषद्
75. तुरीयातीलोपनिषद्
76. तुरीयोपनिषद्
77. तुलस्यपनिषद्
78. तेजोविन्दूयपनिषद्
79. तैत्तिरीयोपनिषद्
80. त्रिपादविभूतिमहानारायणोपनिषद्
81. त्रिपुरापिन्युपनिषद्
82. त्रिपुरोपनिषद्
83. त्रिपुरामहोपनिषद्
84. त्रिशिखिब्राह्मणोपनिषद्
85. त्रिसुपर्णोपनिषद्
86. दक्षिणामू॥युपनिषद्
87. दत्तात्रेयोपनिषद्
88. दत्तोपनिषद्
89. दुर्वासोपनिषद्
90. क. देव्युपनिषद् (पद्यात्मक एवं मन्त्रात्मक)
    ख. देव्युपनिषद् ज़िवरहस्यान्तर्गत)
91. द्वयोपनिज़द्
92. ध्यानविन्दुपनिषद्
93. नादविन्दुपनिषद्
94. नारदपरिव्राजकोपनिषद्
95. नारदोपनिषद्
96. नारायणपूर्वतापिन्युपनिषद्
97. नारायणोत्तरतापिन्युपनिषद्
98. नारायणोपनिषद्
99. निराचम्पोपनिज़द्
100. निरूतोपनिषद्
101. निर्वापोपनिषद्
102. नीलरूद्रोपनिषद्

103. नृसिंहपूर्वतापिन्युपनिषद्
104. नृसिंहष्ठाट्चक्रोपनिषद्
105. नृसिंहोत्तरतापिन्युपनिषद्
106. पंचब्रह्मोपनिज़द्
107. परब्रह्मोपनिषद्
108. परमहंस पिरव्राजकोपनिषद्
109. परमहंसोपनिषद्
110. परमात्मिकोपनिषद्
111. पारायणोपनिषद्
112. पाशुपतब्रह्मोपनिषद्
113. पिण्डोपनिषद्
114. पीताम्बरोपनिषद्
115. पुरुष्ठासूक्तोपनिषद्
116. पैंगालोपनिषद्
117. प्रणवोपनिषद् (पद्यात्मक)
118. प्रणवोपनिषद् (वाक्यात्मक)
119. प्रष्ठनपनिषद्
120. प्राणाग्निहोतोपनिषद्
121. मटुकोपनिषद्
122. वङ्कु चोपनिषद्
123. वाज़्कलनन्तोपनिषद्
124. विल्योपनिषद् (पद्यात्मक)
125. विल्योपनिषद् (वाक्यात्मक)
126. वष्टह्दापालोपनिषद्
127. वष्टहदारण्योपनिषद्
128. ब्रह्मविद्योपनिषद्
129. ब्रह्मोपनिषद्
130. भगवद्गीतोपनिषद्
131. भवसंतरोपनिषद्
132. भस्मजावलोपनिषद्
133. भावनोपनिषद्
134. भिक्षुकोपनिषद्
135. भठाप्रप्योपनिषद्
136. मण्डलब्राह्मणोपनिषद्
137. मन्त्रिकोपनिषद्
चूलिकोपनिषद्)
138. मल्लायुपनिषद्
139. महानारायणोपनिषद्
(वृहन्नारायणोपनिषद्,
उत्तरनारायणोपनिषद्)
140. महावाद्योपनिषद्
141. महोपनिषद्
142. माण्डूक्योपनिषद्
143. माण्डूक्योपनिषत्कारिका
क. आगम
ख. वैतथा
ग. अद्वैत
144. मुलिकोपनिषद्
145. मुण्डकोपनिषद्
146. मुद्रलोपनिषद्
147. मृत्युलाङ्गूलोपनिषद्
148. मैत्रायण्युपनिषद्
149. मैत्रेय्युपनिषद्
150. यज्ञोपवीतोपनिषद्
151. याज्ञवल्क्योपनिषद्
152. योगकुण्डल्युपनिषद्
153. योगचूडामण्युपनिषद्
154. क. योगतत्वोपनिषद्
155 ख. योगतत्वोपनिषद्
156. योगराजोपनिषद्
157. योगशिखोपनिषाद्
158. योगोपनिषाद्
159. राजश्यामालारहस्योपनिषद्
160. राधिकोपनिषद् (वाक्यात्मक)

161. राधोपनिषद् (सुपाठात्मक)
162. रामपूर्वतापिन्युपनिषद्
163. रामरहस्योपनिषद्
164. रामात्तरतापिन्युपनिषद्
165. रूद्रहदयोपनिषद्
166. रूद्रराजावालोपनिषद्
167. रूद्रोपनिषद्
168. लक्ष्म्युपनिषद्
169. लाङ्गूयोपनिषद्
170. लिङ्गोपनिषद्
171. बज्रपंजरोपनिषद्
172. वज्रसूचिकोपनिषद्
173. वनदुर्गोपनिषद्
174. वाराहोपनिषद्
175. वासुदेवोपनिषद्
176. विश्रामोपनिषद्
177. विषिणहृदयोपनिषद्
178. शरभोपनिषद्
179. शाध्ययनीयोपनिषद्
180. शाण्डिल्योपनिषद्
181. शारीरकोपनिषद्
182. शिवसंकलयोपनिषद् (1)
183. शिवसंकलयोपनिषद् (2)
184. शिवोपनिषद्
185. शूकरहस्योपनिषद्
186. शौनकोपनिषद्
187. श्यामोपनिषद्
188. श्रीकृष्णपुरुशोत्तम सिद्धान्तोपनिषद्
189. श्रीचक्रोपनिषद्
190. श्रीविधातारकोपनिषद्
191. श्रीसूक्तम्
192. श्वेताश्वतरोपनिषद्
193. षोषोपनिषद्
194. संकर्षणोपनिषद्
195. सदानन्दोपनिषद्
196. सन्ध्योपनिषद्
197. संन्यासोपनिषद् (अध्यात्मक)
198. संन्यासोपनिषद् (वाक्यात्मक)
199. सरस्वतीरहस्योपनिषद्
200. सर्वसारोपनिषद्
201. सद्दवैउपनिषद्
202. संहितोपनिषद्
203. सामरहस्योपनिषद्
204. सावि॥युपनिषद्
205. सिद्धान्तविद्वलोपनिषद्
206. सिद्धान्तष्ठिाखोपनिषद्
207. सिद्धान्तसारोपनिषद्
208. सीतोपनिषद्
209. सुदर्षनोपनिषद्
210. सुवालोपनिषद्
211. सुमुख्योपनिषद्
212. सूर्यतापिन्युपनिषद्
213. सूर्योपनिषद्
214. सौभाग्यलक्ष्म्युपनिषद्
215. स्कन्दोपनिषद्
216. स्वसंवेद्योपनिषद्
217. हयग्रीनोपनिषद्
218. हंसषोढ़ोपनिषद्
219. हंसोपनिषद्
220. हेरम्बोपनिष

Bibliography

"Dharmasastra Anka". 1996. Hanuman Prasad, Poddar, and Chiman Lal, Goswami, eds. *Kalyan* (January: Annual).Gorakhpur: Geeta Press.

"Upanishad Anka". 1949. Hanuman Prasad, Poddar, and Chiman Lal, Goswami, eds. *Kalyana*. 23(1). Gorakhpur: Geeta Press.

Ahmad, Ilyas. 1937. *The First Principles of Politics*. Allahabad: The Indian Press.

Altekar, A.S. 1972. State and Government in Ancient India. Delhi: Motilal Banarasidas.

Aralikatti, R.N.2000. "Vaikhanasa Agama: Its literature". *Sapthagiri* (January). Tirumal Tirupati Devasthanams.

Aurobindo.1997.*The Renaissance in India with a Defence of Indian Culture*. In *The Complete Works of Sri Aurobindo*. 20. Pondichery: Sri Aurobindo Ashram Trust.

Bandhopadhyaya, N.C.1927. *Development of Hindu Polity and Political Theories*. Calcutta: R. Cambray.

Berolzheimer, Fritz. 1912. *The World's Legal Philosophies*. Translated from the German by Rachel Szold Jastrow. Boston:Boston Book Company.

Bhattacharya,D.C. 1962. "The Nibandhas" in S.Radhakrishnan, ed. *The Cultural Heritage of India*.II. Calcutta: Ramkrishna Institute of Culture.

Carlyle, A.J. and Carlyle, R.W. 1950. *Medieval Political Theory in the West*. London: William Blackwood.

Das A.C.1907. "Limited Monarchy in Ancient India." *Modern Review*. II (October).

Dikshitar, V.R.R.1929. *Hindu Administrative Institutions.* Madras: University of Madras.

Gajendragadkar, P. B. 1969. "The Historical Background and Theoretical Basis of Hindu Law." In S.Radhakrishanan, ed. *The Cultural Heritage of India.* II. Calcutta: Ramkrishna Institute of Culture.

Friedmann, W. 1952. *Law and Social Change in Contemporary Britain,* London: Stevens and Sons Limited.

Ganguly, Joydev. 1972. *Dharmasastra in Mithila.* Calcutta: Sanskrit College.

Ghosal, U.N. 1959. *A History of Indian Political Ideas.* Bombay and London: Oxford University Press.

Hopkins, Edward W. 1884.*The Ordinances of Manu.*London: Trubner & Co.

Jolly, Julius.1889. *The Minor Law Books.* Max Muller, ed. *The Sacred Books of the East.*33.Oxford: Clarendon Press. http://www.sacred-texts.com/sbe/

Kane, P.V.1968.*The History of Dharmasastra (Ancient and Medieval Religious and Civil Law in India).*Poona: Bhandarkar Oriental Research Institute (Five volumes).

Keith, A.B. 1970. *The Religion and Philosophy of the Veda and Upanishads.* Delhi: Motilal Banrasidass.

Keith, Arthur Berriedale. 1914. *The Veda of Black Yajus School entitled Taittiriya Sanhita.* Cambride: Massachusetts.

http://www.jimblog.net/wp-content/uploads/sacredtexts/hin/yv/index.htm

Macdonell, Arthur, and Keith, A.B. 1912. *Vedic Index of Names and Subjects.* London: John Murry.

Macdonell, Arthur.1900. *A History of Sanskrit Literature.* New York: D.Appleton and Company.

Mahabharata. Gorakhpur: Geeta Press, 1957.

Maine, Henry. 1861. *Ancient law: Its Connection with the Early History of Society and Its Relation to the Modern Ideas.* New York: Henry Holt and Company.

Mishra, P.S. "Foreword." In Sri Chandrashekharananda, Saraswati. *Hindu Dharma.* Bombay: Bharatiya Vidya Bhawan.

Muller, Friedrich, Max. 1959. *A History of Ancient Sanskrit Literature So far As It Illustrates the Primitive Religion of the Brahmans.* London: Williams and Norgate.

Muller, Friedrich, Max, ed. 1879-1910. *The Sacred Books of the East.* Oxford: Clarendon Press. http://www.sacred-texts.com/sbe/

Pargiter, F.E. 1962. *Ancient Indian Historical Tradition.* Patna: Motilal Banarasi Das.

Pound, Roscoe.1922. *An Introduction to the Philosophy of Law.*New Heaven: Yale University Press.

Prasad, Beni. 1974. *Theory of Government in Ancient India.* Allahabad: Central Book Depot.

Radhakrishnan, S.1940 (1969).*Eastern Religion and Western Thought.* London: Oxford University Press.

Vardachariar, S. 1946 *The Hindu Judicial System,* Lucknow: Lucknow University Press.

Saraswati, Svami, Pujya Sri Chandrasekharendra. 1991. *The GuruTradition.* Bombay: Bharatiya Vidya Bhawan.

Sarkar, B.K.1937. *The Positive Background of Hindu Sociology. The sacred Book of the Hindus.* XXXII. Allahabad: Panini Office.

Sarkar, Benoy Kumar. 1921. "The Hindu Theory of the State." *Political Science Quarterly.* 36 (1):79-90.

Sarkar, Benoy, Kumar.1969. "Some Basic Ideas of Political Thinking in Ancient India." In S.Radhakrishnan, ed. *The Cultural Heritage of India.* II. Calcutta: Ramkrishna Mission, Institute of Culture.

Sharan, Parmatma. 1983. *Ancient India Political Thought and Institutions.* Meerut: Meenakshi Prakashan.

Vivekananda, Swami. 2001. *The Complete Works of Swami Vivekananda.* Calcutta: Advait Ashram (9 volumes).*The Cultural Heritage of India.* II. Calcutta: Ramkrishna Mission, Institute of Culture.

SOURCES OF ANCIENT INDIAN LAW

Series Editor

PATRICK OLIVELLE

DHARMA

Studies in its Semantic, Cultural and Religious History

Ed. by PATRICK OLIVELLE

ISBN : 978-81-208-3338-8

•

DHARAMSŪTRAS

The Law Codes of Āpastamba,
Gautama, Baudhāyana and Vasiṣṭha

Text & Tr. PATRICK OLIVELLE

ISBN : 978-81-208-1739-5

•

DHARMASŪTRA PARALLELS

Containing the Dharmasūtras of
Āpastamba, Gautama,
Baudhāyana and Vasiṣṭha,

Ed. & Tr. PATRICK OLIVELLE

ISBN : 978-81-208-2970-1

•

THE NĀRADASMṚTI

Critical Edition and Translation

RICHARD W. LARIVIERE

ISBN : 978-81-208-1804-0

Also by PATRICK OLIVELLE

AŚOKA

In History and Historical Memory

ISBN : 978-81-208-3402-6